MW00477480

Complete Horoscope

2023

Monthly astrological forecasts for 2023

TATIANA BORSCH

receive new responsibilities or a promotion right where you are, which will significantly improve your financial situation.

Money. Overall, 2023 is a fairly positive time for your bank account. Most Aries will have an opportunity to improve their material situation, which is reflected in all other areas of your life, as well.

The best months of the year for you are January, the second half of May, June, the second half of September, and December.

Most of your expenses will take place in August, the second half of October, and November. They may be directly related to business, or possibly matters involving your family or home.

Love and family. Your personal life can be divided into different halves. During the first half, you will enjoy stability and predictability, which will be replaced by turbulent passions during the second half.

Couples on the rocks will have to deal with challenges once again, and this time, they will involve money or other material items. This is especially likely during the fall and winter of 2023 – October, November, and December. You may be discussing divorce, but that only applies if you have had a longstanding grudge with one another. There may be a love triangle involved, and you will be forced to make a choice.

Couples who get along might be focused on major construction projects, and closer to the fall, they may invest a lot of resources into this. One partner will be in agreement with this, and the other will not. Naturally, that will lead to arguments, which will begin in October and November, but be over by the holidays.

Single people have a great chance of meeting their better half in 2023, and acquiring real estate, as well.

Health. Much of the year, you will enjoy the support of Jupiter, which is a powerful source of energy, meaning that you have no reason to fear falling ill. However, during the difficult autumn, in October and November, it is worth being attentive to your body and avoiding any injuries, while also being more careful behind the wheel.

If you are elderly or weakened by chronic disease, take care, because there is a high likelihood of a recurrence. Take protective measures, and if you need it, seek the advice of a doctor.

Taurus

Your motto this year is "it's okay to dream". This is the year when your dreams will come true, and all of your virtues are both in demand and appreciated.

Work. You will be able to divide 2023 into two very different periods. During the first half, you will have to tackle problems that cropped up during the fall and winter of 2022, while also laying the groundwork for a new cycle that will begin in May.

As 2023 begins, business owners and managers may be busy with various administrative tasks, perhaps setting up a business or expanding one.

January, April, and the first half of May will be the most difficult months, when you may be involved in thorny negotiations with colleagues from other cities or abroad, while also resolving financial quandaries. February and March will run smoothly, when the most painful matters will have been resolved, one way or another.

In May, Jupiter, the planet of success, will be in your sign, and which means that you will start to see a clear improvement in everything you do. Business owners can count on launching new projects, and employees can expect a new job.

The second half of 2023 will not be calm by any means. In October and November, you may experience serious opposition from partners or perhaps outright competition from people hoping to take your place in the sun. However, luck is on your side, and your position is strong, which means you will manage to repel any attacks.

Money. Financially, the most difficult time of the year will be January. You will have to settle old debts and invest money in your business development, while also grappling with difficult household matters. Here, it may help to remember that everybody hurts sometimes.

During the second half of the year, things will quiet down, but there's no need to break out the rose-colored glasses. You will still have expenses, and they may be related to work, professional matters, or possibly various events within your family.

Love and family. You will see two different trends in your personal life. Many Taureans will be busy setting up a new home or engaged in major repairs where they live now. That is good news for couples who have a robust, stable relationship.

Alternatively, you might be facing divorce or separation and therefore forced to find a new place to live.

In many cases, a new love interest may be the reason for a difficult situation for couples who have already been through a rough patch. The fall and winter are particularly telling, and there is a high likelihood of conflict here.

For much of the year, your personal relationships will be unpredictable and stormy, which may leave you feeling exhausted as 2023 draws to a close.

You may make peace with relatives if you had a recent quarrel, and that includes family members living in other cities or abroad. Here, you count on improvements in May, June, and July.

Health. During the first half of the year, you are feeling sluggish, and you would be wise to keep an eye on that in late March and April. Be careful when traveling and driving in January and October.

During the second half of the year, things will be more stable, but there is a chance of something extreme taking place in October and November.

During the first half of the year, January may be the most difficult month, when you will have to contend with problems from 2022. That may include your relationship with friends, the powers that be, and financial matters. However, by February, all of this will be resolved.

The summer will be smooth sailing, and things will start to grow more complicated in the fall. Employees will have to deal with dissatisfied managers, while business owners will face off with official bodies. Most likely, this will involve real estate and you will have to be agile as you maneuver in order to fix this. As long as Jupiter is on your side, however, you will get what you want.

Money. Financially, 2023 is a great time for you, and a significant improvement from 2022. The best time for any material matters will be May, July, August, and September.

Love and family. Your personal life is no walk in the park. You are in the midst of a difficult but very necessary process that will lead you to reconsider your relationship with an old partner and in some cases, that may lead to a separation.

You may have a new love interest from among your old connections. November may be a critical time for you, when all of your red lines will be crossed.

Of course, this is for couples who have been on the rocks and need to turn the page on the past in order to move forward.

Couples who get along will be busy this fall grappling with various difficult tasks related to their home, and they may be moving to a new apartment, or possibly even a new city or abroad.

Single people might count on a new encounter in 2023, but that will not lead to a long-term romance except in the luckiest cases.

Health. This year, you are more energetic than you were in the past, and that is most noticeable in April and May. January and November will be the hardest months for your health.

Virgo

Hold on! You are embarking on a turbulent year in all areas of your life. This might be beneficial to you, as you have to crack a few eggs to make an omelet.

Work. This year, you might have to understand that the time has come to begin a new chapter in your professional life. Both business owners and employees can expect major changes. In many cases, that will involve overhauling your entire lifestyle – expect a move to a new city or even abroad.

Alternatively, you may be totally renewing your business or taking on new responsibilities with a new organization. You will not feel these changes until May or June, and the first part of the year may still feel somewhat confusing and involve difficult organizational tasks to prepare for the changes underway.

From May to October, you will be very busy, and that is generally a very good thing. But by the fall, many of your achievements will be in doubt once again.

In some cases, this may involve auditing bodies, or possibly business partners from afar or foreign laws.

You will manage to get a handle on this all quickly, and by the holidays, most of your problems will be resolved in your favor.

Money. Financially, the first half of the year is difficult and will be until May. February may be the bright spot here, when you are highly likely to receive a large sum of money.

During the second half of the year, things are looking much more optimistic, especially in May, June, and late September and October.

Love and family. Slowly but surely, you are feeling alienated in your personal life, as things cool off with your spouse or long-term partner, if you have had problems in the past.

Severe Saturn, which has been in the sector of the sky responsible for relationships for some time, is demanding you answer for your past mistakes. If there are not many of them, you will be alright, but if you have a trail of guilt behind you, take a long, hard look at your behavior and reassess. Otherwise, you might expect a separation.

In families that get along, you might be working on home improvements, and the first half of the year will be particularly telling, when you may see major repairs or perhaps even buy new real estate.

In some cases, you will move to another city or abroad. Those planning this major undertaking can count on something happening in the spring or summer of 2023.

Over the fall, you will face some obstacles, as moving abroad involves dealing with foreign laws and other challenges.

Alternatively, you might face someone hostile in your circle, which you will feel the most in October or November.

In the fall of 2023, you might have to grapple with various problems involving relatives. Expect a quarrel with a family member, and November may be the most difficult time for this.

Health. When it comes to your health, the most difficult time is from January to April. Here, you need to take care of yourself and remember that health comes first, and the rest will follow. Be very careful if you are weakened or elderly – at the first sign of illness, don't try to be your own doctor and instead turn to a professional.

During the same period, you may feel fatigued even if you are otherwise healthy. Women should see a cosmetologist more often or at least take better care of themselves at home.

After May, things will improve. Jupiter will transition to a friendly sign, which will be reflected in all areas of your life, including your mood and self-esteem.

In October and November, be more careful when driving and traveling.

Libra

Do what you must, and the rest will fall into place – that is your motto all year long. By following it, you will achieve your goals and confirm your own rules to the game of life.

Work. This year, you will have to resolve a series of important and difficult tasks. From January to May, business owners and managers will have to grapple with problems that arose in 2022. First of all, that involves your relationship with business partners in other cities or abroad, which may have reached a critical phase in the recent past. You will put an end to this drama at some point from January to March, at which point tempers will cool.

In order to smooth over delicate issues, you may have to turn to an ally or intermediary – their influence will significantly improve things, but they are unlikely to solve this for you. During the first half of the yar, you can expect new business partners with excellent opportunities, which will give your business the impetus it needs to achieve new development and progress.

In May, Jupiter will shift, and you will see a new chapter in your life. Many Libras will think about expanding their business and be considering new locations and spaces that would be most favorable to them.

Overall, things are going according to plan, but in October and November, you will have to deal with a serious lack of funds. Perhaps your grandiose projects require a lot more money than you initially planned, and you will not manage to resolve this quandary until 2024.

Your relationship with colleagues and subordinates will require another kind of attention all year long. You may have to start with a clean slate, and that is exactly what severe Saturn, which has been in the sector of the sky responsible for work, is urging you to do.

Those with legal trouble will manage to overcome this challenge favorably during the first half of the year with the help of knowledgeable attorneys and influential people in your corner.

Employees will not see any major gains this year. During the second half of the year, you will have to think about whether you want a new job, but that will not transpire until 2024. Many will decide to open their own business during the second half of the year and make initial steps in that direction.

Money. Financially, you would be wise to prepare for the unexpected, both good and bad. The end of February will be kind to you, as will March and July. You will overcome most of your troubles in the fall, especially November, when financial issues will cause you a lot of headaches and lead to misunderstandings with your business partners or loved ones.

Love and family. Your personal life will be rich, romantic, and exciting. Single people will meet someone intriguing and this time, things look very serious. A long-term, sexy romance or a happy marriage – what could be better?

During the second half of 2023, you can expect large-scale household tasks on the agenda. You may be purchasing a new home, summer home, carrying out repairs, or other related activities. A partner who is doing well may pay an important role in all of this.

You can expect some arguments over money, and when you work on home improvements in the fall, conflict is also likely, especially in late October and November. However, by the holidays, everything will be smoothed over, and you will see that you did everything right.

Health. In 2023, you are less energetic than you could be, so take care of yourself however you need. During the second half of the year, you may tend to gain weight, so think about following a balanced diet right away and remember the importance of exercise and physical activities.

Scorpio

In 2023, you are able to move forward. Your ruler, Mars, is leaving a stressful zone, and that means that you will continue to reboot your life.

Work. During the first half of 2023, you are busy with your professional future. Here, you can expect the end of March and April to be especially interesting times. Employees might get a promotion or additional responsibilities, and the stars see this as a particularly helpful development. Your paycheck will match this honor.

Business owners and managers of every level will be thinking about expanding their business and new projects, and here, you will bring new colleagues on board to help you reach your goals.

Not everything will turn out as planned, however. In January and early February, many Scorpios will have to contend with problems that began last fall, in 2022. This may be financial troubles or issues involving certain business partners. However, by March, most of the worst will be resolved, one way or another.

During the second half of 2023, after May, when Jupiter moves into Taurus, things will change. You have new business partners on the horizon, and they will have significant influence on your work. However, you need to be cautious when building a relationship with them, as the fall is likely to bring some hard times here.

You may not like your new colleagues' position, as they are thinking only of themselves, while you have your own wants and needs. All of this will lead to conflicts, which are highly likely in October and November.

From September to November, employees might face stiff competition, but your position is strong, and the occasional clash is no match for you.

During the last month of the year, many Scorpios will have resolved all of this.

Your connection with colleagues in other cities or abroad will develop with varying success. Some things will work out, and others will require more efforts on your part.

Money. This year, you might concentrate your efforts on achieving material stability, and many Scorpios will manage to do just that. The most favorable months for you are the end of March, April, late July, August, and December. January, February, October, and November will be tough.

Love and family. This year, your personal life seems like an obstacle course. During the first half of the year, you will not see any major developments here. However, beginning in May, things will start to change, and naturally, that is a good thing.

Those in a stable marriage will be pleased with their spouse's success, which will only grow. You might face some difficult household tasks, too – repairs, rehabbing an old home, or buying a new one.

Single people can count on an interesting encounter in the spring or summer of 2023. This person might be someone from your past and you have decided to start up right where you left off.

The fall will bring disagreements for couples, whether they are married or not. Perhaps you need to make a change, but no one is willing to do it. However, this time, there won't be any revolutions. After an outburst, your relationship will go back to business as usual.

Your children will bring you a lot of trouble, as they will not be having an easy time, and you will have to provide both moral and financial support.

Health. You will have to focus on your health during the first part of the year. During this time, old illnesses may resurface, or new ones may unexpectedly appear. The stars advise you to live a healthy lifestyle all year long and take better care of yourself in general. This is a perfect year to say goodbye to bad habits, work out, and otherwise busy yourself with healthy activities.

Sagittarius

You are looking at a year of success, ambition, and material and creative achievements. Your longstanding dreams and plans are finally coming to life, and the stars predict that you deserve it all!

Work. You can divide 2023 into two very different periods. From January to May, things will be hectic, busy, and full of energy. This is good for renewing old ties and making new acquaintances.

Starting in February, many Sagittarians will become very popular in their circles and will find themselves in high demand. Business owners and managers will be able to present their ideas and projects to official bodies and the general public, and you won't have to wait long for success.

You will see special success if you work in the creative fields – actors, artists, musicians, writers, and anyone who works with words. Your popularity will grow, as will your income.

January will be one of the most difficult months in the first half of 2023. Here, many Sagittarians will have to overcome challenges that began during 2022. By February, however, everything will be resolved here.

There will be a shift in the mood during the second half of 2023. You will be able to take the bull by the horns and grapple with difficult, all-consuming, but promising work. You will have to put in some elbow grease, and this will continue into 2024.

Business owners and managers will be able to carry out their ideas, and employees will see a new job or promotion where they are now. However, that does not mean that things will get easier. In August, you can expect disagreements with colleagues in other cities or abroad, who may shirk their responsibilities, and you will have to put in the extra work in order to get things back on track.

During the fall, especially October and November, you will face other challenges. Business owners and managers are advised to prepare for an audit or inspection, as well as problems on your team. An associate may turn out to be less reliable or professional than you need them to be. Here, it is worth looking for some new associates, in order to avoid any problems at this crucial moment.

During this time, you may experience some unpleasantness if you are an employee. That may include intrigue on your team, as well as hidden and outright hostility. But there is nothing left for you to do – there has always been competition, and there always will be. The stars recommend that you do your job, avoid distractions, and by mid-December, things will fall into place.

Money. Financially, this year is stable for you. You will have regular income, and during the second half of the year, it will grow significantly. Overall, 2023 is a good time for you, materially speaking. In February, March, and April, you may be lucky in the lottery – your ruler, Jupiter, might lend a hand.

Love and family. The first half of 2023 is promising where your personal life is concerned, especially from February to April. Here, you might meet new people, have a good time, and even start a passionate romance. It may not last very long, but it is sure to bring some joy to your life. During the second half of the year, any feelings of romance will simply fade away, but there will be room for an office romance.

During this time, parents will be pleased with their children's success, as they are on a very positive streak.

In many families, you will welcome new children or grandchildren.

Your relationship with your parents or an elderly relative will become much more difficult. That may be due to an illness or perhaps a serious argument.

Health. During the first half of 2023, you will feel under the weather in January, only to perk up from February to April. If you want to change your look, work on your style, or get any plastic surgery, there is no better time to do it.

During the second half of the year, your health will become more complicated, and the fall will be particularly difficult – from late October through November, when you will have to take more precautions. You might experience the usual cold or infection, and there is also a risk of injury, so be more cautious when driving or traveling.

During the second half of 2023, you would be wise to quit any bad habits, start working out more often, or work on your appearance. That will help you avoid a whole host of problems, you will look better, and restore you in both body and mind.

Capricorn

The time has come to take care of yourself and those you love. That is what the stars are urging you to do in 2023. Your home is your castle, and right now, that's what you need to keep in mind.

Work. This year is relatively smooth sailing for you. No major career changes are on the horizon, but you are sure to have a lot of work on your hands. During the first half of the year, you will see a continuation of the events from 2022.

Business owners and managers will still be expanding their business, and that will involve a whole host of administrative tasks. That may involve repairs and other events related to acquiring facilities, land, or other real estate. In some cases, that may be taking place in another city or abroad.

A few problems that began last fall will still be felt in January. This will be one of the hardest periods of 2023. However, closer to March, the most difficult matters will be resolved, one way or another, and they won't bother you anymore.

Your connections with colleagues from other cities or abroad will be moving along with varying success, however, here is where you will manage to recover much of what was lost.

Employees will manage to dedicate more time to their family, and perhaps things are so stable and calm at work, and many of your headaches from last year are no longer so pressing.

During the second half of the year, you will experience a dynamic, creative period. You will have a wonderful opportunity to demonstrate your talents to a wider audience, along with official bodies.

Those who work in creative fields – actors, musicians, artists, and anyone who works with words – will see particular success.

During the second half of the year, the most difficult months for anything work-related will be November and December. During this time, you will experience disagreements with friends, like-minded people, or those highly placed in society. However, by the holidays, all of this will be behind you.

Money. Financially, you will be ready for the unexpected, whether good or bad, though there more be more of the bad. You will be spending constantly, and the end of July will be particularly egregious, as will August and November. The astrologist predicts that much of this will be in your personal life, family, or due to your children's needs.

Love and family. 2023 will bring many events to your personal life. During the first half, many Capricorns will be busy setting up their home, maybe for themselves, or possibly for their children.

Your children bring you joy, and they are finally on the positive streak you have been waiting for. They will need your efforts, however, whether financial or other forms of support. In many families, you will welcome new children or grandchildren.

Couples will feel like they are on a rollercoaster this month, and that will be most palpable during the period from August to November. If you have any unresolved issues in your relationship, they may spill over this time, and force you to make a decision – it's now or never. Remember that a happy ending isn't only for fairytales, and sometimes, we get one in real life, too. The most important thing is to remember that it's all up to you.

Health. All year long, you are feeling energetic and even illnesses from 2022 will quickly fade away.

Aquarius

In 2023, Jupiter will change position twice, which means that there are changes underway in your life. The stars predict that you are ready!

Work. The main trend during the first half of 2023 is building connections with colleagues in other cities or abroad. You may renew an old partnership and get ready for travel or laying the groundwork for bigger things.

Business owners and managers will make plans related to expanding their business, and in some cases, that will take place in another region of your country, or perhaps further afield. These events will be in full swing by the second half of the year, and in some cases, that will involve a move and opening up shop in a new location.

The first half of 2023 will be a good time for studies, picking up new skills, and learning new things. During the second half of the year, you will be busy with large-scale household projects, such as construction, various transactions involving land, and other events related to real estate.

Not everything will run so smoothly during the second half of the year, however. In August and September, you might run into disagreements with business partners, who may say one thing, think another, and do something completely different altogether. Keep an eye on this from the very start and build a protective relationship with your business partners. That way, you will avoid a lot of problems, which are likely in the summer and fall of 2023.

From October to November, business owners might clash with various official bodies, while employees might face off with management. Try to build a relationship so that you always feel protected. When signing any important documents, be sure to read all the fine print, including the unpleasant parts. Your business has been climbing mountains lately, and that always attracts competitors and envious folks. Remember that and watch your back.

Money. Financially, this is a good time for you. The only exception may be January, when you will see a continuation of the problems that began in the fall and winter of 2022. Most likely, they involve your children or loved ones.

Saturn, which has been in the financial sector of your sky for some time, is calling for frugality and caution for anything related to money. In 2023, risk is contraindicated, and you are more likely to see losses than gains.

Love and family. The major events of 2023 will take place in your personal life. During the first half of the year, you will see significant improvements to your relationship with relatives and your relationship with your children will smooth over, as well.

Many Aquarians will be thinking about a new home or a move, and you may start making this happen. That may involve a new apartment, or perhaps heading to a new city or abroad.

In many families, you will have to deal with elderly relatives, and the fall will be especially difficult, from late October through November.

After the stress of 2022, couples will be turning the page on a better chapter. If you recently separated, during the first half of the year, specifically from February to April, you are likely to encounter someone new and start a romance, which will make you forget all your past woes.

Health. In 2023, you are feeling energetic and have no reason to fear falling ill.

Pisces

A new cycle that you began in 2022 is continuing in your favor. Saturn is moving into your sign, which will mean discipline and responsibility. Be ready for setbacks as part of this harsh test.

Work. During the first half of 2023, you will be busy with work, new goals, and new ideas. You may be seeing your current long-term projects continue with success, whether you are a business owner or manager. The most optimistic months for you here are March, April, and May.

You may see pleasant changes, and for employees that may include a new job or a significant promotion where you are now, with a corresponding pay raise.

The most difficult period in the first half of 2023 will be January. During this time, you may still be grappling with thorny issues that appeared in the fall or winter of 2022, and that might include disagreements with a business partner, or difficulties related to real estate. However, by March, most of this will be resolved.

In May, Jupiter will change position and open new horizons. You will step up your communication with colleagues from other cities or abroad, and you might renew old ties or perhaps meet new colleagues.

Business owners and managers will be thinking about opening their business in another city or abroad, and you may find yourself frequently on the road or even moving.

Employees can count on working in another city or abroad, or perhaps frequent business travel.

However, there is always a fly in the ointment. Here, that will be some opposition that will arise during the fall of 2023. In October and November, many Pisceans will have to deal with audits and inspections, or possibly legal difficulties. Your partnership with colleagues from other cities or abroad will give you pause, as well. There may be issues involving business partners, or perhaps your work will clash with the laws of another country or even claims from leadership. However, any troubles that crop up during this period will be favorably resolved by the second half of December.

Money. 2023 is a great time for your bank account. You will have regular income and significantly more of it, too. Many Pisceans will reach the next level, and that should last for a long time. Your expenses will likely be related to major purchases, perhaps related to work, or alternatively, your personal life.

Love and family. Your romantic life is stable. If in 2022, you met someone important, now, your relationship may be on the upswing. If you do not have a partner yet, there is hope of meeting someone, and you can count on this relationship in the spring or summer of 2023. In many cases, that might happen on a business trip or among people who have come from afar.

If you are planning a move to another city or abroad, you can be sure to see that happen from May to September. The fall will probably not be particularly favorable for this, as you will be putting out all kinds of fires. That includes logistics, laws in other countries, and difficulties involving someone in your circle.

From October to November, you might face problems involving relatives. That may be a quarrel with a close relative, or perhaps a difficult situation has beset someone you love. You will only resolve this just before the holidays.

Health. In 2023, you will be changing the way you think about your body. Severe Saturn, which has long been in your sign, will force you to leave behind bad habits, take care of yourself, and do what you can to lead a healthy lifestyle.

January

New York Time			London Time		
Calendar Day	Lunar Day	Lunar Day Start Time	Calendar Day	Lunar Day	Lunar Day Start Time
01/01/2023	11	12:58 PM	01/01/2023	10	12:31 PM
02/01/2023	12	1:32 PM	02/01/2023	11	12:56 PM
03/01/2023	13	2:10 PM	03/01/2023	12	1:27 PM
04/01/2023	14	2:53 PM	04/01/2023	13	2:05 PM
05/01/2023	15	3:42 PM	05/01/2023	14	2:51 PM
06/01/2023	16	4:36 PM	06/01/2023	15	3:45 PM
07/01/2023	17	5:32 PM	07/01/2023	16	4:45 PM
08/01/2023	18	6:31 PM	08/01/2023	17	5:50 PM
09/01/2023	19	7:30 PM	09/01/2023	18	6:56 PM
10/01/2023	20	8:29 PM	10/01/2023	19	8:04 PM
11/01/2023	21	9:28 PM	11/01/2023	20	9:11 PM
12/01/2023	22	10:28 PM	12/01/2023	21	10:19 PM
13/01/2023	23	11:29 PM	13/01/2023	22	11:28 PM
15/01/2023	24	12:32 AM	15/01/2023	23	12:40 AM
16/01/2023	25	1:38 AM	16/01/2023	24	1:54 AM
17/01/2023	26	2:47 AM	17/01/2023	25	3:11 AM
18/01/2023	27	3:56 AM	18/01/2023	26	4:28 AM
19/01/2023	28	5:05 AM	19/01/2023	27	5:42 AM
20/01/2023	29	6:08 AM	20/01/2023	28	6:46 AM
21/01/2023	30	7:02 AM	21/01/2023	29	7:38 AM
21/01/2023	1	3:55 PM	21/01/2023	1	8:55 PM
22/01/2023	2	7:49 AM	22/01/2023	2	8:17 AM
23/01/2023	3	8:28 AM	23/01/2023	3	8:48 AM
24/01/2023	4	9:01 AM	24/01/2023	4	9:13 AM
25/01/2023	5	9:32 AM	25/01/2023	5	9:34 AM
26/01/2023	6	10:01 AM	26/01/2023	6	9:54 AM
27/01/2023	7	10:30 AM	27/01/2023	7	10:14 AM
28/01/2023	8	11:00 AM	28/01/2023	8	10:35 AM
29/01/2023	9	11:33 AM	29/01/2023	9	11:00 AM
30/01/2023	10	12:10 PM	30/01/2023	10	11:29 AM
31/01/2023	11	12:52 PM	31/01/2023	11	12:04 PM

You can find the description of each lunar day in the chapter "A Guide to The Moon Cycle and Lunar Days"

Aries

You recently went through a difficult period, but it seems that there is a light at the end of the tunnel. As always, you can keep your head held high!

Work. During the first 20 days of January, you will be busy with work and the holidays will be but a memory.

Entrepreneurs and managers will be able to conclude a difficult period at work, which may have been caused by colleagues from other cities or abroad, or possibly unresolved legal problems.

Despite all the setbacks, during the last ten days of the month, the sky will clear – you are on the right track and victory will be yours. You can lean on your close partners, old friends, and most importantly, Jupiter, which is now on your side.

After January 12, when your ruler, Mars, finally begins moving in a straight line, you will find an opportunity to reach a smooth path of prosperity and development. Your relationships with colleagues from other cities or abroad, which may have been shaky in the past, will improve considerably.

After lengthy negotiations, employees might count on a promotion or an entirely new job. You can be sure of protection from old friends or mentorship from someone highly placed in society. In any case, you might not get what you want this month, but soon – from February to April – things will go your way. January is just a springboard for improvements and development later on.

Money. When it comes to finances, January is looking pretty good. Though you are spending a lot, you have more money than expenses and will be able to cover it all.

Expect to receive the greatest sums on January 1, 2, 11, 12, 21, 22, 28, and 29. Many of your expenses will take place during the second half of the month, but they will be predictable and reasonable.

Love and family. You can count on improvements in all areas of your personal life in January. Difficult situations with relatives are coming to a favorable resolution.

In many situations, this may involve relatives living in other cities or abroad, and your relationships are slowly improving.

You might also find yourself back in the arms of an old flame who now lives far away, or perhaps an old friend. You can expect things to become clearer during the last 10 days of January and all of February.

Health. January is one of the best months for you, energy-wise. You are healthy, full of vitality, and ready to climb mountains.

The only downside this month is meeting challenges while traveling and behind the wheel. The trickiest period is during the first 20 days of the month.

If you want to travel somewhere far from home, be very careful with your documents and following the law in other countries. Better yet – pick a destination where you have been before, in order to avoid any nasty surprises.

Taurus

January can be described as a period of worries and surprises, which promise to be very happy. In sum, things are slowly getting better, and things are charging ahead!

Work. January marks a turning page in your life – from all of the turbulence of 2022 to a new era that you can better predict and understand.

Your ties to colleagues in other cities or abroad will become extremely important. Entrepreneurs and managers at every level can expect negotiations to get off to a rocky start, and then take a turn for the better in late January or February. Many will have to rebuild their business and make some adjustments, which will continue all year long.

Employees will find an opportunity to strengthen their position where they are, but don't expect anything to happen until 2024. However, you will see the silver lining in late January and early February.

Money. Throughout the fall and winter of 2022, your finances were looking wobbly. That may have been due to challenges at work, or perhaps in your family or personal life. Aggressive Mars has been in the financial sector of your sky for some time, and as it moved into retrograde, you were thrown off balance.

After January 12, things are improving, and during the last few days of January, the 30-31, you can count on a nice stream of income. That upward trend will continue through February, too.

Love and family. You are looking at changes in your personal life. Families that get along will see improvements to their living conditions and can count on acquiring new real estate. For now, you are only in the planning phases, but throughout 2023 you will be taking steps in this direction.

Couples whose relationships are on shaky ground might finally sort out their financial disputes – who owes what to whom and what belongs to whom. Even if the first half of January is a time of stress, during the second half, you are sure to find a way out of this quagmire.

Couples might end a stormy period by separating, but at least things will be clear. That may be the best solution, and you will meet someone new during the second half of the year.

Health. You are feeling energetic in January, but the stars still recommend being careful when traveling and driving. If you want to visit another city or head abroad for a winter vacation, pick a place you have been before, in order to avoid any disappointments or other unpleasant situations.

Those who are elderly or weakened should keep an eye on their health, and if there is a problem, see a trained specialist rather than trying to treat yourself.

Gemini

Throughout January, you will be a ball of emotions, with a lot of doubts and ups and downs. This comes as no surprise – the position of the planets is the culprit, here. However, closer to the end of the month, the planets will calm down and so will you, as you find the right path.

Work. During the first 20 days of January, expect some tough times at work. You might find it best to just take some time off and get your affairs in order both at home and at work. Slowly but surely, things will start to look up again though, and by the end of the month, everything will be clear. You can expect to see greater ties to old friends and colleagues in other cities or abroad, and you might even take a trip or start planning one.

After the difficult fall and winter in 2022, which were characterized by conflicts with the powers that be or an unstable situation in the workplace might have thrown you for a loop, late January and February are looking much sunnier.

You might count on support from all sides and greater self-confidence and the feeling of being on the right track. You will get just a glimmer of these favorable trends in January, but they are sure to take shape as time goes on.

Employees who are out of work can count on a new job opportunity somewhere else. Negotiations on this are likely at the end of January and in February, and the stars predict things will go your way.

Money. January is not a great time for your bank account. You will be spending constantly, possibly due to a thorny situation at work, or perhaps because of issues in your personal life. Your income is low, and you might not have any at all. Things will not improve until February or even March.

Love and family. Though the lion's share major events of the fall and winter of 2022 took place in your personal life, here, you now can count on a long saga coming to an end.

If you have been at war with someone close to you for some time, things might come to an end, one way or another. In many cases, you might simply separate, and grapple with everything that entails. That may mean hashing out how to divide up your property, issues with housing, or other unpleasant conversations. But you have to put an end to this somehow, so do it now.

In other, less turbulent situations, you may find a path toward reconciliation. If your love is still alive, it is worth letting bygones be bygones and start over with a clean slate! In late January and early February, you can expect a clear opportunity to do just that.

Health. Most of January will have you feeling sluggish. You have been carrying a burden for a long time now, and the consequences may finally catch up with you. The stars suggest taking care of yourself, relaxing, and most importantly – getting enough sleep. For Geminis, that is the greatest factor when it comes to your mood and well-being.

Cancer

The first month of the year is extremely important for you. You have been living under pressure from the stars for some time now, and slowly but surely, things will lighten up and you can expect a new chapter – just what you had been waiting for.

Work. Your relationship with partners and foes alike will take on new significance in January. You may still be facing a lot of confusion and uncertainty, here. Negotiations you had been waiting for will have mixed success. Your colleagues will change their views, and that may drag on for most of the month.

Those facing legal troubles this month can count on a light at the end of the tunnel. Remember, it can only get better from here! This month you will be on track to resolve longstanding problems, but they will not be truly over until late February or even March. For now, you are calm as you carry on negotiations, and ignoring any setbacks or inconsistencies.

During the first 10 days of January, employees might go on vacation, as work will be slow after the holidays. If, for various reasons, you do not have a decent job to do right now, closer to the end of the month you will find new opportunities, and in March and April, you can count on a positive result.

Money. January is a mess for your finances. You cannot expect any great income, but your spending will be huge. That may be related to work or debts, or possibly resolving personal issues. Do not expect any windfalls until mid-March, so in the meantime, save your pennies and track each expense.

Love and family. If you have faced problems in your personal life, at least some of them are likely to crop up again this month. Throughout January, your spouse may be acting insincerely and inconsistently, which is not conducive to constructive dialogue. Be patient and hold tight. By the end of the month, things will be clear, though you may not be on the path to reconciliation if your marriage was already on the rocks. There will be opportunities for a compromise to resolve the thorniest, most difficult issues.

Couples who get along will tackle problems together, which is more than enough.

Health. Aggressive Mars has been in the sector of the sky related to health for some time now, and that means that you might occasionally feel sluggish and tired.

Those who are elderly and weakened should be careful this month – there is a high likelihood of infection, colds, or the reappearance of old, chronic illnesses.

Those who are young and healthy would do well to lead a healthy lifestyle and make sure to get enough sleep.

Leo

Despite the occasional hurdle, you are moving closer to your goal. The worst is over, and you're almost there!

Work. Jupiter is changing positions, and that is reflected very favorably in your work. This month, however, you should be content with very little – holding necessary negotiations and bringing an old friend into your business.

The best time for that kind of event is the second half of January, and especially the last week of the month. You will be busy with work, relationships, and possibly dealing with old debts, whether financial or moral in nature.

A challenging relationship with a friend or someone who lent you support in the past is looking closer to being resolved. After a difficult fall and winter in 2022, when many important connections seemed to fall apart for various reasons, you will have new opportunities to reach an understanding and peaceful resolution to your problems. In some cases, that may involve bringing on allies who can act as an intermediary.

Employees are thinking about a new job or moving up where they are. A little later, at the end of March, or possibly in April or May, you will have a wonderful opportunity to bring your ideas to life. Right now, though, there is nothing stopping you from laying the groundwork for future success.

Money. Your finances are looking healthy in January. Money will be coming in regularly, and you can expect somewhat more of it, too. Expect the greatest sums on January 1, 2, 11, 12, 20, 21, 28, and 29.

Love and family . January is characterized by a blast from the past and a sense of nostalgia. During the last 20 days of the month, you will meet up with old friends, and people who you have not seen for a long time. You might rekindle things with a former flame.

January is a great time for reconciliations and making up after a longstanding quarrel, especially the last 20 days of the month. If you do, sunnier days are ahead, and old grudges are not worth blighting what should be a bright future.

Health. In January, you are feeling a bit under the weather, and you might experience mood swings, lethargy, and fatigue. The elderly and those who are weakened might experience a reappearance of old illnesses, as well as colds and infections.

In many families, a loved one will be ill, and you will have to come to their aid – both in words and deeds.

In sum, keep an eye on your loved ones, on yourself, and maintain a healthy lifestyle, which includes getting enough sleep.

Virgo

In January, your greatest task is to do the right thing and help those in need – and you can! The idea that nice guys never win could not be further from the truth!

Work. The first 20 days of January are likely to look rather gloomy at work. First of all, everyone is sluggish coming back from the holidays, and secondly, Mercury, your ruler, will be in retrograde until January 19, while Mars will be in retrograde until the 12th.

That means that any major changes in the workplace that you began in the second half of 2022 are still underway, and you will be able to safely deal with it all during the last 10 days of the month. If you run into any resistance from management or disagreements with your partners, everything will fall into place closer to the end of the month.

Entrepreneurs and managers at every level will face the difficult task of renewing their business.

Employees might leave their current job to look for something new. The last 10 days of the month are best for this endeavor, or all of February. It is highly likely that you will have to continue working where you are for some time, but that is temporary. Keep that in mind as you seek out greener grasses.

Money. The first 20 days of January are ruinous for you, financially speaking. You will be pouring money into your home and professional goals. However, Virgos will be able to count on a welcome surprise – a gift from a loved one, or perhaps a small prize.

The last 10 days of the month are looking more stable and prosperous. Everything will return to normal, and you can expect the greatest sums of money on January 30 and 31.

Love and family. The first 20 days of January are likely to find Virgos busy with children and loved ones. You might take a trip or meet with relatives and old friends.

The stars strongly advise you to pay close attention to your relationship with your spouse or partner. Jupiter, the planet of good fortune that has been propping up your marriage sector, is moving to another sign, and you will have to deal with any challenges on your own. Remember that when it comes to love, the less you demand, the more you get, and act accordingly.

Health. January sees you bounding with energy, and you have no reason to fear falling ill. It is a good time for any trips to the spa or various minor cosmetic procedures but avoid the first 20 days of the month for any plastic surgeries or major procedures, as Mercury and Mars will both be in retrograde.

Libra

You've just survived some difficult days, but that is all coming to an end. It should be smooth sailing from here on out, and things will be much more predictable, too. But don't let your guard down – there are still a lot of risks out there!

Work. Busy entrepreneurs and managers at every level will spend a significant part of January smoothing over relationships with partners from other cities or abroad. This will not be an easy task after everything that happened during the spring, summer, fall, and winter of 2022. However, nothing lasts forever, and now is the time to make those issues a thing of the past.

In January, you will be making important streps toward reconciliation, and, though there may be some loose ends to tie up, any progress is better than none. You might have strong allies who put their best foot forward helping you and your opponents reach an understanding. Those grappling with thorny legal issues over land or other real estate might also count on a satisfying compromise.

The first 20 days of January are likely a time for laying the groundwork, while the last 10 days, you might be able to turn all that work into positive results.

Any business travel planned in January might turn out to be very successful, though the stars recommend being careful when it comes to following any administrative laws to the letter and keeping an eye on your documents.

Money. January is a neutral month for your finances. Rather than your own sources of income, you can count on support from a loved one or family member. Business is suddenly booming for your spouse or life partner, and the whole family is reaping the benefits.

Love and family. If you are mostly focused on your personal life, here, you can count on resolving longstanding problems. Most likely, it involves misunderstandings with relatives who live in other cities or abroad. In the last 10 days of the month, you can count on a favorable resolution to some tricky problems.

Those whose marriages are on the rocks will reach an agreement on real estate, which has been a sticking point for some time, now. Your relationship with your children will soften as you reach greater understanding, and this positive trend will continue into February.

Those who are single or have been disappointed by their personal life can count on meeting someone new in late January or February. In many cases, it will be a fateful meeting.

Health. In January, you are feeling full of energy, but the stars still recommend being careful when traveling and driving. The riskiest time is the first 20 days of the month. If you are planning any trips abroad during this time, plan everything to a T and do not ignore foreign laws.

Scorpio

In January, you are feeling vigorous, though it is a time of ups and downs. Try to stay positive, and everything will fall into place!

Work. In January, you will barely be at home. Entrepreneurs and managers will be consumed by detailed organizational tasks, which, after the events in the fall and winter of 2022 will be absolutely necessary.

During the first half of January, things will be hectic and not particularly productive, but closer to the end of the month, you can count on a positive outcome.

Those with connections in other cities or abroad will find themselves at odds with partners and foes alike. It might be over people overlooking their moral or financial obligations. Or possibly, the sticking point is not money, but land or other real estate. Both parties will be able to come to a compromise in the last 10 days of January or February.

During the first 20 days of February, you might have negotiations or meetings about planning an event.

Closer to the end of the month, employees will be negotiating a new job, and a little later on, they will get the results they desire. You might also strengthen your position where you are and find yourself with new duties or responsibilities.

Money. Financially speaking, January is likely to be tough. You will be bleeding money, and that may be related to business, debts, or growing your company, or possibly due to obligations with your home and family. This is nothing new to you, it is a continuation of the fall and winter of 2022. However, now, you can count on support from your spouse, parents, or other loved ones.

Love and family. In January, many Scorpios are spending time with their family, relatives, and loved ones. In the first 10 days of the month, you might take a trip and see family living in other cities or abroad.

Complicated real estate transactions are dragging on and might take up a significant chunk of the family budget. However, the worst is behind you, and now you can finally busy yourself with more pleasant tasks, like how you will arrange your home, apartment, or summer house.

Your relationship with someone special is seeing a lot of ups and downs, and if you feel that things are currently hanging by a threat, be more careful and sensitive. If the love is gone, however, that point is moot.

Health. In January, you are active, healthy, and full of life. The stars recommend being careful when driving or traveling. Pluto, a harsh and uncompromising planet, has been in the sector of the sky responsible for roads, cars, and any other means of transport for a few years, now. That means you might find yourself facing problems on the road, your car breaking down, and other difficulties. For now, the stars recommend being cautious and vigilant.

Sagittarius

You are entering a very active period, characterized by luck and popularity. But first, you need to close the chapter on an important yet difficult period in your life, and January is the time to do that.

Work. During the first 20 days of January, entrepreneurs will be working hard to smooth things over with partners. During the fall and winter of 2022, some people that you may have counted on in the past may have behaved inconsistently, or even become hostile. The cause may be money, land, real estate, or other major property, and each side has its own opinion of what went wrong.

Any argument will have to end at some point, though, and this time, you are likely to find a compromise closer to the end of January or in February.

You may have to bring in intermediaries first, though, perhaps some well-meaning colleagues from other cities or abroad. Their role will be priceless in any business this month.

Employees are on a positive streak, this month. They might be making new plans, coming up with new ideas that will eventually come to life in the future. While others are relaxing, many Sagittarians are focused on work this month, and soon, they will reap the rewards.

Money. January is not a bad time for your finances. You will have steady income, and a little more than usual, too.

Expect the largest sums to come in on January 2, 11, 12, 20, 21, 28, and 29. You will have a lot of expenses this month, and most of them will be related to the holidays, children, and loved ones. However, closer to the end of the month, you bank account will finally be in the black.

Love and family. If your personal life takes up more of your time than work, and this is the area where you felt the most pressure during the fall and winter of 2022, here, you can count on a change for the better.

Divorcing couples will reach an agreement on dividing up their apartment, summer house, or other real estate. Even if you are not able to avoid separation, your financial issues will be resolved, one way or another. Relatives, children, or someone close to you might help you reach an agreement.

Some couples may have a chance to reconcile, and if there is any love left, it is worth taking advantage of that opportunity. You can also count on relatives' support here.

Don't underestimate your children's influence, with everyone's combined efforts, you may just manage to calm down your better half.

Health. During the first 20 days of January, you are feeling less than energetic, so be careful to avoid winter colds, infections, and be sure to lead an extra healthy lifestyle.

Capricorn

It seems you are once again planning a real estate transaction, and as usual, things are very serious! Ride the wave!

Work. For many Capricorns, the holidays will be over, and you will be back to work by January 4 or 5.

All month long, entrepreneurs and managers of every level will have to grapple with problems on their team. The disagreements may have begun earlier, in the fall or winter of 2022. There may have been a mutiny, or perhaps someone behaving unscrupulously or simply being incompetent. The situation is now coming to an end. You will have to reach an agreement with someone, but it is not worth counting on certain individuals.

Employees may once again be seeing changes at work, which may have begun in the summer of 2022. For now, things have stabilized, though some will decide to leave, and others will find great benefits to staying where they are.

The best time to resolve your greatest and most complicated work-related problems is the last 10 days of the month. The first 20 days, you would do better to study the situation and discuss it in detail. Many things may look unclear and uncertain during this time.

Money. Overall, your finances are stable. You will have a steady income, thanks to Venus, which is moving into the financial sector of your sky all month.

Expect the greatest sums to come in on January 3, 4, 13, 14, 22, 23, 30, and 31. Your expenses are low, and mostly related to your personal life – vacation and your loved ones' needs.

Love and family. You are seeing changes in your personal life once again. They may look differently – it all depends on your past relationship and your future plans. Partners who have a strong relationship will solve problems related to their housing or other real estate together.

Those who are ready to split up will also be dealing with housing-related issues, either giving them up or dividing them.

Your relationship with relatives is also shifting. Longstanding disputes and other problems are coming to a close. One or both sides will eventually realize that a bad peace is better than a good war, and act accordingly.

It is hard to say what is in store for those who are dating. Their relationship might not be defined yet, or perhaps it will come to some kind of close. There may be some minor disagreements, and getting over them will require wisdom, patience, and understanding. But the most important factor is love, and the rest, they say, will follow.

Health. In January, you are not feeling very energetic. And there is a strong chance of old or unexpected diseases rearing their ugly heads. If you had health problems in the fall and winter of 2022, you may still be dealing with lingering troubles. This will not last, and the stars predict changes for the better.

Aquarius

In January, will find yourself a recluse, limiting your own interests due to home and family obligations. Sometimes, you just have to grin and bear it!

Work. This is not the best month for you at work. The best that entrepreneurs and managers can do is spend time getting their affairs in order and think about ideas for the future. You are sure to have many!

During the last 10 days of January, you will find yourself very busy at work, when new, interesting, and promising opportunities arise, and one way or another, they will be related to partners in other cities or abroad.

For both businesspeople and employees, that means expanding opportunities, frequent travel, and opening their business to other cities or abroad. All of this will begin in the near future, and now is a good time to get ready for the changes to come.

Money. Despite the great opportunities ahead, your finances are a source of stress this month. Expect a lot of expenses, mostly related to your family, your children's needs, or a loved one. Your income is low, and by the end of the month, your account will be in the red.

Love and family. January is a month full of celebrations and time with family. Your relationship with your children may be your greatest source of concern. In some cases, there may be real difficulties to deal with, and fixing them will take time and be hard on both your nerves and your wallet. In other, less stressful cases, you will have to spend a lot of money on your children's education and well-being. You are well aware of which category you fall into, and it will be determined by what happened in the summer, fall, and winter of a turbulent 2022.

For most couples, this is a challenging month, too. Problems from the recent path will crop up once again, and in some cases, you will simply have different outlooks on life, different value systems, and in others, it will simply be a disagreement over money. Once again, you know which description fits your situation best, as you have seen this before, in the summer, fall, and winter of 2022.

You are seeing a lot more of your relatives now, and you may be in touch with some who live in another city or abroad.

Health. This month, you are less energetic than usual, so be careful and take care of yourself. The risk of falling ill is fairly high right now, and you may see a reappearance of old, chronic problems.

Pisces

You are right in the middle of everything this January – friends, loved ones, a multitude of family obligations – when it rains, it pours! But you can handle it all with aplomb!

Work. Generally speaking, you are on a positive streak. Entrepreneurs and managers will be making new plans related to expanding their business and new financial opportunities. For now, things might just be in the planning stage, but in the very near future, you will make them come to life.

In some cases, your business expansion may be related to acquiring new production facilities or moving to a new office. Most likely, these bothersome tasks began in the fall or winter of last year and are finally coming to a close.

Your social circle may be expanding, too. In the first half of the month, you will see old friends, and closer to the end of the month, expect to make some new ones.

Remember that the last 10 days of the month is the best time for anything work-related, and the first 20 days are better for assessing your position and getting together with old friends and like-minded people. You might take a trip or be in contact with a colleague from afar.

Money. Your finances are not looking their best in January. You have a lot of expenses, and right now, they may be more than you earn. However, things will improve significantly later on, perhaps even by February.

Additionally, you can count on support from loved ones, your better half, or your parents.

Love and family. You will have some fateful events in your personal life this month. Many families will be busy with improving their home, repairs, or even building a new house. Most likely, these are tasks you began last year, and they are coming to a close.

You might be pouring most of your financial and organizational resources into a loved one.

During the first 10 days of January, many Pisces will find the time to take a trip. This will be a chance to relax from both work and household responsibilities.

Health. In January, you are feeling energetic and have no reason to fear falling ill.

.

February

New York Time				London Time		
Calendar Day	Lunar Day	Lunar Day Start Time		Calendar Day	Lunar Day	Lunar Day Start Time
01/02/2023	12	1:38 PM		01/02/2023	12	12:48 PM
02/02/2023	13	2:30 PM		02/02/2023	13	1:39 PM
03/02/2023	14	3:26 PM		03/02/2023	14	2:37 PM
04/02/2023	15	4:24 PM		04/02/2023	15	3:41 PM
05/02/2023	16	5:23 PM		05/02/2023	16	4:47 PM
06/02/2023	17	6:22 PM		06/02/2023	17	5:54 PM
07/02/2023	18	7:22 PM		07/02/2023	18	7:02 PM
08/02/2023	19	8:22 PM		08/02/2023	19	8:10 PM
09/02/2023	20	9:22 PM		09/02/2023	20	9:19 PM
10/02/2023	21	10:24 PM		10/02/2023	21	10:28 PM
11/02/2023	22	11:27 PM		11/02/2023	22	11:40 PM
13/02/2023	23	12:33 AM		13/02/2023	23	12:54 AM
14/02/2023	24	1:40 AM		14/02/2023	24	2:09 AM
15/02/2023	25	2:46 AM		15/02/2023	25	3:22 AM
16/02/2023	26	3:50 AM		16/02/2023	26	4:28 AM
17/02/2023	27	4:47 AM		17/02/2023	27	5:24 AM
18/02/2023	28	5:36 AM		18/02/2023	28	6:09 AM
19/02/2023	29	6:19 AM		19/02/2023	29	6:44 AM
20/02/2023	1	2:09 AM		20/02/2023	1	7:09 AM
20/02/2023	2	6:55 AM		20/02/2023	2	7:11 AM
21/02/2023	3	7:28 AM		21/02/2023	3	7:35 AM
22/02/2023	4	7:58 AM		22/02/2023	4	7:56 AM
23/02/2023	5	8:28 AM		23/02/2023	5	8:16 AM
24/02/2023	6	8:59 AM		24/02/2023	6	8:38 AM
25/02/2023	7	9:32 AM		25/02/2023	7	9:02 AM
26/02/2023	8	10:08 AM		26/02/2023	8	9:30 AM
27/02/2023	9	10:49 AM		27/02/2023	9	10:03 AM
28/02/2023	10	11:34 AM		28/02/2023	10	10:44 AM

You can find the description of each lunar day in the chapter "A Guide to The Moon Cycle and Lunar Days"

Aries

You do what you think you need to do, and follow your heart, too. But there's no better feeling than when both things coincide!

Work. The various challenges you took on in 2022 are either resolved or close to a favorable end. You are once again turning to things you had put off and making future plans. You are sure to see positive, long-term, and impressive results.

Right now, you have support from many people, and you are looking for the right people, new partners, and renewing old ties in February.

Difficult relationships with colleagues in other cities or abroad will finally become predictable this month. You might even have constructive negotiations and a successful trip. You are likely to pick up some old partnerships too, right where you left off.

By turning to some old friends for support, employees find themselves accomplishing remarkable things. That means either a promotion where you are or an entirely new job. Hold onto your hats! Your time has come!

The best time for any work-related events is from February 1 to 23. The last week of the month will be less active and better for reflecting on everything you have learned.

Money. Financially speaking, February is a time of ups and downs and contradictions. You will have money, but there are no escaping expenses. There is not much you can do to avoid this. After all, change is never free.

If you are not part of the working world and do not have your own business, you will find yourself spending many of your resources on friends, loved ones, and children. Keep in mind that your expenses this month will be useful, and even pleasurable.

Love and family. Your family situation is also stabilizing. Thorny issues related to your relatives are nearly resolved, and you might take a trip and see family members who live in other cities or abroad.

Minor disagreements are likely during the first 10 days of February, but they will be favorably resolved in the second half of the month.

Couples can expect some hiccups during the first 10 days of the month. Some old wounds may rear their heads again, and you will be forced to get to the very root of your problems. You will manage, though you should try to manage any personal issues with kid gloves. Of course, that advice is good any time, especially for you!

Single people can expect a fateful encounter, and it is most likely to take place while you are traveling or among people from far away.

Health. During February, you are healthy, energetic, and ready to move mountains. During the last few days of the month, however, all the hecticness may finally catch up with you, leaving you feeling fatigued.

Taurus

A long, brilliant path is opening up just ahead. A new, promising future lies ahead, but you need to be 100% ready for it!

Work. February is one of the busiest months of 2023 for you. You will have a lot of work to do, and monumental tasks, but this will pay off in dividends. In the coming months, business owners and managers will need to grapple with a lot of work, most of them will be related to restructuring and preparing your business for new projects already looming on the horizon.

Both employees and business owners are advised to toe the line when dealing with managers and the powers that be. If you show too much ambition during the first and last 10 days of the month, it might be misinterpreted and lead to trouble. You want to avoid any problems right now, so avoid letting any minor ambitions or petty misunderstandings cast a shadow on your success.

Many Taureans are thinking about buying real estate and taking major steps in that direction. In some cases, which will be related to expanding your business.

Money. Your bank account is looking good this month. You have more money coming in, and that is directly related to your success at work.

During the first and last weeks of the month, you are likely to run into some major expenses, but you will still find yourself in the black once the month is over.

Expect the largest sums of money to come in on February 1, 10, 11, 18, 19, 27, and 28.

Love and family. In many families, the main event this month will be acquiring new real estate, major repairs, construction, and other tasks related to your living space. For now, things are still in the planning stage, but they will come to life very soon.

Couples will find themselves going through a rough patch. During the first 10 days of February, you may experience conflicts, and you may even decide to just exit stage left – there is a limit to how many problems and how much heartache one can take. The ball is in your court, but if you feel worse without your partner than with them, you might just give it another go. Your thoughts and feelings are stuck in the past, but that won't be forever!

Health. In February, you are feeling energetic and have no reason to fear falling ill.

The elderly or those weakened by chronic illness are advised to take care of themselves and find the time to relax, since all year long you will have to be responsible for your own body!

Gemini

You will reach a turning point in February. Any doubts and hesitations will be a thing of the past, and the road to the future lies ahead – and this time, there are no potholes or speed bumps.

Work.

You are on a positive streak at work. You can expect a new job or major project, soon. That might be in the next two or three months, but you are already attending negotiations, meetings, and taking the necessary steps to prepare for it in February.

Your relationships with partners in other cities or abroad are moving along nicely, and you might be involved in promising negotiations or a successful trip.

Despite the fact that this month is busy and full of success, be careful during the first 10 days – you might run into some minor difficulties with management or partners from other cities or abroad. If you are planning on traveling, the best time would be mid-February or the end of the month. The period from February 2 to 7 is not particularly auspicious. Petty disagreements may pop up from February 21 to 23. The main significance of any work-related events this month will involve friends or friendly, highly placed individuals. Their support will be *sine qua non.*

Money. Despite the positive developments at work, when it comes to money, you can expect a lot of problems this month. Your income will not be particularly high, but you will still have enough to live on.

Your expenses will be fairly typical in February and involve travel, relationships with friends, fulfilling your obligations – all of this is hard on your wallet.

Expect some money to come in on February 2, 3, 13, 14, and 20-22.

Love and family. Don't expect any huge shifts in your personal life this month. Separated couples may come to feel some pangs of regret but are still unlikely to reconcile. Don't expect to meet anyone new right now – but the time will come, and soon.

Many Geminis will travel this month, and that is likely to turn out well. You may see old friends who live in other cities or abroad, or relax in the company of some fascinating people

Couples who get along may count on taking a trip together somewhere far from home, and even if you experienced some minor quarrels in the past, they will soon vanish without a trace.

Health. This month, you are feeling much more energetic than before, and if you experienced any illnesses recently, you can expect a speedy recovery.

The stars recommend being careful when traveling or driving from February 2 to 6, and also from the 21st to the 26th.

If you do not have any pressing need to travel then, whether for work or personal life, it is best to postpone your trip to another time.

Cancer

It is not worth rushing things this month. The planets are together and lined up, and each one has a gift for you. However, you will need to get ready for that, both physically and spiritually, and that is your task for February.

Work. February is an excellent time to relax and handle various administrative tasks. You can calmly get your affairs in order and lay the groundwork for a busier period, which will begin in late February or March.

Your relationship with colleagues from other cities or abroad is moving along nicely, and you might take a successful trip.

Though this is a relatively calm and overall successful period, during the first 10 days of the month, you might have to deal with problems from the past. They may involve unresolved legal issues, or possibly minor difficulties with colleagues from far away.

Be careful and do not let problems from the past influence your life today. Take things as they come, and don't forget to cross your T's and dot your I's.

Money. Your financial situation is improving, but the past may rear its ugly head every now and again. You may find yourself paying off old debts or friends to whom you owe a favor.

You will also be spending on your family and your children's needs, as well as those of loved ones, and close to the end of the month, your bank balance may end up in the red.

Expect the largest sums to come in on February 4-6, 14, 15, 23, and 24.

Love and family. Things are moving ahead nicely in your personal life. Your relationship with your spouse or partner is stable, and even if you run into a few disagreements, which is very likely in early February, they won't ruin the rest of the month. The cause of these arguments will be opposing views over your living space, jealousy, and general resentment.

By mid-February, you will have resolved all of this favorably, and life will be back to normal.

Many Cancers will find the time to relax in February and head somewhere far away or just spend time doing as they see fit.

Single people and those who have been let down by love in the past might count on an interesting encounter this month. Whether or not it turns into a romance depends on you, but there is a chance of things lasting.

Health. This month, you are feeling sluggish, so lead a healthy lifestyle and chose nearby destinations as much as you can when traveling.

Leo

Life is constantly moving forward, and that is clearer than ever in February. The obstacle course is over, or at least things are likely to be much calmer.

Work. You will constantly be in the limelight in February. Meetings and negotiations will be endless, and overall, everything will turn out well enough. However, some people may deal with arguments, once again due to differing views on business, or some sort of financial obligations.

Employees may disagree with managers or the powers that be, and this time, it is not worth digging your heels in. Avoid being sharp or bossy, and instead tame your pride and listen to your foes.

All relationships will become difficult during the first 10 days of the month, and the way things pan out is still to be seen. In any case, you are on the cusp of a new, relatively positive period – though it won't begin until April or May. For now, it is worth remaining modest.

Money. Financially speaking, February is full of ups and downs. On one hand, you might have some money coming in, but you will also have to settle some debts and fulfill your various responsibilities, both moral and financial. Expect the largest expenses to take place during the first 10 days of the month, and for some money to come in on February 7, 8, 16, 17, 25, and 26.

Love and family. When it comes to your personal life, February is a challenge, to say the least. Warring couples will find themselves arguing for the umpteenth time, and those who get along will face conflicts with those close to them.

Couples who are dating will also find that things are not quite working out as planned. Aggressive Mars is in conflict with the planet of love, Venus, and this may be reflected in your relationship becoming more complicated. Misunderstandings, jealousy, and demands of one another are to be expected. If that describes you, try to keep a cool head and don't let emotions run your life.

These recommendations are particularly important for those whose relationship is merely hanging by a thread. This time, that thread may finally snap, leaving you all alone. If that doesn't sound so scary, after all, then do what you feel you need to. In any case, the ball is in your court, and the stars have your back. There are a lot of fish in the sea, after all.

Health. This month, you are feeling a bit down, so take extra steps to care of yourself.

Virgo

The changes continue, both at work and at home, though your life is looking much more calm, predictable, and like something you can handle. The chaos you felt before is now a thing of the past.

Work. February moves quickly, and you will be busy and productive. Business owners and managers of every level are likely to be preparing for some changes in their business. Everything you do in February will have a major impact on your professional status and become the cornerstone of your future success.

Real estate transactions will turn out in your favor, and that is directly related to expanding or reorienting your business.

In some cases, you may be planning to expand to other cities or abroad.

Employees will find that their employers are restructuring this month. In some cases, they will remain where they are, while in others, they may soon find themselves seeking a better place for their talents, and it is worth taking that into consideration this month.

Despite the positive and relatively productive atmosphere in February, during the first 10 days of the month, you may run into some obstacles. That may be due to business partners in other cities or abroad, or possibly involve resolving legal disputes. In either case, however, the quandary is sure to be resolved in your favor.

Money. In February, your finances are looking strong. You will have a steady income, and noticeably more of it. Expect the largest sums to come in on February 1, 10, 11, 18, 27, and 28. Your expenses are low, reasonable, and predictable.

Love and family. In your personal life, your partner will take initiative this month. If he or she suggests moving to a new home, apartment, or abroad, so be it. Real estate transactions will be at the top of many families' agendas.

The first 10 days of the month are likely to present some challenges for you emotionally. During this time, spouses may have opposing views of various domestic issues, and experience differing moods, as well. Things will get complicated if you have a history of misunderstandings or shared business.

In other cases, you may be grappling with jealousy or different demands of one another. Expect some knock-down, drag-out fights during the first 10 days of the month, which will then fade into nothing.

The situation is similar for unmarried couples.

Children are a source of happiness, and they are experiencing positive changes in their own lives. Many families will be expecting new children or grandchildren.

Health. In February, you are feeling a bit tired, but this will not cause any serious trouble, as long as you lead an exceedingly healthy lifestyle and take utmost care of yourself. February is a great time to quit any bad habits or undergo any wellness procedures.

Libra

February is a time of great beginnings, achievements, and decisive steps in all directions. Buckle up and hold on tight!

Work. This month, you will finally find yourself on an even path as you develop your ideas and projects. Business owners and managers of every level can count on successful negotiations with people with whom you recently found yourself in a deadlock. This most likely involves colleagues from other cities and abroad, who have been behaving unintelligently, if not with outright hostility for some time. Now, you are likely to finally reach an agreement with them. The best time for this is the last 20 days of the month.

During the first 10 days of the month, expect less success, and possible disagreements over work-related issues, which you will overcome sometime later. You might bring in intermediaries or allies to help you with this, though remember your opponents may do the same. Things are sure to improve in any case and knowing that is already a lot.

Another source of difficulty in February may be your relationship with a subordinate, and any manager or person responsible for major projects should take that into account. They may not be carrying out your instructions and ideas, which is sure to harm your business.

Alternatively, you may simply have to take on some of the work yourself.

Business travel planned for February will turn out very favorably.

Money. Financially speaking, February is relatively neutral. Your income is stable, and your expenses are modest and reasonable.

Much of your spending this month is likely to be related to your home, family, and children's needs.

Love and family. There are a lot of developments in your personal life, right now. Parents are still concerned about their children. A lot of your family budget may go toward them.

Your relationship with a relative, and possibly someone who was close to you in the past, may be less than ideal. However, you will make some progress, here, and gradually, the major disagreement will be resolved, and things will return to normal.

Couples will have a rough first 10 days of the month, and conflict between Mars and Venus may lead to arguments, disappointment, and taking offense. Get through this period, and the heavens will eventually calm down and look quite differently.

Single people and those who have been disappointed in the past are sure to meet someone new. You might have a torrid affair, and if you are ready for a long-term, stable relationship, nothing is stopping you, either.

Health. You are healthy in February, energetic, and leaving a great impression on everyone fate throws your way. During the first 10 days of the month, be careful when traveling or driving.

Scorpio

This month, time will move more slowly, and you will be more preoccupied with your family. If you feel like relaxing, now is the time! The work will always be there, tomorrow.

Work. Incurable workaholics will get a lot done, this month. For example, you might get your office in order and conduct various real estate transactions. You might also resolve financial issues, whether closing out debts or handling previous obligations.

New business and responsibilities are also on the horizon. If you already know about that, nothing is stopping you from calmly preparing for a major leap, which you can expect to take in March or April 2023.

Your relationship with various partners has been difficult in the past, and that may be due to real estate or other large property. This time, however, things are looking calmer and much more surmountable.

Money. Your finances are seeing a lot of ups and downs – you are spending a lot on your children's and loved ones' needs. You won't find yourself broke, however, as you will continue to see a regular income that is sufficient to meet all of your needs.

Love and family. In many cases, the major events this month will take place at home and within your family. Couples who get along might be busy improving their home, investing time, money, and resources in the endeavor.

Your children are a source of joy, but their development and education require a lot of resources, too. This is necessary and important, and if you don't handle it, who will?

Unmarried couples can expect the first 10 days of February to be a difficult time, and they may experience emotional outbursts, misunderstandings, and arguments. The stars recommend not taking it to heart and believing that all things will fall into place. And they will.

Health. In February, you are not particularly energetic. You need to take care of your body and take any measures you need to avoid any winter colds and infections.

Sagittarius

Your colorful life will once again be stable and predictable this month. That doesn't have to mean it is boring, though! Quite the contrary! You are busy and dynamic as ever, and once again charging ahead!

Work. You are on a positive streak at work. Difficult relationships with partners have been keeping you up at night for some time, now, but they are now resolved, and favorably. The best time for this is the last 20 days of the month. During the first 10 days, you may encounter arguments related to large property, land, or real estate. Somewhat later, closer to the middle or end of the month, things will calm down.

You are seeing a lot more of colleagues from other cities or abroad in February, and you may take a trip that changes the nature of that relationship, for the better, of course.

If you are offered a new job or new project this month, it is worth taking. New offers will be large-scale and labor-intensive, but they will bring you accolades and respect.

Money. Financially speaking, February is a good time for you. You will be making regular income, and slightly more of it, too. Of course, there is no way to escape expenses, but most of them will be pleasurable, anyway. Travel, seeing others, and satisfying the needs of your home, children, and loved ones do not come cheap. Remember, that is what money is for. The best investment you can make is in children, friends, and loved ones.

Love and family. Your personal life is busy this month, but not easy. Fighting couples might once again find themselves arguing over shared property, likely their residence, during the first 10 days of the month.

This is nothing new. Things are closer to a favorable resolution, but the warring parties are going to have to stop, take a deep breath, and a long, hard look at the problem at hand.

Couples who get along may have a difficult time resolving issues related to home improvement, this month.

Your children are a source of joy, and positive changes are on the horizon in their lives, in the near future.

Single people can count on a torrid affair this month, though its end depends only on your current plans and intentions.

Many Sagittarians will enjoy sudden popularity and find themselves in-demand in both wider and closer circles.

Trips planned for February are likely to be extremely successful, especially if they take place during the last 20 days of the month.

Health. All month long, you will be dynamic, energetic, and very attractive, and everyone fate sends your way will notice.

Capricorn

Once again, money is on your mind. Here, there is nothing you can do about it – for you, material success is a must.

Work. This month, many Capricorns are consumed with the busywork of expanding their business, especially upper-level managers and business owners. However, not everything will go as planned. During the first 10 days of February, you can expect petty work-related disagreements and conflicts with colleagues and subordinates.

Those planning to do business with partners from other cities or abroad will face obstacles during this time.

These issues are unlikely to have lasting consequences, and during the last 20 days of the month, they are sure to be favorably resolved.

Employees might argue with gossipy colleagues during the first 10 days of the month. The stars remind you that silence is golden and avoid adding to the intrigue – it's better this way.

During the last 20 days of the month, things are much more promising. Many of your problems will disappear, and your work will continue to move forward in your favor.

Money. February is a good time for your wallet. Money will be coming in regularly, and you will have enough of it to cover your growing expenses.

Expect the largest sums to come in on February 1, 9-11, 18, 19, 27, and 28.

The largest expenses will take placed during the first few days of the month, and the stars predict that they will mostly be related to your children's needs.

Love and family. Your personal life will be sharply focused on your living space, this month. Many Capricorns will be busy with home improvements, whether for themselves or their children. You may also acquire more real estate.

Unmarried couples will go through a rough patch until February 10. Arguments are likely, and you may be the cause. Try to keep a lid on your emotions and avoid throwing any temper tantrums. At least remember that your actions have consequences.

During the first 10 days of the month, you may experience problems when it comes to your relatives. The cause may be something that came up in the recent past, so there is nothing new here.

For various reasons, trips planned for the first 10 days of February might not take place or might turn out differently than you had expected.

Health. For most of February, you are feeling sluggish, so try to take care of yourself and lead a healthy lifestyle.

Aquarius

February is a great time for communicating and resolving major issues, both at home and at work. Take the reins and move down your chosen path.

Work. The last 20 days of February is the best time for anything work-related. During this time, you are capable of anything. Expect the most success during arguments, negotiations, and discussions – you will be able to shift any situation to your advantage.

Your relationship with colleagues in other cities or abroad is moving along nicely, and you might take a successful trip.

Those hoping to open a business in another city or abroad might see their dreams come true. In other cases, you may already have a business located far away, and suddenly feel the drive to grow it further.

If you want to try something new, launch a new career, or seek happiness somewhere else, you might start making plans. In some cases, they may not come to fruition until April or May, but the boldest steps will begin this month.

Employees will begin an easy, but very successful streak at work – they are gaining both responsibility and respect.

Money. Financially speaking, February is a rather favorable month. Money will be coming in regularly, and you will even have somewhat more of it.

Venus, the planet of small joys, will spend most of the month in the financial sector of your sky, which always means small, but very pleasant material surprises.

Expect the largest sums to come in on February 2, 3, 12, 13, and 20-22.

Most of your expenses will take place during the first 10 days of the month, and the astrologist predicts that they will be related to your personal life, children, and loved ones' needs.

Love and family. Your personal life is looking positive in February. You may experience some minor disagreement during the first 10 days of the month, but they are sure to be resolved favorably. During this time, many Aquarians will be busy with issues related to real estate, and this may look very differently, depending on what took place in your recent past.

During the last 10 days of the month, single people can count on meeting someone new, and that is likely to take place while traveling or among people from far away.

February is also a time of great creativity. The last 10 days of the month are very promising for anyone who works with words – writers, journalists, or comedians. Wherever you are in the world, you will stand out for your wit and sense of humor, and anyone fate sends your way is taking note.

Health. This month, your energy is right where it needs to be, and you have no reason to fear falling ill. This is a great time for any cosmetic procedures, updating your wardrobe, or changing up your entire image.

Pisces

You are about to begin a calm, romantic, and even sensual month. Indulge in relaxation, good friends, and anything else your sensitive soul desires.

Work. If you want to busy yourself with work this month, or simply can't get away from it, you will be able to calmly deal whatever comes your way.

Managers and business owners should keep in mind that during the first 10 days of February, they may face various problems with partners from other cities or abroad, or see old legal issues suddenly rear their heads once again. These inconveniences will not have any significant consequences, but they will remind you of some problems in your recent past.

The last 20 days of the month, things are looking up. You will be busiest and most successful from February 20 to 28. You may expect new job offers or invitations to conduct new business.

Money. February is kind to your finances. You will have regular income, and significantly more of it during the last 10 days of the month. During this time, Jupiter and Venus, the most favorable planets in the sky, will be in the financial sector of your sky, which means that you may see a windfall. Buy a lottery ticket, go to the races, or otherwise test the capricious financial Fortune!

Love and family. February is a positive time for your personal life. Couples, whether married or not, may be focused on their future home, and though some roadblocks are likely during the first 10 days of the month, they will not cast a shadow over the atmosphere of the entire month.

Your relationship with relatives will improve significantly this month, and you are likely to be the one leading the charge. If you recently had a sudden argument or a relationship has cooled, you will be able to fix things.

Any trips planned for February will be very successful. Overall, February will be harmonious and calm, allowing you to smooth over all of the ups and downs of a very difficult 2022.

Health. You are feeling a little less energetic this month, and that will be especially noticeable during the Full Moon on February 4-5. Elderly people and those who are weakened are advised to take it easy and take care of themselves during this time. Those who are young and healthy should keep in mind that our bodies are especially vulnerable during the last month right before our birthdays.

This is the time to be kind to yourself, break any bad habits, visit a cosmetologist, massage therapist, and, if you can, visit a health resort or spa.

March

New York Time			London Time		
Calendar Day	Lunar Day	Lunar Day Start Time	Calendar Day	Lunar Day	Lunar Day Start Time
01/03/2023	11	12:24 PM	01/03/2023	11	11:33 AM
02/03/2023	12	1:19 PM	02/03/2023	12	12:29 PM
03/03/2023	13	2:16 PM	03/03/2023	13	1:31 PM
04/03/2023	14	3:15 PM	04/03/2023	14	2:36 PM
05/03/2023	15	4:15 PM	05/03/2023	15	3:44 PM
06/03/2023	16	5:14 PM	06/03/2023	16	4:52 PM
07/03/2023	17	6:15 PM	07/03/2023	17	6:00 PM
08/03/2023	18	7:15 PM	08/03/2023	18	7:09 PM
09/03/2023	19	8:17 PM	09/03/2023	19	8:19 PM
10/03/2023	20	9:20 PM	10/03/2023	20	9:31 PM
11/03/2023	21	10:25 PM	11/03/2023	21	10:44 PM
13/03/2023	22	12:31 AM	12/03/2023	22	11:58 PM
14/03/2023	23	1:37 AM	14/03/2023	23	1:11 AM
15/03/2023	24	2:40 AM	15/03/2023	24	2:18 AM
16/03/2023	25	3:37 AM	16/03/2023	25	3:16 AM
17/03/2023	26	4:28 AM	17/03/2023	26	4:03 AM
18/03/2023	27	5:12 AM	18/03/2023	27	4:41 AM
19/03/2023	28	5:50 AM	19/03/2023	28	5:10 AM
20/03/2023	29	6:23 AM	20/03/2023	29	5:35 AM
21/03/2023	30	6:54 AM	21/03/2023	30	5:57 AM
21/03/2023	1	1:26 PM	21/03/2023	1	5:26 PM
22/03/2023	2	7:24 AM	22/03/2023	2	6:17 AM
23/03/2023	3	7:55 AM	23/03/2023	3	6:38 AM
24/03/2023	4	8:27 AM	24/03/2023	4	7:01 AM
25/03/2023	5	9:03 AM	25/03/2023	5	7:28 AM
26/03/2023	6	9:43 AM	26/03/2023	6	9:00 AM
27/03/2023	7	10:27 AM	27/03/2023	7	9:38 AM
28/03/2023	8	11:16 AM	28/03/2023	8	10:25 AM
29/03/2023	9	12:10 PM	29/03/2023	9	11:19 AM
30/03/2023	10	1:07 PM	30/03/2023	10	12:19 PM
31/03/2023	11	2:05 PM	31/03/2023	11	1:24 PM

You can find the description of each lunar day in the chapter "A Guide to The Moon Cycle and Lunar Days"

Aries

March is usually not a very good month for you – but this year is an exception! The stars are aligned, and Venus and Jupiter are both in your sign – that could be better?

Work. For the most part, March is a time for relaxing, making family-related decisions, and romance. However, if you are an incurable workaholic and, in your world, work comes first, you will still be able to accomplish a lot for your own business, even during this fairly lazy month.

The best time for any work-related events is the first or last 10 days of the month, when you will be able to make decent money, hold necessary meetings, and surround yourself with like-minded individuals, or simply the right people.

During the second 10 days of March, things are not so rosy. During this time, you might receive unpleasant news from a colleague from another city or abroad, and it may involve gossip or outright deceit.

During this time, much of what your partners or opponents would like to keep under the table might come to light, and you will find yourself dealing with it during the last 10 days of the month, which promise to be more favorable. However, you are in a strong position – in the end, you will achieve clarity and assert your own rules in the game of life.

Employees might also face trouble at work. During the middle of the month, you are likely to face unexpected audits, which will throw a wrench in your usual working process. However, everything will turn out just fine, as the last 10 days of March are expected to be a quiet, calm time.

Any business travel should be planned for the first 20 days of the month.

Money. Financially, March is a very favorable time for you. You will have regular income, and you might receive some unexpected surprises, too. This is especially the case for the first and last 10 days of the month.

Love and family. March is a very positive time for your personal life, as well. It is the perfect time for relaxing with your family, relatives, and loved ones. You might plan a trip for a week or two to get away from work, gain new perspective, and restore your body and soul.

This is also a great time for single people – your chances of meeting your soulmate are very high this month! Your time has come!

Your relationship with relatives may grow more complicated once again, and that is most likely during the second 10 days of the month, when some family members' secrets suddenly emerge. Later on, however, you will be able to smooth things over thanks to your own efforts.

Any leisure travel should be planned for the first or last 10 days of the month. If your plans overlap with the second, more difficult 10 days of March, be careful with your documents and try to avoid any jaunts to difficult, dangerous destinations.

Health. As usual, your energy is lagging in March. If you take care to lead a healthy lifestyle, however, there is no reason to fear.

March is also the ideal time for any cosmetic procedures or plastic surgery.

During the second 10 days of the month, take extra care when traveling or driving.

Taurus

March is a great time for bringing your plans to life, whether at home or at work! Dive right in!

Work. This month will bring you a lot of luck. It is a time to bring your ideas to people who have the power and influence to make them happen, and to bring on friends and other like-minded people. Remember, everything you do in March will have a long-term positive impact, so *carpe diem!*

The best time for anything work-related is the first and last 10 days of the month, when you will receive all the support you need, both officially and behind the scenes – and the latter may most effective.

The second ten days of March will bring some disagreements with a friend or like-minded individual. The problem may be financial in nature, but you will manage to fix things immediately.

Employees may receive promises for a future promotion, and some time later, this will come to fruition.

Money. March promises a lot of financial ups and downs. On one hand, you will not find yourself broke, but you will also have some major expenses. You may have to pay back old debts, help a friend out, or give into the demands of someone with power and social influence.

On the other hand, some of your hard-earned cash may go toward parties or birthday celebrations, which are sure to be plentiful in March. Naturally, there is also no escaping expenses related to your home, children, or family.

You will not find yourself ruined, however, as money will continue to come in, both from official sources and somewhat more through unofficial channels.

Love and family. March is also a good month for your personal life. Those with families will be busy with home improvements, and right now, you will manage to get through the fussy details quickly, without any setbacks or obstacles in your way.

Single people and those who are dissatisfied with their personal life can count on a new romance, which you will keep a secret from those around you.

Those with a stable partner will be delighted with their children's success, and may will think about expanding their family. The best time for this is the last 10 days of March.

Health. In March, you are healthy, energetic, and attractive to everyone Fate sends your way. You will not start to feel any fatigue from this busy period until after the New Moon on March 21-23, so try to relax a bit more during this period, and make sure you get enough sleep.

Gemini

March is a positive and somewhat unusual month for you. During this time, you will be able to channel your energy – and right now you have plenty of it – into achieving your most important ideas. Success is coming your way, and Fortune is on your side!

Work. March is one of the best months of the year for you at work. This is a great time to launch large-scale projects, and also to make new friends. This is the case for all Geminis, regardless of their field. Employees can count on a promotion right where they are, or an entirely new job at a larger, more promising organization.

Someone highly placed in society might play an important role in your life this month. His or her support will be timely, effective, and most importantly, provided in good faith.

There's no way to avoid it – March is a time when your professional dreams become reality. Keep that in mind and aim higher!

Your relationship with colleagues from other cities or abroad is developing with mixed success – some things are going well, others are not. Most of your disagreements will take place in mid-March, before everything falls into place. Any travel planned for March is sure to leave you feeling satisfied.

Money. March is also a good month for your bank account. You will have a regular income, somewhat higher than previously.

Expect the largest sums to come in on March 1-3, 11-13, 20, 21, 29, and 30.

Some of your expenses this month might be typical, but alternatively, you might find yourself spending on friends, nights out, and romantic dates.

Those with families will be spending on their children, their development, and education. All of your expenses in March will either be pleasant or serve an important purpose.

Love and family. March will have a strong focus on your professional and social life, and you may not have much time left over for your personal life. However, people who live for love, and those who have been looking for a partner for some time might count on an interesting encounter that is likely to brighten their life. That person might be part of your circle of friends or a new job.

Alternatively, you may start to see an old friend in a different, more romantic light. In short, there will be opportunities, and it is up to you how you use them.

Those with families will be delighted to see their children succeed and enjoy a positive streak.

Health. This month, you are bounding with energy, and this will only become more apparent the more active you are. The word "tired" might just vanish from your vocabulary altogether. In any case, be careful traveling or behind the wheel from March 16 to 18.

Cancer

This month, you may find yourself spreading your wings. Use them to grab the bull by the horns and steer things in the right direction. Things haven't been so good for you in a long time, so be bold as you charge forward and don't look back!

Work. Your professional future is looking up this month. The chances of seeing your ideas come to life are high, but this time things will be different. The dark days have come to an end!

Managers and business owners might strengthen old ties with colleagues in other cities or abroad, and make new contacts, as well.

During the first and last ten days of the month, you may see some important agreements and contract signed. They may continue into the future and symbolize a new era in your professional life, which is sure to be much more exciting and successful.

Employees are highly likely to find the job of their dreams and dive right in. Over the next several months, you will be so busy that you will simply not have any free time for other things.

But nothing is ever perfect, not even at work. The fly in the ointment may be problems from the past rearing their ugly heads once again. Each specific case may look differently – it may be legal issues, or possibly related to old debts.

In any case, however, you have already addressed the most acute matters, and all you have to do is keep cool while you put everything else in order. Be careful during the second 10 days of March!

Money. March is a decent month for your finances, and most importantly, there are many very real possibilities ahead.

Expect the largest sums to come in in March 4, 5, 13-15, 22, 23, and 31.

Your expenses are low, predictable, and reasonable.

Love and family. Not much is happening in your personal life, for now. Couples who get along will be making future plans and elated at the possibilities that lay before them. This is the case whether you are married or not.

Happy couples might take a trip together, which will bring them closer together.

You might meet some new and interesting people, but these relationships are unlikely to grow into anything beyond friendship.

Romantic liaisons are also a real possibility this month, but they may end up being work-related. In some cases, your supervisor's attention may go beyond a professional relationship. Only you will know whether that is a good thing or not.

Health. This month, you are healthy, energetic, and have no reason to fear falling ill. If you had a serious illness in the fall and winter, you may still be grappling with some of the effects. Mid-March is the most difficult time for you, and you are likely to feel worse.

Be very careful when driving a car or traveling. During the second 10 days of the month, you are highly likely to run into some unpleasant surprises.

Leo

All month long, you might feel strongly dependent on your environment, and also on people whose views are hostile and in contrast to your own. Don't wallow in it, however, this is only temporary. Freedom is looming on the horizon.

Work. March is full of contradictions at work. The astrologist sees you on a difficult dividing line. You might need to take a break rather than running forward. This is always a good idea when you finish one task and begin another.

It will be easier to step into the future if you first deal with the past. You might find that early spring is the perfect time to do just that.

Business owners and managers will begin difficult negotiations on shared business or projects, as well as related financial matters.

One new and fresh aspect of this process will involve developing strong ties with colleagues in other cities or abroad. In 2023, it is worth betting on these relationships and developing your business with their assistance.

Employees might take some time off or a few days to busy themselves with a new job search. You won't have to wait!

The best time for anything work-related is the first or last 10 days of March. During the second 10 days, you might see problems from earlier months rearing their heads once again. They may involve financial or moral claims from like-minded individuals, friends, or the powers that be. Fortunately, this unpleasant situation is unlikely to last long, and with worst already behind you, you will be able to resolve them in the near future.

Money. March is a very difficult time for you, financially speaking. Many Leos will have to settle old debts and set aside money for a new future. In cases of conflicts with partners over shared business, it is worth thinking about giving up your share in exchange for fair financial compensation. The stars recommend that you keep things simple and avoid dragging grudges into the future.

Expect to spend the largest sums of money from March 12 to 20, before things improve.

You may receive some help in the form of real estate transactions, loans, or credit.

Love and family. Those who are dedicated to the home may spend the entire month busy with household problems. If you are planning a move, you are likely to be immersed in various real estate transactions.

Any sale, exchange, or acquisition may be of equal interest to those who are planning a move abroad, as well as those simply moving to a new home.

Alternatively, you might complete major repairs.

If you recently had a serious argument or breakup, these issues may be related to the separation, division of property, or, most likely, seeking a new residence.

Health. During the first 20 days of March, you are feeling a bit sluggish, and you might experience fatigue, exhaustion, or anxiety. During this time, be kind to yourself and avoid any infections or colds. During the last 10 days of the month, you will perk up.

Virgo

This month, you are still between a rock and a hard place. The ball is in other people's court. Be a team player if you can, and if you can't, wait for an opportunity to move forward on your own.

Work. You are looking down a month full of meetings and active networking. You will be busy negotiating with partners, and the topic at hand may be future business development or financial in nature.

Business owners and managers at every level might be striving to expand their business and seek out new resources for this endeavor.

Your efforts will pan out – during the first and last 10 days of the month, you can count on constructive negotiations and a nice amount of money.

During the second 10 days of March, you may run into minor disagreements with partners about your business organization, but by the last 10 days, this will be a thing of the past.

Employees are likely to encounter disagreements with management, competitors, and problems on their team during the second 10 days of March. The stars recommend avoiding any open confrontation. The results will be better if you tread lightly and remain diplomatic.

The most important events in March will be related to colleagues from other cities or abroad – you might be developing a lot of ideas with their direct participation and support.

Any travel planned for this month will be a success.

Money. March is a great time for your finances, but the money in question is unlikely to be yours. Rather, you can count on financial support from partners, beneficial loans, or successful credit transactions.

Those who are not part of the working world will receive financial support from a loved one, parents, or a spouse. You might also profit from a successful real estate transaction.

Love and family. Your personal life is very busy this month.

Couples who get along will be busy working on their home and with various real estate transactions. Many will be planning a move – perhaps to a new home, or, more extravagantly, to another city or even abroad. If this is the case, March is a great month to get ready for this massive undertaking. Your loved one will be able to manage a lot and take on a great deal.

Things will turn out somewhat differently for those who recently decided to separate or divorce. You will spend March deciding who owes whom what. The stars predict you will be pleased with the outcome.

Health. This month, you are feeling a bit under the weather, and those who are elderly or weakened should be particularly cautious. Take care of yourself and if you need to, see a specialist and avoid trying to be your own doctor.

Libra

March is an unusual month for you. There is no better time to unravel some of your life's most complicated mysteries, intrigue, or anything analytic! In short, you are playing Sherlock Holmes more than just a little!

Work. In March, you will have to figure out how to fulfill the responsibilities you have taken on and how to get your partners to follow through with what they promised you. At first glance, it seems simple – you have plenty of well-wishers, strong arguments, and the facts are on your side.

Though it's smooth sailing during the first 10 days of the month, with no setbacks or problems, during the second 10 days, things will suddenly become more difficult. Most likely, the problems will involve partners from other cities or abroad whose hostility has been palpable for some time. This time, you will once again have to respond to various demands, workplace misunderstandings, and other issues that you cannot ignore.

This time, however, things will be resolved quickly – by the last 10 days of March, expect calm waters once again.

Managers and business owners are advised to keep an eye on their subordinates. You might have to overhaul your team and get rid of those who are not willing to support you. The sooner, the better off you will be.

Money. March is not particularly exciting when it comes to your bank account. Your income is stable, and your expenses are low. If you need it, you can count on help from loved ones who are on a successful streak.

Expect the largest sums to come in on March 1-3, 6. 11, 12. 20, 21, 29, and 30.

Love and family. March is a great time for you to tackle any issues in your personal life. Single people and those who have been let down by love in the past can count on a fateful encounter. Let nature take its course, don't try to force anything, and the stars will have your back.

Couples who get along will work together to overcome issues related to relatives who are currently experiencing difficulties.

The second 10 days of the month will be the most challenging, but by the last 10 days, many issues are likely to be resolved in your favor. This may involve your in-laws and your partner playing a key role in smoothing things over.

Any trips planned for March will be a success, especially during the first or last 10 days of the month.

Health. In March, you are not exactly bounding with energy, so lead a healthy lifestyle and take care of yourself to avoid any spring infections or colds.

March is also a great time to quit bad habits, visit a beauty salon, and take some time to enjoy nature. Despite how busy you are, you will be able to find two or three days to relax.

Scorpio

This month, you will have a great opportunity to make some of your ideas happen, as reality and your wishes coincide. That does not happen very often, so don't let it pass you by, luck is on your side!

Work. March is one of the best months of the year for you at work. Entrepreneurs will be busy with new projects, and employees will be considering a new job offer. You are likely to engage in negotiations on this during the first and last 10 days of the month, and you will come out convinced that this is just what you need. Your career is making leaps and bounds, but you are likely to be extremely busy – you have a busy month ahead and will barely even have time to think.

The good news is that you will not have to deal with any major work-related issues of your own, as you already dealt with them long ago.

All month long, you can expect to make new connections at work, which will be both useful and pleasant. Some of them are sure to lend you a hand in the future.

Money. March might be a time of contradictions when it comes to your wallet. You will have an income coming in, but you may find money burning a hole in your pocket. The largest expenses will come during the middle of the month, and the stars predict that they may be related to your children or a loved one.

Expect the largest sums to come in on March 4, 5, 13-15, 22, 23, and 31.

Love and family. March is a great time for your personal life. Single people and those who have been disappointed in the past can expect an affair with a new colleague. This will not cause trouble at work, on the contrary, it will give you more drive than before.

You may finally cut the cord with a former flame, and the second 10 days of March will be the most difficult period, when you can expect conflicts, possibly over opposing worldviews, different value systems, or financial woes.

During the second 10 days of the month, parents may end up spending large amounts of money on their children's needs.

Health. In March, you are healthy, spritely, and unlikely to experience any sickness. If, however, you were seriously ill during the fall and winter of 2022, you need to take extra care. Your ailments may resurface during the second 10 days of March.

Sagittarius

March is sure to be a busy and hectic time for you, but also very positive. You will need to focus on your family, work, and those around you. As a servant of two masters, however, you will manage and, as always, succeed in everything you do!

Work. The stars' influence in March means this is a better time for relaxing and resolving personal issues, though those who can't imagine life without work are advised to slow down a bit and keep cool as you settle professional matters.

During the first 10 days of the month, you might receive new invitations that lead to positive financial results, whether you are an employee or business owner.

During the first and last 10 days of March, you will be busy with meetings, networking, and friendly get-togethers. You can leverage this all for your business – meeting new people, expanding your circle, and meeting people who are both pleasant and useful to you.

Those who work in creative professions will see the most success, as their popularity and influence grow.

Money. March is not bad for your finances. You will have a regular income, in addition, you can also count on some pleasant material surprises. This may be prizes, gifts, or even an unexpected winning lottery ticket.

Love and family. The stars predict that the major events in your life this month will be personal, romantic, or family-related.

Many Sagittarians will meet new people, and they may include a new romance. This will be a torrid, passionate affair, but where will it take you? What is it? A fling, a game, or real love? It is not worth fretting over, at least for now. Enjoying what is in front of you is the best thing you can do.

Those with stable family lives will be delighted by their children's success, as they embark on a successful streak at work.

Many families will welcome new children and grandchildren.

March is also a time of celebrations and fun. You may become very popular and in high demand in your circle, so expect parties, birthday celebrations, and events. The whirlwind of events will take over your life, and you are sure to attract the positive attention of those whose opinion you value. They know, remember, and love you – what could be better?

Spouses who get along might be working on home improvements, and you can expect some minor spats during the second 10 days of the month.

Couples who are divorcing or splitting up may run into past problems resurfacing. This time, things will be settled peacefully, likely because the worst is already behind you. Any loose ends will be dealt with calmly, without arguments, demands, or insults.

Health. This month, you are feeling energetic enough and have no reason to fear falling ill.

April

New York Time			London Time		
Calendar Day	Lunar Day	Lunar Day Start Time	Calendar Day	Lunar Day	Lunar Day Start Time
01/04/2023	12	3:04 PM	01/04/2023	12	2:30 PM
02/04/2023	13	4:04 PM	02/04/2023	13	3:38 PM
03/04/2023	14	5:04 PM	03/04/2023	14	4:46 PM
04/04/2023	15	6:05 PM	04/04/2023	15	5:56 PM
05/04/2023	16	7:07 PM	05/04/2023	16	7:06 PM
06/04/2023	17	8:11 PM	06/04/2023	17	8:18 PM
07/04/2023	18	9:16 PM	07/04/2023	18	9:32 PM
08/04/2023	19	10:23 PM	08/04/2023	19	10:47 PM
09/04/2023	20	11:30 PM	10/04/2023	20	12:02 AM
11/04/2023	21	12:34 AM	11/04/2023	21	1:11 AM
12/04/2023	22	1:33 AM	12/04/2023	22	2:12 AM
13/04/2023	23	2:25 AM	13/04/2023	23	3:02 AM
14/04/2023	24	3:10 AM	14/04/2023	24	3:41 AM
15/04/2023	25	3:48 AM	15/04/2023	25	4:12 AM
16/04/2023	26	4:22 AM	16/04/2023	26	4:38 AM
17/04/2023	27	4:53 AM	17/04/2023	27	5:00 AM
18/04/2023	28	5:22 AM	18/04/2023	28	5:20 AM
19/04/2023	29	5:52 AM	19/04/2023	29	5:40 AM
20/04/2023	1	12:15 AM	20/04/2023	1	5:15 AM
20/04/2023	2	6:23 AM	20/04/2023	2	6:02 AM
21/04/2023	3	6:57 AM	21/04/2023	3	6:27 AM
22/04/2023	4	7:35 AM	22/04/2023	4	6:56 AM
23/04/2023	5	8:18 AM	23/04/2023	5	7:32 AM
24/04/2023	6	9:06 AM	24/04/2023	6	8:15 AM
25/04/2023	7	9:59 AM	25/04/2023	7	9:07 AM
26/04/2023	8	10:55 AM	26/04/2023	8	10:06 AM
27/04/2023	9	11:53 AM	27/04/2023	9	11:09 AM
28/04/2023	10	12:52 PM	28/04/2023	10	12:15 PM
29/04/2023	11	1:52 PM	29/04/2023	11	1:23 PM
30/04/2023	12	2:51 PM	30/04/2023	12	2:30 PM

You can find the description of each lunar day in the chapter "A Guide to The Moon Cycle and Lunar Days"

Aries

This month, you will not be defending your boundaries so much as expanding them. And everything will work out for you!

Work. April is one of the best months of the year, when the planets come together and bring many opportunities. That may mean renewing old ties and making new acquaintances that are incredibly useful to your business development. You will discuss your projects with new business partners and old colleagues, and most importantly, find the money you need to make this happen. This applies to business owners or managers at any level.

Employees can count on support from management – right now, you are able to come to your bosses with any request or suggestion, and they will most likely allow you to convince them. Overall, roll up your sleeves and get to work, and you will not have to wait long for success.

Money. Financially, April is a great time for you. Your achievements this month may have a major effect on your wallet in both April and May. Nearly all Aries can count on significantly higher income, whether from your usual salary or unofficial sources.

That may include profits from various real estate transactions, credit, or support from loved ones. This month, you are so lucky with money that any efforts you put into this direction are sure to lead to success.

Love and family. Those focused on their personal lives may be busy improving your home this month. That could be construction, repairs, or other efforts that will continue, and you can expect help on all fronts, here.

Couples might look toward the past and reconsider their relationships. If you recently had a quarrel, this month, you will manage to overcome it all, reach an understanding, and a path toward reconciliation. But if you are feeling any shreds of guilt, apologize, and you can expect a positive reaction from your partner.

Those with problems involving their children will also have a good opportunity this month to smooth things over. This is a great time for making amends!

Health. In April, you will feel a strong surge of energy, despite the heavy workload, and you will feel better than ever. Naturally, you have no reason to fear falling ill.

Taurus

Right now, you hold exclusive potential, and the stars recommend that you think about something large-scale. Success is guaranteed in whatever you do, so hold on!

Work. This month, you are able to count on those around you. You are getting incredible support from friends and those who are highly placed in society, as well as the stars! You can be sure of your own luck, and your circumstances are working for you.

April is a great time for making decisions on difficult issues involving official bodies, where someone from your circle might serve as an intermediary.

You are on a lucky streak if you are an employee, too. You are getting ready for changes, and this can only be a good thing. Near the end of the month or perhaps in May, you might get a promotion, but in early April you are getting ready to promote your own interests at work. If you recently had a disagreement with management, you will be able to resolve it in your favor this month.

Money. Financially, April is neutral. Your income is steady and in line with your spending, but there is nothing unexpected, here. You might get some good surprises, which could be material benefits in the very near future, or possibly some moral or financial help.

Love and family. Your personal life is busier than ever this month! A recent encounter will quickly turn into a fiery romance, and if you have not yet found a partner, you can count on expanding your circle of friends and possibly making an interesting new acquaintance. Most likely, it is someone from your group of friends, so don't miss any outings, and be sure to look your best.

Those who already have a partner will also be making new friends, this month. Uranus, which is in your sign, might totally overhaul your feelings. If that is your case, be careful and test your feelings for your current partner, as well as your new acquaintance. Remember that not all that glitters is gold, and act accordingly.

Health. In April, you are feeling a lot of ups and downs. You might have bursts of energy followed by bouts of fatigue and the desire to seek tranquility and relaxation. Do not ignore your body's needs, and take some time out, as you will certainly have the opportunity to do so. A few days away from it all are sure to restore your body and soul.

Gemini

You can expect a busy, extremely positive month. The stars recommend that you take things into your own hands and boldly translate words into deeds. The ball's in your court!

Work. April is a great time for nearly all Geminis, regardless of what field you work in. Ideas you have been marinating for some time are finally coming to life.

Business owners and managers are getting their projects off to a good start; your great ideas are coming to life.

Employees can count on a promotion, or if they recently received one, they will be strengthening their position. You might also receive new and unexpected offers from a bigger, more promising organization.

Your connection to colleagues in other cities or abroad will go more smoothly this month, though the crux of the issue is not yet resolved, and you will have to come back to the drawing board once again.

New acquaintances are likely this month, and that will be a benefit to you at work. You might receive support from friends, highly placed individuals, or even official bodies. Overall, your time has come, and you deserve it!

Money. Your financial situation is also better, but that is no surprise given how things are going at work. You will have regular income, and significantly more of it than usual. Expect the largest sums on April 8, 9, 17, 18, and 25-27.

Your expenses are predictable and reasonable, even pleasant.

Love and family. Most of April's events will take place at work, and your personal life may be on the back burner. However, given your liveliness, you might manage to juggle both areas of your life.

Single people might find a new passion among their circle of friends or at a new job. Only time will tell how long it lasts, but there are chances that things will continue.

Those with families will be pleased to share their success at home and at work as well as their financial success. This will partially compensate for all the time you are spending away from your loved ones.

Health. This month, you are strong, energetic, charming, and sexually attractive. Naturally, you have no reason to fear falling ill.

Cancer

Forget about your problems, being cautious, and predicting things. The more open-minded you are right now, the more successful this time will be. A new life is knocking at your door!

Work. You have been waiting for things to look up at work for a while now, and that is happening now. April is a good time to start new projects, change jobs or even the direction of your career.

Your relationship with colleagues in other cities or abroad is moving along with great success, and you might take a successful trip. Those looking to open a business somewhere new are closer than ever to seeing that dream through.

Difficult relationships with a business partner, friends, or like-minded individuals will improve somewhat. Things are probably not entirely resolved, but you will cover a lot of ground in April, and it is worth taking advantage of that. You might once again be dealing with financial loose ends or moral or financial debts.

This month is practically the ideal time to start going to school, look for new information, and decide on your future goals. So, decide what you want and don't waste your time!

Money. Your finances are looking better, but not so much that you can stop worrying about money altogether. However, each day, you are getting a better understanding of your financial situation and things are looking up. Expect the largest sums to come in on April 1, 2, 10-12, 19-21, 28, and 29.

Love and family. Single people and those who have been let down by former love affairs might pack their bags and head to a new city or even abroad. There is a high likelihood of romance this month, and that will probably take place on a trip or with people from faraway.

If you are planning on learning something new this month, you will find yourself in fateful company, and you might have an unusual and interesting encounter with someone.

Couples, whether married or not, will take a trip together, and that is the best way to strengthen your relationship. You may face a dilemma – relax or get to work, in which case, the best thing is for you to first finish your projects and then reward yourself with a trip somewhere.

Health. In April, you are feeling much better, and any illnesses from March will quickly fade away.

Leo

You are probably not starting April with a clean slate. You have plans, ideas, and most importantly, the will to make them happen. Patience and hard work are all you need.

Work. In April, you might find yourself heavily dependent on business partners or people with whom you have a connection based on various projects and circumstances. However, this has happened before, and each time, you have managed to work your way out of a sticky situation. That is the case now, as well. You are able to strike an agreement with your partners, though it will not be easy.

That may be due to financial troubles in your shared business, and you will have to back up your arguments with facts, as no one is going to fork over any money until that happens. Alternatively, and worse, you might be splitting up your business and spend a lot of time haggling over shared obligations, both moral and financial. In April, however, things will get easier, and toward the middle of the month, you will find a compromise that both sides can live with.

Your connection with colleagues in other cities or abroad is developing with varying success, and you might take a trip, which is best planned for late April.

Money. Financial matters are finally working their way out of a dead-end, but for now, that does not concern you personally. You might receive favorable credit, various types of loans, or support from business partners or profit from various real estate transactions.

Those who are not part of the working world can count on help from their spouse, parents, or loved ones. Many families will take out credit.

Love and family. Your personal life is seeing a continuation of the processes that began in the recent past. That may involve construction, repairs, or acquiring new real estate either for yourself or your children.

Couples who are divorcing will sit down at the negotiating table this month and things will go more smoothly, possibly even productively.

One more thing this month – this is a great time for anyone who is looking to grow their family. The likelihood of pregnancy is very high right now, which any women hoping for a baby should keep in mind.

Health. In April, you are feeling sluggish, and you can expect mood swings and bouts of sadness. In order to get through this, take a few days off of work and spend some time doing what you always dreamed. A trip somewhere faraway will help you relax and see things from a new perspective.

Virgo

All month long, you are able to demonstrate your speed, discipline, and hard-working nature. These qualities, along with your detail-oriented ways, are sure to lead to incredible results. Go for it!

Work. Your main task this month is to convince your business partners of your amazing ideas and that they should make an investment. The stars predict that this is necessary if you want to develop your business. If you don't have reliable colleagues, it is worth focusing on finding some. April is a perfect time for this. You can expect new acquaintances, meetings, and negotiations in which you catch the eye of the people you need. Be bold as you strive for your goals, and it is reasonable to take on a bit of risk right now. Remember that a lot is riding on your ability to sell your ideas, so stock up on arguments and back them up with facts where you can. The stars are on your side.

Close to the end of the month, you will spend more time communicating with colleagues in other cities or abroad, and you might take a successful trip. Your ideas might interest a partner from afar.

Money. Despite your clear success when it comes to networking this month, things are not so smooth when it comes to money. But don't get too down about it – you will have money soon. Everything you do in April will pay off, perhaps not overnight, but in a little bit. You are unlikely to end up bankrupt in April, though you will probably have less to spend than you had planned on.

Love and family. There are a lot of changes in your personal life. Couples who get along are able to reach mutual understanding and agree with one another. Your loved one will be on a winning streak, which is reason for you to celebrate.

Those who recently separated or lost a loved one might count on a favorable resolution to your material problems this month, as well as a new person in your life.

You have been waiting for stability in your relationship, and now, the time has come, and this goes for all Virgos, whether you are married, in a long-term relationship, or just beginning a new romance.

Closer to the end of the month or maybe in May, you can expect to go on a trip, and it will be a great success.

Health. In April, you are not feeling as energetic as usual, and that will be most noticeable during the New Moon on April 1 and 2, as well as the Full Moon on April 15-17. During these times, try to take care of yourself and take whatever measures you must.

Libra

April is a great time for slowing down, taking a close look at things, and analyzing your work. It is also a great time for both business and personal meetings. Plan things well in order to keep up!

Work. Business owners and managers will have to work on getting their teams in order. Upper management may be inspecting things, or you can expect new associates, which will take up most of your time at work this month. Business owners and managers will have to cut ties with those weighing them down and take a long, hard look at who is conscientious and professional. You have been thinking about this for a while now, but the time has now come for you to overhaul your team

and administrative issues. Some Capricorns will be busy setting up facilities to expand their business, and you will be able to assess your capabilities and get a clear-eyed view of the location you have selected.

In some cases, you might count on support from relatives, and this is especially true if you have a family business.

Employees might consider various options for employment in a company that has many ties to other cities or abroad. The stars welcome any opportunity to study somewhere faraway.

Money. Your financial situation is gradually normalizing. The major expenses that were so frequent during the last few months are no longer an issue. Saturn, the planet of limitations, discipline, and modesty is now in the sector of the sky responsible for finances, and that may drive a sense of responsibility in anything related to money. Keep a close eye on your budget and avoid any unnecessary spending. But given your cautious nature, you probably don't need to be told.

Love and family. If the major events of this year are taking place in your personal life, this is where you will see a shift. Many Capricorns will be busy with various real estate transactions, possibly related to a move to another city or abroad, or alternatively, simply to a new home. Most likely, all of these related events in April are in the planning phase, and it will take some time for your plans to come to life.

Your relationship with your children is more predictable, and the worst is probably behind you. Ahead, expect smooth sailing and for the difficulties of the last few months to be over.

Divorcing couples might manage to discuss material issues in relative peace, and if you can, try to deal with the thorniest issues this month, while you have an opportunity for both sides to reach a compromise.

Your relatives' influence in family problems can only be positive right now.

Couples will have a calm April, and things will be predictable. You might discuss the future of your relationship or possibly living together.

Health. In April, you are feeling energetic. You are active, vibrant, and able to bring your ideas to life in business and at home.

Aquarius

All month long, you will be active, curious, and enterprising. This will be reflected in all areas of your life, from the political to the personal.

Work. April is a generally positive month for networking with management, as well as resolving any legal problems from the recent past.

You will once again discuss difficult issues related to real estate, land, and other major property, and then manage to resolve them in your favor. You might see financial compensation or perhaps a sale following mutual agreement. Any compromises here look very reasonable, which is both desirable and likely.

Your relationship with colleagues in other cities or abroad will be moving along with varying success. Business owners might reach an agreement that will lead to a nice financial payoff.

Money. April is one of the best months of the year for your bank account. In addition to your usual salary, you can expect income from various real estate transactions. That may be related to your job, or possibly events in your personal life.

Expect the largest sums to come in on April 8, 9, 17, 18, and 22-27.

Love and family. Your personal life is peaceful and predictable. This month, you will need to deal with various household matters that have been pending since the winter, and possibly much earlier. This may involve tasks related to buying a new home, summer home, or apartment. This may become more prominent in your life close to the end of April and it will continue into May.

Your relationship with relatives is becoming very important, and you might see family that lives in other cities or abroad.

Mars and Venus will be in your sign during the first 10 days of April, and Saturn will be there, too. This all means that you can expect to rekindle a former flame, reconnect with an old friend, or meet with a lover who lives in another city or abroad.

Fate will give you many opportunities to find love, and you would be wise to use them if you are currently unattached.

Health. This month, you are feeling much more energetic than usual, but Saturn's transiting through your sign means that you should lead a healthy lifestyle and avoid overeating or drinking to excess.

Those with chronic cardiovascular disease should keep an eye on their health.

Pisces

This month, you will be able to tackle any task with inspiration and ingenuity. That gives you a chance to succeed in anything, whether political or personal. You have a lot to do, but anything worth doing is difficult!

Work. In April, issues that were a thorn in your side before are now favorably resolved. That may involve old legal troubles that kept you up at night for some time. Alternatively, you are smoothing over a tough relationship with colleagues in other cities or abroad. You will not avoid every argument, but close to the end of the month, your partners who live faraway will reach a compromise. You will give it everything you've got, and your efforts will pay off.

You might take a successful trip or plan one.

For anything work-related, the second half of April is ideal. Here, you will see positive changes in areas that have posed a challenge in the past, and you will see that nothing is insurmountable.

Money. Financially, April is looking very promising for you. You will have regular income, and significantly more of it. You might even say that this is the first glimmer of the success that awaits in the very near future. Expect the largest sums on April 1, 2, 10-12, 19, 20, 28, and 29.

Love and family. In your personal life, things are going great. Your relationship with relatives has seen some challenges, but you are now close to a resolution. You might be the one to take the first step, and your family member is sure to respond in kind.

Single people might have a fateful meeting while traveling or among people from somewhere faraway. You might both be on the road when this happens! If you recently me someone and began a romance, now is the time to think about how to strengthen your relationship. You might have serious talks while on a trip, and this is especially likely during the last 10 days of April or in May.

Health. Jupiter and Neptune are both in y our sign, which means a powerful burst of energy, and it's up to you how you decide to use it. In any case, you have no reason to fear falling ill.

May

New York Time				London Time		
Calendar Day	Lunar Day	Lunar Day Start Time		Calendar Day	Lunar Day	Lunar Day Start Time
01/05/2023	13	3:52 PM		01/05/2023	13	3:39 PM
02/05/2023	14	4:53 PM		02/05/2023	14	4:48 PM
03/05/2023	15	5:56 PM		03/05/2023	15	6:00 PM
04/05/2023	16	7:02 PM		04/05/2023	16	7:14 PM
05/05/2023	17	8:09 PM		05/05/2023	17	8:30 PM
06/05/2023	18	9:18 PM		06/05/2023	18	9:47 PM
07/05/2023	19	10:25 PM		07/05/2023	19	11:00 PM
08/05/2023	20	11:27 PM		09/05/2023	20	12:06 AM
10/05/2023	21	12:22 AM		10/05/2023	21	1:01 AM
11/05/2023	22	1:10 AM		11/05/2023	22	1:43 AM
12/05/2023	23	1:50 AM		12/05/2023	23	2:16 AM
13/05/2023	24	2:24 AM		13/05/2023	24	2:43 AM
14/05/2023	25	2:55 AM		14/05/2023	25	3:05 AM
15/05/2023	26	3:24 AM		15/05/2023	26	3:25 AM
16/05/2023	27	3:53 AM		16/05/2023	27	3:45 AM
17/05/2023	28	4:23 AM		17/05/2023	28	4:05 AM
18/05/2023	29	4:55 AM		18/05/2023	29	4:28 AM
19/05/2023	30	5:31 AM		19/05/2023	30	4:55 AM
19/05/2023	1	11:55 AM		19/05/2023	1	4:55 PM
20/05/2023	2	6:11 AM		20/05/2023	2	5:27 AM
21/05/2023	3	6:57 AM		21/05/2023	3	6:08 AM
22/05/2023	4	7:48 AM		22/05/2023	4	6:56 AM
23/05/2023	5	8:44 AM		23/05/2023	5	7:53 AM
24/05/2023	6	9:42 AM		24/05/2023	6	8:55 AM
25/05/2023	7	10:41 AM		25/05/2023	7	10:01 AM
26/05/2023	8	11:40 AM		26/05/2023	8	11:07 AM
27/05/2023	9	12:39 PM		27/05/2023	9	12:14 PM
28/05/2023	10	1:38 PM		28/05/2023	10	1:22 PM
29/05/2023	11	2:38 PM		29/05/2023	11	2:30 PM
30/05/2023	12	3:39 PM		30/05/2023	12	3:40 PM
31/05/2023	13	4:43 PM		31/05/2023	13	4:52 PM

You can find the description of each lunar day in the chapter "A Guide to The Moon Cycle and Lunar Days"

Aries

May bring flowers and new beginnings alike. This month, keep in mind that the more quietly you move, the further you will go.

Work. During the first half of the month, things will move slowly, but it is also a time of great responsibility.

This is most likely related to accounting or distributing finances. You may negotiate with partners regarding major financial or administrative matters, as well.

Until May 15, Mercury will be in retrograde, which means that you may experience difficulties and setbacks. The stars recommend being cautious, responsible, and never rushing things.

In the end, everything will go as planned, and the delays will allow you to correct any errors and ensure that you are meticulous as you can be.

Employees might raise the issue of a raise, bonus, or benefits, and following some discussions, your wishes will be granted.

Many will continue to expand their business, and a significant part of your expenses will include work-related purchases, as well as various real estate transactions. You may need to get a loan or otherwise obtain funding for this purpose.

Money. This month, your finances are doing well. You will have a regular income, in addition to some profits from work you completed in earlier months, or perhaps a bonus or favorable credit.

Expect the greatest sums to come in on May 1, 2, 9-11, 18, 19, 28, 29.

Love and family. If your personal life comes first, you may find yourself immersed in a variety of household tasks. Many will be busy setting up their living space, which will occupy a lot of your family's resources or those of a relative. It is likely you will be able to cover these costs on your own, however.

Your relationship with your family is harmonious, and noticeably better these days.

Many Aries will take some time off from work in early May and perhaps travel, relax, and maybe even engage in some important business networking.

Mercury will be in retrograde until May 15, and this is a good time to renew old ties, meet up with former classmates, friends, and acquaintances you may have fallen out of touch with for various reasons.

Though you may meet new people during this period, they are unlikely to be reliable. Expect them to make a swift exit from their life, leaving nothing but less-than pleasant memories.

Health. This month, you are feeling somewhat sluggish, but it won't get worse than that. You can engage in self-care – perhaps a massage, a trip to the cosmetologist, or simply relaxing with a good book on a soft couch. The first half of May is the best time for any of this.

Taurus

This month, your most important task will be forming clear opinions on important, key issues. That will require time, and remember that the more quietly you move, the further you will go.

Work. During the first half of the month, expect difficulties and confusion. On one hand, you may find work disrupted by delays, red tape, and other inconveniences, while treacherous Mercury moving into retrograde is sure to have an impact on your work, as well.

This is also a good time to examine your projects for flaws and take the right steps to correct them.

During the second half of the month, things will improve greatly, and you can expect to find yourself very busy with work. You have been continuing the process of expanding your business recently, and those efforts will be managers' and business owners' primary concern all year long.

Employees will walk a tightrope between home and work responsibilities, but they will succeed in both realms. You might hold lengthy negotiations regarding a transfer to another, more prestigious and important position. That may not come to pass in May, but the stars predict that is the direction in which you are heading.

Your relationship with colleagues in other cities or abroad is developing nicely, and you might even renew a former partnership.

Money. This month, financial matters may be on most Taureans' minds. After all, you have regular income and somewhat more of it coming in. Expect the largest sums on May 3, 4, 11, 12, 20, 21, 30, and 31.

Love and family. Major developments are also taking place in your personal life in May. Spouses with a happy marriage will continue to work on their home, and that may involve large-scale repairs, or possibly a new construction or simply purchasing a comfortable apartment.

In some cases, you may do that in another city or even abroad.

Spouses whose marriage is on the rocks might see drastic changes. You may reexamine your shared values and end this uncomfortable process with a separation.

It is not worth desperation, however. There are many fish in the sea, and you will find the right person for you!

Your relationship with relatives living in other cities or abroad might suddenly become more active, with frequent calls, visits, or trips to see someone living far away.

Health. In May, you will be healthy, energetic, but inconsistent and agitated. The stars recommend getting enough sleep and finding the time to relax somewhere sunny and with a warm beach. You will likely have the opportunity to do just that.

Gemini

There's no way around it, May is not the best month for you this year. But it is not a particularly bad month, either. If you have a clear goal, follow it, and if you have any doubts, then hold on for a couple of months and think things through.

Work. The first 20 days of May are not the best for you at work. Your ruler, Mercury, is in retrograde until May 15, and you are sure to feel the effects professionally.

You will not expect any breakthroughs at work, but you can examine your current projects and make corrections and changes or additions as needed. That might just be what May is for, in your case.

It is possible that the people you need are not where you expect them to be, and you may also run into red tape.

Both business owners and managers, as well as responsible employees may need to prepare for inspections from auditing agencies.

Many Geminis might run into secret intrigue or open rumors alike, so keep your finger on the pulse of what is happening at work and protect yourself.

Alternatively, if everything at work is under control, you might take some time off in early May to spend time with yourself, your loved ones, and family. You will definitely have the chance to do just that.

The best time of any work-related events is the last 10 days of May. During this time, many of the problems that cropped up during the first half of the month will be favorably resolved.

Money. Despite a few hiccups at work, you do not have any financial problems on the horizon. You have an income, as well as expenses, most of which are expected from May 21 to 25.

Love and family. There may be a variety of developments in your personal life.

Many Geminis may decide to improve their home and start taking steps in that direction. There are various plans on the table now – some will opt for major repairs, while others will be thinking about a new home, apartment, or summer home in the next few months.

The most dedicated of all will take the bull by the horns this month already, while others may wait for different periods from 2023 to 2024.

Unmarried couples might seriously think about the future of their relationship this month. Is it time to take a step forward, for example, living together? Or is now not the time?

The stars recommend not rushing anything and thinking things through. It is not worth making any decisions while Mercury is in retrograde. Take a break and wait a couple of weeks. By then, the solution may be clearer.

Health. This month, you are feeling sluggish, and the elderly and those who are weakened are advised to take special care of themselves. Troubled times are ahead, when old, chronic illnesses are likely to make a reappearance.

Cancer

In May, the steady charge forward that characterizes most of late 2023 for you will see some hurdles. This is not a problem – in order to prepare, you need to take the time to think things through and protect yourself.

Work. Things will move slowly during the first half of May. On one hand, it may be due to delays in communication, the people you need

care of yourself and don't try to test your body with any excess.

Libra

May is a time of anxiety and transitions for you. You may be a subtle and romantic Libra, but right now you are shouldering something unusual for you – household and domestic tasks.

Work. During the first 20 days of May, you may run into some hurdles at work. Don't expect a breakthrough at work, but you might be planning things and giving your work a thorough review.

Business owners and managers should focus on finances and keep a scrupulous record of everything.

You might make large expenditures on expanding your business, maybe acquiring land or facilities for that purpose. You can expect a lot of work to deal with all year long. The stars welcome any negotiations with partners, banks, and other financial institutions.

Your relationship with colleagues in other cities or abroad is noticeably improved, and you might be holding discussions that seem lengthy, but will bring positive results.

Employees be busy with family matters, which are also going through a time of transitions.

The last 10 days of May are the best time for anything work-related, when things will move forward smoothly and efficiently.

Money. Financially, you are doing great in May. You might not be making your own money, but you can count on funds from business partners, favorable credit, and help along the way.

You might also get support from your spouse or a loved one.

Love and family. There are major changes in your family life, right now. Many Libras are totally or partially changing up their residence. For example, you might be moving to a new home, buying an apartment, summer home, or working on major repairs.

Some Libras are already making strides in this direction this month, while others will be busy with this project all year long.

Many families are experiencing difficulties related to children. Adult children may be growing emotionally distant, while you need to watch small ones like a hawk!

After a lot of ups and downs, unmarried couples might decide to live together and be discussing both romantic and financial issues.

Any trips planned for the first 20 days of May will go well, as long as you select a destination you have been to many times before.

Health. In May, you are not as energetic as you have been, so lead a healthy lifestyle and remember to get enough sleep!

Scorpio

Many Scorpios are die-hard individualists and value their personal freedom above all else. However, in May, things are changing. But now, there is no way around it – it is time to be part of a team. Embrace your new role, maybe you'll even like it!

Work. This month, you have new, important partners on the horizon, and might also find yourself renewing old business relationships. Their influence will be positive on your professional life. Colleagues, both new and old, will bring you new and exciting opportunities, so consider their invitations with the attention they deserve and study it all carefully.

You may spend May on negotiations, and though things will be difficult at the beginning of the month, by the end, you will be seeing the results you want.

Employees might see greater popularity within their circles. This is only getting started in May and will continue in the future.

Your relationship with colleagues in other cities or abroad is growing and becoming more positive; you may take a trip or receive a visit from a colleague who lives far away.

Money. May is not a particularly exciting month for your finances. Everything is going as planned, and there are no surprises on the horizon.

You may receive support from a spouse or loved one whose own business is on the rise.

Love and family. Your personal life is looking very sunny. During the first 20 days of the month, you might renew your relationship with friends and relatives living in other cities or abroad.

During the second half of May, you might meet new people, which is a special gift for those who have been looking for a partner for some time.

You are embarking on a period during which not only will you manage to steer a torrid romance your way, but you may also get a long-term relationship out of it. You might meet this person while traveling or among people who have come from far away.

Parents should keep an eye on their children, as the young ones may run into some difficulties at school or unexpectedly fall ill, and older ones may distance themselves or start a difficult period in their lives.

This advice applies not only to May, but to the entire year.

Health. This month, you might feel serious fatigue from all of the work you have been doing lately. Find the time to get away and relax. This will be possible during the first half of May.

Sagittarius

May is a time of hard work, responsibilities, and challenges for you. You are impatient by nature, and any setbacks tend to set you off. However, this time, remember that patience and hard work are all you need to guide your every move.

Work . The last 10 days of May are the best time for anything work-related. The first 20 days are not exactly bad, either – during this time, many Sagittarians will be putting the finishing details on projects they began earlier, making corrections, and fixing any mistakes.

You might run into various types of hurdles – perhaps the people you need won't be there for you, or you will simply have to deal with red tape.

One way or another, things will press forward, and in the end, you will reach your goal.

Employees might expect a new job offer, and after some hard thought and discussing your options, you will accept it. The stars recommend taking a sober look at your strengths and opportunities, as a new job or business will require skills, responsibilities, and dedication. It's a lot of work, but it's well worth it.

You are growing closer to colleagues in other cities or abroad, some more than others. You will manage to reach an agreement on some things, while others will still be up in the air. Success here is for the future, so be patient. By 2024, most of these problems will have resolved themselves.

Money. Financially, May is a great time for you. You will have regular income, and somewhat more of it than usual. The good news is that this positive change will continue into the future. Expect the largest sums to come in on May 1, 2, 9, 10, 18, 19, 28, and 29. This month, your expenses will be related to your children and loved ones.

Love and family. Everything is stable in your personal life. Your relationship with your family is warm and harmonious, and if you have to deal with any difficult issues related to your home, you will resolve them favorably. Your children bring you happiness and will also take up the lion's share of the family budget.

The last 10 days of May will be a good time for couples. If you have a steady partner, things are serene and calm. If you are single, you can count on meeting someone interesting from your circle of acquaintances.

Many Sagittarians will run into problems with their parents and elder relatives. Take care of your loved ones, especially if you worry about their health. In case of conflict, try to smooth things over.

Health. In May, you are not as energetic as you have been, so try to lead a healthy lifestyle and do not forget to get enough sleep.

During the last 10 days of May, you are entering a period during which you might start to really work on your fitness. Avoid any bad habits and start going to the gym or join a dance club!

Capricorn

May is a challenging and unusual time for you. You may be an incorrigible workaholic, but the stars urge you to busy yourself with your love life or family. This month will be interesting but emotionally taxing.

Work. Though most of the month will have you busy with your personal affairs, you will not stop working altogether. The best time for work-related matters is the last 10 days of May, when all of your working processes will be close to complete, whether you are an employee or business owner.

During the first 20 days of the month, you may run into some problems and obstacles. You may get a way to relax, and if you do stick around at work, the people you need will not be nearby.

The good news in all of this is that you will renew your ties with your business partners in other cities or abroad. Most likely, these are connections you made some time ago, and which for some reason petered out.

Those busy with expanding their business might complete the initial tasks related to this.

Money. Financially, May might be difficult for you. You can expect major expenses, higher than your income, mostly related to your personal life and home and children's needs.

Your children may be responsible for the lion's share of this spending.

Love and family. Your personal life is at the heart of it all this month! Perhaps you will manage to keep a lid on your innate conservatism and try your hand at something romantic. It will not be difficult for you to steal the hearts of those around you with your brilliant wit and talents on full display. This is a great chance to find just the right person, if you haven't found him or her just yet.

Those with families will be immersed in their children's affairs, and this will likely involve a serious investment in their education and training.

The first 20 days of May are a good time for renewing your relationships. For various reasons listed above, the last 10 days are a good time to meet new people. For the rest of the year, your life will become much freer, more interesting, and romantic.

You might finally get a handle on your household issues, and finally able to focus on much more pleasant tasks.

Health. In May, you are healthy, energetic, looking great, and impressing everyone Fate sends your way.

Aquarius

May will have you busy with family and household matters. You might not really want to deal with these things, but the time has come!

Work. Many Aquarians will focus on relaxing and family during the first 20 days of the month. Business owners and managers at every level, however, might be busy with serious work restructuring their business, future development, and expanding their territory. The first 20 days of May may be a time for negotiations, studies, and discussing your future plans.

This is also a good time for ironing out the kinks and revising projects. All month long, you will be working on difficult tasks that will require your utmost attention and care.

During the first 10 days of the month, you may run into some obstacles or find that the information or people you need are simply not there. Don't rush things – that is not a good idea right now, but during the last 10 days, things will speed up a bit and you will see that you chose the right path.

Money. May is a neutral month for your finances. Your income is modest, but your expenses are under control. Things are going as planned, and you will not run into any surprises.

Love and family. Many Aquarians will find that the most important events this month take place at home or with their families. The time has come to change up your living space, and that may mean a whole new residence, or simply some major repairs.

In some cases, this may involve acquiring new real estate in another city or abroad. Young people and those uninitiated to this long, laborious process might seek help from their parents or elder family members.

Couples may decide to live together and hunt for a house or apartment.

Health. In May, you are not as energetic as usual, so take care of yourself. Many Aquarians have a tendency to gain weight, which will be a recurring theme all year long. If that is not part of your plans, think about a diet and actually following it.

Pisces

In May, you might think about making some serious changes in your life. Only you can decide what they will look like, but the stars advise that change is imminent.

Work. In May, your professional activities will take your attention somewhere far away, perhaps abroad. That may involve picking up old partnerships, or possibly a move or opening business in another city or abroad.

Negotiations on this topic may drag on all month long, but the most positive aspects will shine through during the last 10 days of May. During the first 20 days, you can expect setbacks at work, whether due to red tape or difficult colleagues in other cities or abroad. By the last 10 days of May, however, things will settle down and you will find the right path.

Any travel planned for May is sure to turn out successfully, especially if you have been to the same destination before. The same goes for old partners you may begin corresponding with once again.

Money. Financially, May is looking great. You will have a regular income, and this will continue into the future. Expect the largest sums to come in on May 7, 8, 15-17, 25, and 26.

Love and family. Your personal life looks agitated and turbulent.

Some Pisceans will make plans related to a move, and that may be to another city, abroad, or possible simply a new home. For now, you are in the planning stage, but during the year, these plans are sure to come to life.

Many Pisceans might take a trip to a place you have been before for a spring break.

Your relationship with relatives is much more active than before. You might take a trip together or see your family members living in another city or abroad.

Health. This month, your spirit might turn out to be much stronger than your body. Take care of yourself! Saturn is firmly and permanently ensconced in your sign and is telling you the same.

This advice is particularly important for those who are elderly or weakened.

June

New York Time				London Time		
Calendar Day	Lunar Day	Lunar Day Start Time		Calendar Day	Lunar Day	Lunar Day Start Time
01/06/2023	14	5:50 PM		01/06/2023	14	6:07 PM
02/06/2023	15	6:59 PM		02/06/2023	15	7:24 PM
03/06/2023	16	8:08 PM		03/06/2023	16	8:41 PM
04/06/2023	17	9:14 PM		04/06/2023	17	9:52 PM
05/06/2023	18	10:14 PM		05/06/2023	18	10:53 PM
06/06/2023	19	11:06 PM		06/06/2023	19	11:41 PM
07/06/2023	20	11:50 PM		08/06/2023	20	12:19 AM
09/06/2023	21	12:27 AM		09/06/2023	21	12:48 AM
10/06/2023	22	12:59 AM		10/06/2023	22	1:11 AM
11/06/2023	23	1:29 AM		11/06/2023	23	1:32 AM
12/06/2023	24	1:57 AM		12/06/2023	24	1:52 AM
13/06/2023	25	2:26 AM		13/06/2023	25	2:11 AM
14/06/2023	26	2:56 AM		14/06/2023	26	2:33 AM
15/06/2023	27	3:30 AM		15/06/2023	27	2:57 AM
16/06/2023	28	4:08 AM		16/06/2023	28	3:27 AM
17/06/2023	29	4:51 AM		17/06/2023	29	4:04 AM
18/06/2023	1	12:39 AM		18/06/2023	30	4:49 AM
18/06/2023	2	5:40 AM		18/06/2023	1	5:39 AM
19/06/2023	3	6:34 AM		19/06/2023	2	5:42 AM
20/06/2023	4	7:31 AM		20/06/2023	3	6:43 AM
21/06/2023	5	8:30 AM		21/06/2023	4	7:47 AM
22/06/2023	6	9:29 AM		22/06/2023	5	8:54 AM
23/06/2023	7	10:28 AM		23/06/2023	6	10:01 AM
24/06/2023	8	11:27 AM		24/06/2023	7	11:07 AM
25/06/2023	9	12:25 PM		25/06/2023	8	12:14 PM
26/06/2023	10	1:25 PM		26/06/2023	9	1:22 PM
27/06/2023	11	2:27 PM		27/06/2023	10	2:32 PM
28/06/2023	12	3:31 PM		28/06/2023	11	3:44 PM
29/06/2023	13	4:37 PM		29/06/2023	12	4:59 PM
30/06/2023	14	5:46 PM		30/06/2023	13	6:15 PM

You can find the description of each lunar day in the chapter "A Guide to The Moon Cycle and Lunar Days"

Aries

June will bring you a surge of energy, along with the wisdom to use it where you need it most. With this in your arsenal, you can move mountains!

Work. June is not a time to sit back and relax for most Aries. You are in touch with colleagues in other cities or abroad, and you might take a successful trip. But not everything with your faraway partners is going smoothly. You may face challenges that have roots in the past and have unexpectedly reared their heads once again. This time, however, you will overcome things more quickly. Let the past remain in the past, and you are sure to reach a mutually beneficial partnership.

Many Aries, especially business owners and upper-level managers, will have to deal with important day-to-day matters this month. Things will run smoothly, and you will avoid any setbacks or trouble.

Employees will have a great opportunity to increase their income. That may be a promotion that includes a higher salary, or perhaps a job at a new, more promising organization.

Money. June is a great time for your wallet. Many Aries will be pleased to see a higher income, and that is likely to remain the case in the future.

Expect the largest sums to come in on June 5, 6, 14, 15, and 23-25.

There are always expenses, and most of them will be related to leisure, your children, and loved ones this month.

Love and family. There are changes underfoot in your personal life. Your relationship with relatives is growing closer, and you might travel together or meet with family members living in other cities or abroad. If you have any old grudges, they will be smoothed over.

Your children are a source of joy but expect to spend a large share of the family budget resolving their problems during the second half of the month.

Couples may swing from one extreme to another. Unexpectedly, you will discover that your viewpoints clash on certain subjects. Issues over your shared finances and other material issues or different value systems will come as a surprise. You may find yourself arguing all month long, but there is hope that you will get through it.

The stars recommend that you don't get greedy or ask for too much if you want to keep the problem small. What's more, you had money before, you still have it, and it is not going anywhere in the future.

Single people and those who have been disappointed by past relationships can count on meeting someone new and a torrid romance. Whether things pan out depends on your plans and intentions, but there is a chance your relationship might continue.

Health. In June, you are feeling energetic and have no reason to fear falling ill.

Be especially careful when driving and traveling from June 15 to 18.

Taurus

Jupiter, the planet of success, is in your sign, which means that Fortune is on your side. Let Fate take you where it wants and take it as it comes.

Work. For some time now, you have been working toward the major step of taking your business to the next level, and now, push comes to shove. Expect to spend the next three years working actively toward your future. Some of the changes will begin this month, already, while others will come later, but they will affect almost everything. Business owners may hold negotiations on taking things to the next level and other, more promising projects, while employees at every level may be discussing a new job.

Moreover, be careful with those around you – this includes your friends, and someone highly placed in society. Not everyone will be pleased with your success, and both envy and competitiveness are everywhere.

This may involve finances or material responsibilities.

Money. Financially speaking, June is a prosperous time for you. Money will be coming in regularly, and there will be significantly more of it, too. Expect the largest sums to come in on June 7, 8, 16, 17, 27, and 28.

Love and family. Your personal life is moving along in due course, right now. Couples who get along will take important steps regarding home improvement, and they will be pleased with the results.

Closer to the end of the month, or perhaps in July, many Taureans will go on a trip, where they will see old friends and rekindle old ties.

Single people have excellent chances of a fateful encounter. This time, it is more than just an affair with a messy ending, but something capable of taking on a life of its own. June is a great time for this, but so is almost all of 2023. Your time has come!

Health. In June, you are feeling energetic and are unlikely to experience any illness!

Gemini

Jupiter's path is creating lots of change in your life. The time has come to stop, take a step back, look around, and put in reinforcements wherever you can. This goes for both work and love.

Work. In June, you will have to look back and assess everything you've accomplished and determine your future prospects.

Business owners and managers will be able to finish the lion's share of their organizational tasks, something that will take up nearly all of 2023. You will be taking on more responsibility, and your tasks will become more difficult, so you will need to develop a business strategy and some tactics to cope.

However, despite the challenges, you will be able to rebuild, and some time later, you will fully enjoy your position in the sun. This goes for both employees and business owners.

Moreover, during the first 10 days of June, Geminis who are part of the working world will encounter some resistance from the powers that be or a critical manager.

Most of the issues will be pop up during the last 10 days of June, but you try to do everything you can to smooth things over, and you will be largely successful, too.

Your relationship with colleagues from other cities or abroad is developing with varying success – some things look optimistic, while others are going to require some more work.

Money. Your finances are looking stable this month, but that's all. You have predictable income and expenses, and there are no surprises here.

Expect the largest sums to come in on June 1, 2, 10, 11, 6-12, 19, 20, 28, and 29.

Love and family. Your personal life is bringing you to a point when you will have to seriously consider how you want to set up your home, or possibly get a new place to live. Most likely, you have thought about this for a while, and the time has come. The most decisive Geminis may be taking their first steps in this direction right now, while others will wait until sometime later in 2023.

Your relationship with relatives who live in other cities or abroad is suddenly keeping you a lot busier, and you are making plans to travel. You will run into some obstacles, though, most of which will take place during the last 10 days of June. You will manage to figure things out, but no one will be able to do that for you.

Couples, whether married or not, will travel together, and the stars recommend you plan things well.

Health. This month, you are feeling sluggish, so take care of yourself and take precautionary measures if you are elderly. If you are young, be sure to get enough sleep.

Cancer

In June, you are going to have to work hard to set some boundaries between work and your personal life, with special focus on the latter. You have traveled a long, winding road, and the time has come to take stock of what you have achieved and set your eyes on new goals.

Work. The last 20 days of June are the best time for anything work-related. During this time, you will see colleagues from other cities or abroad, and you may renew an old partnership. You can count on a lot of help here from old friends or people who are highly placed in society. Carefully check the terms of cooperation before signing any documents, especially the financial parts. You can't afford the luxury of keeping your head in the clouds right now.

This advice goes whether you are a business owner or employee, and whether you are talking about a new project or a new job.

Any travel planned for June will be a smashing success, but you will need to invest a lot of resources to achieve that.

Money. Financially speaking, this month is going to have a lot of ups and downs. On one hand, you will not find yourself in the red, but you can expect some hefty spending, most of which will take place during the last 20 days of the month.

During the last 10 days of June, be very careful, as you may see financial losses in addition to your expenses. You may have to settle some old debts, as well.

Love and family . In June, many Cancers will spend a lot of time at home with their family, on romance or their personal lives. You may feel like taking some time off to be with loved ones.

You might travel to see relatives or old friends who live in other cities or abroad.

Couples will experience some tension, perhaps you have both managed to offend each other, or maybe even a serious argument is in store. Try not to make any decisions until you have looked at all the pros and cons and listened to your heart. Don't do anything rash.

If your relationship has been rocky for a while, it is worth taking steps to protect it while you can, at least for a while whether you are married or not.

Health. In June, you are feeling sluggish, so right now, the best investment you can make is an airline ticket to a sunny beach. Alternatively, you might spend some time in nature closer to home.

Leo

You are ready to make a leap, which will take your business to the next level. You are beginning a positive month full of responsibilities, but luck is on your side!

Work. When it comes to work, June is a busy month full of events. Business owners will be eying new, favorable future contracts, while employees will be picking up new responsibilities, either at a more promising organization, or through a promotion right where they are.

Getting a promotion doesn't mean you have won the battle, however. You will have to show you can handle managing, shoulder responsibilities, and more. Despite your success, try to be more modest, and avoid clashing with your superiors and the powers that be, which is counterproductive. The last 10 days of June are the most problematic, and there is a high chance of conflict. Find refuge with your friends and loved ones, who will support you and help you deal with your new responsibilities and challenges.

Money. Financially speaking, June is full of contradictions. You will have regular income and significantly more of it, too. However, your expenses will be on the rise, as well. Your long-term financial outlook is very positive, though, thanks to Jupiter.

Love and family. June brings with it a lot to deal with at work, and you may not have much time left over for your personal life. This is especially the case until June 20, after which, things should slow down a bit.

During this time, you may spend more time with your loved ones, and they are sure to return the favor. You have turned the page on difficult times, and that may lead to a separation, or perhaps ending an old quarrel. This applies to spouses who have faced serious difficulties in the past.

Couples who get along will see their relationship go through a transformative period, so keep an eye on your own shortcomings and take steps to fix them, if you can.

Remember that life does not stop, and changes are everywhere. Keep your finger on the pulse of things and learn fate's lessons as you go.

Health. This month, you are feeling energetic and have no reason to fear falling ill. During the last 10 days of the month, you might feel fatigue from all the stress at work. If that is the case, slow down and take some time for yourself.

Virgo

You are embarking on a period for which you have been preparing for some time. The time for talking is over, now, it's time to act!

Work. June is an incredibly important month for your career. You will be able to confirm your longstanding ideas and ambitious plans.

You might renew contact with old business partners, some of whom may live in other cities or abroad. You are beginning a new period in your career, and maybe your life, which will change literally everything. You may be making important steps in this direction already in June, or maybe it will come later in 2023.

You may be making plans related to a move, opening a business in another city or abroad. Alternatively, you may spend a lot of time traveling for work.

Employees will be negotiating a new job, and this will be very successful. You may already be starting your new job this month, and your old friends will be there to lend a hand. Even if not everything goes smoothly, there will be a solution. The overall trend is looking up, so keep that in mind, keep moving forward, and don't look back!

Money. Financially, June is not bad for you at all. You will have regular income, and significantly more of it. Expect the largest sums to come in on June 7, 8, 16, 17, 26, and 27.

Your expenses are low, and most of them are related to meetings at work, entertainment, or your loved ones.

Love and family. Virgos who are part of the working world might leave their personal lives on the back burner this month, work comes first! But if your personal life is the focus, get ready for some changes, not all of which are going to be positive.

If your relationship is literally hanging by a thread, remember that that thread can break at any time. That may be in June, or perhaps a little later. Severe Saturn has been in the sector of your sky responsible for marriage and long-term partnerships. Consider this a serious stress test for your relationship. Are you ready for it? Either way, there are things for you to think about. If you are facing difficulties with your spouse or partner, turn to friends, whose influence may smooth things over, but they are unlikely to solve this for you.

Health. In June, you are as vibrant as ever, and have no need to fear falling ill.

Libra

You are embarking on a fast-moving, dynamic, and extremely practical month. You want a lot, and nothing is stopping you from getting it! The heavens are on your side!

Work. In June, you are busy with every day, administrative, and financial tasks. Business owners and managers at every level will be holding important negotiations with partners and the results will be positive.

You might be actively cooperating with colleagues from other cities or abroad. You may even go on a successful trip!

Despite the generally positive tone this month, there is no way to avoid trouble entirely. This time, the fly in the ointment might be a difficult relationship with a colleague or your subordinates. They may throw a wrench in your plans, which will slow down everything. This is a longstanding problem, and perhaps you will decide it is time to change things up. This is what severe Saturn, which has been in the sector of your sky related to work, recommends.

Money. Financially, June is a favorable time for you, not so much because of your own resources, but because you will be able to count on material support from business partners, credit, or even income from unofficial sources.

Those who are not part of the working world might count on support from a loved one who is experiencing a positive streak at work.

Some Libras will receive an inheritance.

Expect some expenses related to your children's needs, as well as those of people in your circle. They may be so-called "friends" or people who are highly placed in society. The stars have some advice, here: do not promise too much, because their appetites may grow.

Love and family. Many Libras may be busy with everyday household issues. Major home repairs, selling real estate, buying other property, and other stressful tasks are on the agenda. That may happen in another city or abroad.

Your relationship with your children has been rocky in the past, and most likely, they are already adults, if that is the case. You are well-aware of the reason for this tension, so there is nothing new, here. You may temporarily fall out with a family member, as well.

Couples' relationships are also difficult, this month, and in the worst cases, they may separate. If there is any love still alive, it is worth trying to stick together, but otherwise, whatever happens, happens.

Health. This month, you are not as healthy as you could be, and the time has come to begin taking your well-being seriously.

Those who are young and strong should lead a healthy lifestyle, but the elderly and those who are weakened might take some preventive measures against chronic conditions, which will be prone to resurfacing.

Scorpio

You are alone on your own path, but teamwork is the word of the day. You are aware of the disadvantages you face, but there is also a silver lining – someone else is making difficult decisions for you, so you have less to worry about.

Work. There are changes afoot at work. Most Scorpios will encounter people with power and influence this month, and cooperation with them may be a constant this year, allowing you to make great strides. Be attentive, and when negotiating future working conditions, be sure to dot your i's and cross your t's, especially when it comes to finances. It is clear you have a lot of joint projects to complete, and this will allow you to be successful and avoid most problems.

You will be corresponding more frequently with colleagues from other cities or abroad, and you may bring back a former collaboration.

You may also receive new offers related to travel or a move, so be practical and responsible as you consider them, understanding that this will change your destiny.

In the months to come, it will be much clearer what path you should take.

Money. Financially, June is a month of contradictions. Your income has not changed, but you have a lot of expenses. The astrologist predicts that most of them will be related to your family, especially your children's needs.

Love and family. You are seeing changes in your personal life, as well. Those with families will have to tackle problems caused by their children, and that will involve investing a lot of resources in their care, training, and education. Alternatively, your children may be going through a rough patch, and you will have to help them out in words and deeds.

Those who have been looking for their better half for some time are in for some good news. You will begin a period full of opportunities to build your life. That may be a long-term romance, or perhaps you will soon be walking down the aisle.

Couples who have been together for a while may decide whether to live together, or possibly even to get married. You may begin a love story with an old friend or rekindle things with a former flame. Some Scorpios will see these events take place in June, while others will have to wait for a few months. The important thing is that your time has come!

Many families will be planning on a move. Some will be purchasing a new home, while others will be heading to a new city or abroad.

Health. In June, you are feeling sluggish with this swirl of activity both at work and at home. In order to get away from it all, try to sleep in and remember the healing power of a walk in nature.

Sagittarius

It is time to sit down and focus. You are climbing mountains at work, and as busy as ever. Once again, life is speeding up, but that's just your style!

Work. This month, you can expect to meet new people who will propose some interesting, but labor-intensive projects. They may involve faraway places or new countries, and naturally, that means business travel. There is no reason to turn down the opportunities fate sends your way, and all your hard work will pay off.

However, you also need to take a sober look at your reserves. Sit down with a calendar and create a clear plan and stick to a strict schedule in order to manage it all.

A new job is beckoning employees, and most likely, it will involve a promotion where you are right now. Alternatively, you can be sure of a higher salary.

Money. Financially, June is a great time for you. Money will be coming in regularly, and you will have much more of it. You can expect the largest sums to come in from June 19 to 22. Your expenses are low, and your higher income compensates for everything.

Love and family. Things are less rosy in your personal life than at work. Many Sagittarians will face difficulties with their parents or loved ones. Elderly relatives might fall ill or go through hardships, and you will have to lend a hand in both words and deeds.

Your relationship with your spouse is also not ideal, and you may have disagreements over household affairs. Alternatively, things between you may cool off a bit.

You may even find yourselves separated for totally objective reasons, for example, one of you has to work faraway for some time.

Your ties to relatives are also changing, and you may visit family living in other cities or abroad, or even handle a relative's business.

Health. In June, you are feeling less than vibrant, as you begin a period during which your body requires special care. A healthy lifestyle, rising early, and spending time in the sun will help keep your body strong, your mind clear, and your soul content.

Capricorn

He who would eat the fruit must climb the tree. If that is your motto this month, you will go far.

Work. In June, many Capricorns will have to draw a clear line between their professional and personal lives, and your presence will be sine qua non, here.

Business owners and managers will have to deal with matters related to production, and it is absolutely essential that your team's work be coordinated and coherent, here.

Many will have to smooth over a relationship with colleagues in other cities or abroad, which will require skill and effort on your part. You are sure to succeed in part, and the rest will require hard work. You may need to turn to a mediator or attorney in order to get a full handle on things.

You will need to prepare meticulously for any business travel planned for June, and study all possibilities, including those that are less than favorable. However, despite a few bobbles, things will move forward, and nothing will seriously throw a wrench in your plans.

Money. Your financial outlook is contradictory this month. On one hand, you will have your usual income, but you will also be bleeding money. The astrologist predicts that most of this will be related to your personal life, family, and your children's and loved ones' needs.

Expect to spend the greatest amounts in mid to late June.

Those who work with others' finances – accountants, bankers, and brokers – should be especially careful in June. Avoid any risky financial operations, as they will bring major losses, rather than profit.

Love and family. In June, your personal life is no less important than work. Parents will be dealing with their children's troubles and spend a lot of money on their development and education. Your children will bring you joy, and they are continuing to experience a positive streak.

Spouses whose marriage is on the rocks will clash yet again, this time over finances. Material matters are coming to a head for those who recently decided to divorce.

Your relationship with relatives may be challenging, as well. In some cases, that may mean things have cooled off or someone has been alienated. You are likely to reach a compromise, so there is reason to assess the situation and make the most beneficial choice you can.

Health. This month, you are feeling tired, but if you lead a healthy lifestyle and don't overdo things, you will avoid any complications.

Aquarius

This month, you will have to confine yourself to the things you know and only move along familiar paths. This is not a time for any experimentation! Most likely, this is temporary.

Work. This month, Aquarians who are part of the working world will be busy with financial and everyday matters. You may conduct various real estate transactions, especially if you are expanding your business. That may take place in other cities or abroad.

Your relationship with some partners may be far from ideal, and that is also related to real estate or other major property. Disagreements here may set the tone for the entire month, but conflict is especially likely from June 23 to 27.

At the same time, you will be able to protect your own property and that is legally owed to you. That means fending off any attacks from your foes.

Employees may spend much of June focused on family matters and are advised to just ask for a few personal days rather than coming up with excuses for avoiding work.

Money. It would be a stretch to call your finances stable this month. Most Aquarians will be spending heavily on their children or a loved one.

In mid-June, you may receive a large sum of money from unofficial sources.

You may also profit from real estate transactions or credit. Some Aquarians may receive an inheritance.

Love and family. The lion's share of June's activity will be in your personal life.

Many Aquarians will be fully immersed in setting up their home and may decide to move somewhere more comfortable. Those who recently faced difficulties with their residence or other real estate may have finally found a workable solution.

Additionally, you may face conflict in this area with your partner or someone from your recent past. Now, though, you will be able to protect your property from any unfair claims.

Many families may overcome problems involving their children and any related expenses.

June is a challenging time for couples, whose relationship will be put to a real test. That may be due to problems involving your parents, or possibly unexpected aggression from your loved one. The stars recommend handling either situation with kid gloves, because your partner is certainly not capable of doing that right now. Time heals all wounds, and you are advised to sit tight and avoid any sudden movements.

Health. In June, you are right where you need to be, and have no reason to fear falling ill.

Pisces

Jupiter's movements always bring change, and June is no different. Something that seemed like science fiction is quickly becoming reality.

Work. Once again, most Pisceans are developing their relationship with colleagues in other cities or abroad, this month. You might be renewing old ties, holding negotiations with past partners, or even go on a trip. June 10-19 is the best time for this.

Additionally, business owners and managers at every level may face difficulties involving colleagues. It seems that someone who is supposed to help you will instead throw a wrench in your plans.

Employees are advised to be careful with colleagues and avoid any intrigue on your team. Stay neutral – it is better, this way. You may also have to make a tough decision if you work with colleagues from faraway.

Money. Your finances are stable in June. You will have your regular income and expenses are low. For now, things are looking good.

Love and family. Your personal life is no less important than work, this month. Many Pisceans will be taking care of major issues involving your home. You may be getting a summer home ready, or perhaps looking for real estate faraway. You are noticeably spending much more time with relatives, and you may see family members living in other cities or abroad.

Near the end of the month, you will spend a lot of time with your children. You will be happily reunited, whether you have been separated by time or distance.

Health. This month, you are energetic enough and have no reason to fear falling ill. However, all month long, especially after June 20, you are advised to be careful when traveling and driving.

July

New York Time			London Time		
Calendar Day	Lunar Day	Lunar Day Start Time	Calendar Day	Lunar Day	Lunar Day Start Time
01/07/2023	15	6:54 PM	01/07/2023	14	7:30 PM
02/07/2023	16	7:58 PM	02/07/2023	15	8:37 PM
03/07/2023	17	8:55 PM	03/07/2023	16	9:33 PM
04/07/2023	18	9:44 PM	04/07/2023	17	10:16 PM
05/07/2023	19	10:25 PM	05/07/2023	18	10:49 PM
06/07/2023	20	11:00 PM	06/07/2023	19	11:15 PM
07/07/2023	21	11:31 PM	07/07/2023	20	11:38 PM
09/07/2023	22	12:01 AM	08/07/2023	21	11:58 PM
10/07/2023	23	12:29 AM	10/07/2023	22	12:18 AM
11/07/2023	24	12:59 AM	11/07/2023	23	12:39 AM
12/07/2023	25	1:32 AM	12/07/2023	24	1:02 AM
13/07/2023	26	2:08 AM	13/07/2023	25	1:30 AM
14/07/2023	27	2:49 AM	14/07/2023	26	2:04 AM
15/07/2023	28	3:36 AM	15/07/2023	27	2:46 AM
16/07/2023	29	4:28 AM	16/07/2023	28	3:36 AM
17/07/2023	30	5:24 AM	17/07/2023	29	4:34 AM
17/07/2023	1	2:33 PM	17/07/2023	1	7:33 PM
18/07/2023	2	6:22 AM	18/07/2023	2	5:37 AM
19/07/2023	3	7:21 AM	19/07/2023	3	6:43 AM
20/07/2023	4	8:20 AM	20/07/2023	4	7:50 AM
21/07/2023	5	9:19 AM	21/07/2023	5	8:56 AM
22/07/2023	6	10:17 AM	22/07/2023	6	10:03 AM
23/07/2023	7	11:15 AM	23/07/2023	7	11:09 AM
24/07/2023	8	12:15 PM	24/07/2023	8	12:17 PM
25/07/2023	9	1:16 PM	25/07/2023	9	1:27 PM
26/07/2023	10	2:20 PM	26/07/2023	10	2:39 PM
27/07/2023	11	3:26 PM	27/07/2023	11	3:53 PM
28/07/2023	12	4:33 PM	28/07/2023	12	5:07 PM
29/07/2023	13	5:39 PM	29/07/2023	13	6:16 PM
30/07/2023	14	6:39 PM	30/07/2023	14	7:17 PM
31/07/2023	15	7:32 PM	31/07/2023	15	8:07 PM

You can find the description of each lunar day in the chapter "A Guide to The Moon Cycle and Lunar Days"

Aries

This month, you will have to juggle several projects at the same time. You will also have to choose between leisure and working on your tan and busying yourself with hard work on the household front.

Work. Incurable workaholics – and they are well-represented among Aries – will spend much of July on everyday and administrative tasks. You are likely to continue with major construction, repairs, and many bothersome jobs related to this.

Business owners and managers at every level are advised to be careful with their subordinates – their mistakes may cost you dearly. The last 10 days of July will be the most indicative here, when a colleague's shortcomings will cause unexpected problems. You may also see intrigue from secret enemies and competitors during this period.

Employees will spend most of the month busy with family matters, but during the last 10 days of the month, and you will have to deal with problems on your team stemming from gossipy colleagues. Someone in your circle may bring to light information that you would have rather kept secret.

From July first to 19, things will be quieter. Any events planned during this period will go as expected, without any holdups or problems.

Money. July is a great time for your finances. You will have steady income, and significantly more of it. Expect the largest sums to come in on July 3, 4, 7, 11-14, 30, and 31.

Your expenses are pleasant in July – shopping, relaxation, your children's needs – not only can you afford it all, but it's the best investment in your personal life.

Love and family. Those who are not part of the working world may be busy with their personal lives this month. You are working on improving your household and various tasks related to real estate. This pleasant summer month is a great time for relaxation, which is best planned with your family, relatives, and loved ones.

Some Aries will head somewhere faraway, while others will go to a summer house or visit relatives who live nearby.

Families will be harmonious, and many Aries will be busy with their children's affairs and spend a lot on their unexpected needs.

This month will bring pleasant surprises to couples, as well as unexpected irritation. The stars recommend not being stingy or making any demands of your partner in order to avoid any disagreements.

Health. The elderly or those with chronic diseases should be especially careful during the last 10 days of July. Illnesses may creep up unexpectedly and cause a lot of anxiety during this time.

Taurus

This month, you will manage to accomplish a lot, and your energy will be the envy of even the most decorated athletes. That's the way it should be, because realizing a long-held dream is at stake.

Work. It is hard for you to sit still in July. Business owners and managers will be discussing their plans with colleagues from other cities or abroad and may even go on a trip in order to make them happen.

You may renew your ties with former business partners, old friends, and hold successful, constructive negotiations.

Employees will continue to climb the ladder of success. Jupiter is incredibly strong in your sign, so fear no challenges – you are capable of anything!

The best time for anything work-related is the first 20 days of July. After July 20, your ruler, Venus, will be in retrograde, and you will need to take a step back, look around, and do the things you had put off for later. These may be day-to-day administrative tasks and things necessary to tie up loose ends.

Any business travel planned for July will be a smashing success.

Be careful from July 20 to 23. You may experience unexpected disagreements with friends, or someone highly placed in society. The problem may be either financial or ideological in nature.

Money. July is stable but no more. You have your usual income, and your expenses are low. Most of them will happen during the last 10 days of the month.

Love and family. July is a busy in your personal life, as well. You might go on a trip and meet up with old acquaintances, relatives, and friends who live in other cities or abroad. In many families, things are not so easy right now. The problem is you, and the way you have been conducting yourself, which is irritating your partner. You might be bothered by household issues, your children's behavior, or your partner's unwillingness to do things the way you would like. After July 20 will be the most difficult time, when your disagreements may lead to clashes.

This is not a good time for most couples. It is impossible to predict exactly how things will play out, but you can expect some agitation.

The stars recommend not being selfish and considering your loved one's interests if you want to mitigate any trouble.

Health. In June, you are healthy, energetic, and able to climb mountains. The only thing that might bother you is your weight. If that sounds like you, think about how to eat a balanced diet and don't forget about the healing power of a walk in nature.

Gemini

You are embarking on a very busy month, but your hard work is sure to bear fruit. The astrologer predicts that you know exactly what you want, and you are certain to get it. Well, almost all of it, and that's not so bad, either.

Work. July is a time full of success and you will remember this time for your achievements, especially the financial ones.

Business owners can count on healthy profits from work they completed earlier, while employees will be recognized for their merits, which may lead to a material benefit.

The best time for anything work-related is the first 20 days of the month. After July 21, you might run into unexpected problems with your superiors or official bodies. That may involve real estate or other major property.

You may also experience disagreements with colleagues from other cities or abroad this month. That may be over the laws in other countries, or possibly your partners behaving unreliably. That situation will drag on for a bit, so be patient, and step by step, you will manage to solve this. In the end, you will get what you want!

Money. Financially, this is a great month for you. In addition to your usual income, you can count on profits from unofficial sources, support from your parents or a loved one.

Love and family. Your personal life is characterized by major household projects, most likely involving a new apartment, home, summer home, or other large acquisitions that involve the whole family.

However, in many families, your relationships may feel unstable. You might experience disagreements with your parents or other relatives, especially during the last 10 days of July.

Somewhat later, things will calm down, so try to keep a cool head and avoid making decisions driven by emotions.

Be especially careful when completing any documents related to real estate purchases or repairs and check every detail.

These recommendations are especially important for those who have decided to move to another country. Foreign laws might significantly differ from what you are used to, so assistance from those in the know will prove to be invaluable.

Health. In July, you are feeling a bit run down. Be especially careful if you are elderly or weakened by chronic disease. A health resort, spa, or visit to a specialist might give your body the push it needs this month, and all year long.

Those who are young and strong should try to live a healthy lifestyle and remember the importance of a good night's sleep.

Cancer

This month, you are still busy and active as ever, but things are not turning out quite as you would have hoped. That's not to say you should admit defeat, but you have some things to work on, and you are sure to do just that!

Work. In July, many Cancers are solidifying cooperation with partners and colleagues in other cities or abroad. You may be renewing an old partnership, be in constant contact with associates, or go on a successful trip.

People who are highly placed in society and friends may be involved in all areas of your business this month but be prudent and pragmatic with them. It is worth determining who owes what and who owns what right off the bat.

You are unlikely to arrive at a compromise right away when it comes to the material and financial obligations that are likely to take up most of July, but things will work out on your second attempt, and everything should fall into place.

During the last 10 days of July, you will experience unexpected disagreements with colleagues from other cities or abroad, which will significantly complicate your relationship. You may see old legal problems rear their ugly heads once again. Moving forward, you can say that these issues will indeed be resolved eventually, but it will take some time.

Money. Your finances are seeing a lot of ups and downs in July. On one hand, you will not end up bankrupt, but you have a lot of expenses. They may be due to business, or possibly your personal life. If you are planning any shopping sprees, be sure to take measures to ensure you do not overspend.

Love and family. During the first half of July, things are calm and positive. Many will go on a trip to see friends and relatives who live in other cities or abroad. During the second half of the month, however, expect conflict and strife. You may disagree with either family members or your romantic partner.

In addition to conflict with your better half, you may also have serious arguments with close family members. Things may look messy and chaotic, so keep your emotions in check and if possible, act as a peacemaker and diplomat. Since right now no one in your inner circle is up to that difficult task, the stars might bestow it on you alone.

Keep an eye on your friends. Their appetite might turn out to be extreme.

Health. This month, you are healthy, energetic and have no reason to fear falling ill.

Drivers and anyone traveling should be careful all month long, especially during the last 10 days of July.

Leo

It's a good idea to take a break between so many important activities. That may be just what July brings for you.

Work. July is a better time for relaxing and spending time with family, but for those who cannot step back from work for even a minute, this month will still be useful for you. You will be able to calmly delve into the tasks you had been putting off, especially getting your financial documents in order.

Closer to the last 10 days of the month, that may change. During that time, many Leos will experience financial difficulties. You will have to ask for credit, settle old debts, or possibly patch up some holes in the company budget. No need to worry, though, as things are moving ahead, and you will find the money.

Money. Despite your obvious professional success, things are not easy when it comes to money. Expect the largest expenses during the second half of July. Some will be related to business and old debts, and others will be due to your personal life.

You will not find yourself totally broke, however, and expect the largest sums to come in on July 3, 4, 11, 12, 20, 21, and 31.

Love and family. July will shake up your personal life once again. Divorcing couples may argue over shared property or have moral claims against one another. Your long-term relationship may have been on the rocks for some time, and now, the time has come to finally bring things to a close.

You may have someone new in your life, in which case that is the source of all your problems. However, these relationships may lead to disappointment, so all that glitters is not gold. At least for now.

The stars recommend that you think long and hard about what you really want in a relationship, and what is getting in your way. It seems that now is the time for this is now.

This of course only applies to couples who have been feuding. If everything at home is harmonious, you and your partner will be able to resolve any household or financial issues together.

Health. For most of July, you will feel less than energetic, so find time to relax. The first half of the month will bring you an opportunity to do just that.

Virgo

This month, you will have to turn to others for support. They will be people you love and trust. You are turning a page on the past, but the future is blurry, and you can't go it alone!

Work. Virgos who are part of the working world will have to solve many difficult tasks this month. For business owners and managers, a partner will have become increasingly difficult to deal with, and during the last 10 days of July, that will be more noticeable than ever. You may experience open disagreements, which may turn into an outright conflict.

Those planning a trip or to open their business in another city or abroad may also face challenges this month, and most of them will appear during the first two weeks of July. In September, however, things will all be resolved, thanks to your hard work and perseverance.

In all areas, July is a good month for seeing old friends or people who are highly placed in society. Some of them may become valuable mediators in any conflict involving your partners.

Money. In July, you can expect money troubles, mainly due to a difficult situation at work or problems in your personal life. Remember that sooner or later, we all reveal the thorn in our side, and that may be a clue to how this plays out.

Love and family. Those who managed to avoid any problems at work will be in for an unpleasant surprise in their personal life.

Couples who are on the rocks have arrived at the point that their relationship is literally hanging by a thread. Any misstep, and that thread is sure to break. The last 10 days of the month will be the most difficult time for you, as anything you do may lead to an angry response from your partner. Remember that any conflict could be your last, and act accordingly. However, if the love is truly gone, you can ignore this advice.

Many couples will notice that their relationship needs a lot of tact, attention, and understanding. Keep that in mind if you have any desire to remain together. This applies whether you are married or not.

Health. During the first 20 days of July, you are feeling vibrant and have no reason to fear falling ill. During the last 10 days of the month, however, you may feel run-down after all of the challenges you have been facing, so plan for some time to relax and focus on yourself. This is especially the case for the elderly and those who suffer from chronic illnesses.

Libra

July has its ups and downs for you. You will make achievements, but nothing comes without some baggage. But remember – you never know what you are capable of until you try.

Work. In July, you will have to work hard to defend your place in the sun.

Many Libras will be dealing with unresolved tasks that began in 2022. That includes a relationship with a like-minded person, and various financial obligations. In some cases, it may be problems between the two of you, and it could involve friends or possibly people highly placed in society with material claims, and you will have to settle up. Things will be at their sharpest during the first 10 days of the month, however thanks to your hard work and efforts, you will manage to push through.

During the last 10 days of the month, you will face problems of a different sort. Business owners and managers at every level will face opposition from their subordinates, while employees may have to grapple with an ill-intentioned colleague.

Many Libras will have to contend with secret enemies and those who are in open conflict with you. If this is the case, the last 10 days of the month will be particularly telling. This situation may continue into the future, so keep your fingers on the pulse of what is happening and be sure to keep an eye on yourself.

Money. Despite the trouble at work, you will not find yourself in the red. Your income compensates for your expenses, and close to the end of July, your bank account will be neutral.

Love and family. July is heavily focused on your professional life, and you may not have much time left over for personal matters. In many families, you will be talking about major household changes, and that may keep you busy with your spouse or loved one.

Most likely, you are building a home, apartment, summer home, or buying new real estate. In some cases, this may continue into next year or take place in another country.

Relationships in dysfunctional families are far from ideal. You may see conflict related to money or disagreements over how to raise your children. It is likely that some secrets – either yours or your partner's – will come to light, which will not help smooth things over with your family. If that is your case, be careful and do not behave suspiciously or give anyone any reason to gossip.

Unmarried couples may experience a similar situation, but here, this only concerns partners who have faced many problems in the past.

Health. In July, you are healthy, energetic, and this means you are able to favorably resolve any problems that life throws at you, whether at work or at home.

Scorpio

Once again, this month brings you to an important turning point. Now, you are laying the foundation for a new future, so there is good reason to think everything over and make your calculations ahead of time.

Work. For anything work-related, July is a crucial time for you. This is a busy, dynamic month with a lot of promise.

Business owners and managers at every level will be getting in touch with partners from other cities or abroad and may go on a successful trip.

You may renew your relationship with old partners or meet new colleagues. You have new business and interesting projects on the agenda but be more cautious with everyone fate sends your way. It is not worth being too demanding, but don't give into your partner on everything, either. Find a workable compromise for everything this month, even if it isn't an overnight process.

Employees might be discussing a new job or a promotion where they are, but that is likely to take some time, so don't expect much to happen until mid-September. Naturally, things will work out in your favor. The reason for the delay is your competition and your bosses being busy with other matters.

Money. Your finances are improving, whether you are a business owner or employee.

Expect the largest sums to come in on July 1, 2, 9, 10, 18-20, 28, and 29.

Your expenses are modest, and most are related to your children.

Love and family. Your personal life is looking chaotic and stressful. Parents will face serious difficulties with their children, and that may involve an argument or possibly them finding themselves in a sticky situation. Either way, you will have to lend a hand in words, deeds, and money. But if not you, who else?

Couples will run into disappointments and possibly even a serious argument, leading you to doubt your entire relationship. Expect your personal challenges to reach a crescendo during the second half of July, while the first two weeks will be smooth sailing.

From July 1 to 20, many Scorpios may go on a trip, which will turn out very well. If your family or romantic relationships are causing you trouble, a trip may help smooth things over. The stars recommend that you exercise utmost restraint and ensure that arguments do not spill over into serious conflict.

Health. In July, you are healthy, active, attractive, and it comes as no surprise that any illness will pass you by.

Sagittarius

You are embarking on a quiet, somewhat lazy month, which gives you a chance to stop and take a look around you. Perhaps it's time to stop chasing success for a moment and simply relax?

Work. For anything work-related, July is less than ideal. Most Sagittarians are taking a step back from work and focusing on themselves, their loved ones, and their families. That may be the case during the first 20 days of the month.

Those who for various reasons are unable to get away from work will spend time on organizational tasks, raising funds, and negotiating with partners.

You may also be actively communicating with colleagues from faraway, and things will turn out well for you. Colleagues from abroad or other cities will be evasive or contradictory, which will slow down negotiations. Expect to not get a clear answer on much from them this month.

But despite this, things at work depend on you and what steps you take. Things will pick up for most Sagittarians during the last 10 days of July.

Money. Financially, July is an unstable time for you. Money will be coming in as usual, but your expenses will be high. In most cases, they are related to leisure, household issues, and travel.

Perhaps someone close to you will cover the largest expenses for you, or simply share the burden.

Love and family. July is a great time to focus on your personal life and family. Remember that the office will not slide into chaos if you are gone for a few days. Your main job in July is to strike a mental balance, and it doesn't matter where you do that – in a hammock on a tropical island or at home in nature.

During the first 20 days of July, things will be harmonious and peaceful within families. The last 10 days, however, will be more complicated, and expect conflicts between parents and children and arguments over real estate.

The last 10 days of July will be difficult for couples, too. Your relationship needs to be defined, and you are not the culprit. If your partner is not behaving the way one should in a healthy, positive relationship, you have some things to think about. Think hard about what you really want, and what you don't want. Then, things will fall into place and life will become calmer and easier once again.

Health. In July, you are feeling tired, so take care of yourself and take any measures you must. It might be a good idea to watch what you eat and follow a healthy diet. Do not overwork or overbook yourself and remember that an inner balance is the key to stability at work, at home, and in love.

Capricorn

Expect a positive month, divided into two halves. There's both good news and bad news. But the stars predict that you will manage it all!

Work. During the first 20 days of July, you can be sure to ride a positive streak. During this time, work will move at a comfortable pace, without any hold ups or problems. You will renew your ties with colleagues from other cities or abroad, and you may take a successful trip. You are at the heart of it all – you are surrounded by old colleagues and new friends. Negotiations are going as they should, and you are showing everyone you are positive and knowledgeable. This is a great time for exchanging any information, studies, and communications.

After July 20, things will grow more complicated. During this time, the connections you have built will unexpectedly fail. Initially, this involves colleagues from other cities or abroad. Here, you can expect various misunderstandings, so keep your finger on the pulse of what's happening and consider various options to get back on the straight and narrow.

During the same time, you can expect various financial challenges, which will include unexpected expenses, debts, and spending on hospitality.

Money. Financially speaking, the first 20 days of the month will be neutral. You will have your normal income, and your spending will be reasonable and modest. During the last 10 days of July, however, expect to grapple with business expenses, debts, and spending related to your personal life.

Love and family. Some Capricorns will be more focused on their personal life this month. You may head somewhere with a warm, sunny beach, and spend time with relatives or friends who live in other cities or abroad.

During the first 20 days of July, your relationship with relatives is fairly calm, and if you had any recent misunderstandings, they will be resolved. But don't let your guard down – during the last 10 days of the month, you might find yourself arguing once again. Don't be surprised if all of your family members get dragged into it, as well.

During the last 10 days of July, you might also face problems related to your children. In the best-case scenario, that just means expenses related to their education, studies, and development whether they are still small or already grown. In the worst cases, though, expect to tangle over money with your adult children.

During the last 10 days of July, couples can expect trouble, as well.

Fate's path is at times confusing. Something that seemed clear is not so anymore. The problem might be you and your inner problems and have nothing to do with your partner. If that sounds like you, assess the situation and do not make any final decisions. Venus, the planet of love, is in retrograde, and this is not the time to exert full control over the situation or try to force any understanding. If you have any doubts, just sit tight!

Health. This month, you are feeling sluggish, though you will not fall ill. Close to the end of the month, many Capricorns might feel tired from meetings, negotiations, or being surrounded by people. In late July or August, it will be time to take a break.

During the last 10 days of the month, be extra careful when driving or traveling. There is a high probability of accidents on the road during this time.

Aquarius

July is a busy, practical month for you. Remember that a bird in hand is worth more than two in the bush, and things will be fine.

Work. During the first 20 days of July, you will be very busy with work and forget all about leisure or relaxation.

Business owners and managers can count on support from subordinates, while employees will benefit from well-wishing colleagues. Those busy expanding their business or with various real estate operations might count on positive results during the first 20 days of the month.

After July 20, however, things will not be so rosy. During this time, you might see major disagreements with partners, mostly over money and other material obligations. You are unlikely to reach an agreement over this in July, especially if the situation drags out.

Regardless of what your deceitful opponents say, be careful. Not everything is as people say, and you may have to revisit some issues multiple times.

The astrologist predicts that any disagreements will involve real estate, land, or other large property.

Money. During the first 20 days of the month, things will be looking up. You will have regular income and somewhat more than usual. Expect the largest sums to come in on July 7, 8, 16, 17, 26, and 27.

Major expenses and unexpected financial trouble will wait until after July 20, and they may be related to work or possibly your personal life.

Love and family. In many cases, most of July's events will be centered around your personal life. Couples who get along will work together to tackle difficult issues related to real estate, along with bothersome tasks that will cost you both money and nerves.

In many families, relationships are far from ideal. You may have small disagreements, which will spill over into serious conflict during the second half of the month. You will be fighting over money and differing views on how to improve or divide up your home.

During the last 10 days of July, Venus will be in retrograde, which will bring misunderstandings even among the strongest couples. Unmarried couples can expect the same, especially if they have been together for a long time.

Health. This month, your energy potential is low, so take care of yourself and take the steps you need. Don't forget the importance of self-care, keep a cool head, and avoid stress. Take a few days in nature, to visit a health spa, and get a relaxing massage, which is the best medicine.

Pisces

In July, you seem to be receiving favorable attention from all ends. Wherever you are – on a beach on the Indian Ocean or just in nature near home, it is impossible to not take notice of you!

Work. During the first 20 days of July, you would do best to focus on relaxing rather than stress at work. The exception to this is people working in creative professions – actors, artists, musicians, and anyone who works with words. If that is you, expect a successful tour, recognition, and a handsome financial reward.

If various circumstances have forced you to spend your summer days at work, the stars recommend renewing old ties, and making new connections, as well. You might find yourself talking to old colleagues from other cities or abroad or even going on a trip.

Things will not run so smoothly after July 20. Expect unexpected and unpleasant surprises. Your relationship with some partners will grow much more difficult, and you may see claims against one another and open conflict.

You can expect your relationship with a colleague from faraway to worsen during the last 10 days of July, as well. You may have to reconsider some matters at work and things might drag out, or perhaps some colleagues will suddenly change the rules of the game.

During the last 10 days of July, managers should keep a close eye on their subordinates and avoid taking their word for things. Trust, but verify, in order to avoid mistakes or misunderstandings.

Employees should also be careful during this period and avoid placing too much trust in their colleagues. Stay out of any gossip on your team.

Money. July might be an inconsistent time for your finances. You have a lot of expenses, and most of the time, they are related to your personal life, romance, or your family.

Love and family. The stars predict that during the first 20 days of July, you would do well to relax and spend time with your loved ones. You might take a trip, which will turn out well. Take a few days to visit the beach, or simply take time off of work in order to restore your body and soul.

You might renew ties with old friends or former lovers, or expect to

In early and late August, you may face problems involving friends, like-minded people, or someone with a much stronger position in society than you. The root of this disagreement will be ambition or financial claims.

Your relationship with colleagues from other cities or abroad is developing with varying degrees of success, and by the end of August, you can expect negotiations or a trip.

Money. Financially speaking, August is not particularly auspicious. You do not have much money, but your expenses will be high, probably due to your personal life and your family and children's needs.

Love and family. Your personal life is turbulent and inconsistent. Those with families will be fully immersed in the details of everyday life. You might need to put the finishing touches on a recently purchased home or buy things to decorate your home.

These troublesome tasks might lead to arguments, even in the most loving couples. You may need to reconsider or start over from scratch, but the results will be worth it. In the end, you will get everything you want.

Divorcing and divorced couples will have yet another argument this month. This time, it is over real estate, money, and raising your children.

In many families, you may experience problems involving children, and this will be much more noticeable as August draws to a close. Pay attention to the details and try to help your older children if you see that they need your support.

This is a difficult time for most couples. Your ruler, Venus, will be in retrograde all month, and starting on August 23, Mercury will be in retrograde, as well.

All of this means that something will be brewing in your love life. It is hard to rewrite the rules of a relationship when you are in it. You know what you want from your partner, but that is not always the reality. But if there is anything that makes the relationship worth saving, hold onto those feelings tight. If not, these recommendations are superfluous.

Health. In August, you are feeling somewhat sluggish, and you might be experiencing tiredness and fatigue, low self-esteem, and mood swings. If you really need a break, then take one, let yourself relax and let go. But otherwise, try to eat a healthy diet. This month you have a tendency to gain weight, and you know how hard it is to lose it!

Gemini

This month, your path is long and winding, though you are sure to find a way out of the maze. Make a clear plan of action, follow it, and avoid any sharp turns, both in your love life and at work.

Work. For Geminis in the working world, the biggest issue this month will be your relationship with partners from other cities or abroad. Their inconsistent behavior will put the brakes on your plans and business.

There may be influences behind the scenes, and you might not learn about them right away. Even when this comes to light, you are unlikely to be able to cope with everything in August. Ride it out! Cross each bridge when you come to it, and don't rush things. Remember, haste makes waste.

What's more, all month long, you might face issues with management or the powers that be, which will become more noticeable near the end of August. Remember that insisting or trying to add anything right now will only backfire.

Be cautious, flexible, and follow the ancient Chinese tactic of waiting until your enemy's corpse floats by. Only patience and tenacity will see you through to victory.

Money. Financially, August is not particularly bright for you. You do not have much money, but your expenses will be rather high. Instability at work, at home, and with your family means that your wallet will be rather empty by the end of the month.

Some Geminis might see profits from real estate transactions, either a sale or a favorable exchange. If things are really challenging, you can count on support from older family members.

Love and family. Many Geminis will be preoccupied with household matters this month. You will be setting up a home somewhere new, working on repairs, purchasing items, and decorating.

In certain cases, you may be doing this in a new city or even abroad. If that sounds like you, be attentive to laws, paperwork, and documents. Venus is in retrograde, and by the middle of the month, Mercury will be, too, which will lead to problems with paperwork, documents, delays, and many unpleasant annoyances.

Some families may face various problems involving relatives and elderly family members.

Perhaps a family member will fall ill or face a serious of problems at work, and you will have to come to his or her aid, in both words and deeds. Perhaps you will see a family blowout. Regardless, don't let your emotions rule the day, remain calm, and don't lose sight of your plans. Soon, these difficulties will be but a memory.

Health. This month, there is nothing threatening your health, though the ups and downs and irritations may leave you feeling fatigued by the time September rolls around. Regardless of your circumstances, do not give into your emotions and remember to get enough sleep. Remember that sleep is the foundation of good health.

All month long, the stars recommend that you take extra precautions when traveling and driving. There is a high likelihood of accidents, right now. This applies whether you are traveling for work or pleasure.

Cancer

"Money can't buy you happiness, but lots of money can," is surprisingly appropriate this month. Your ability to handle both projects and money has always been your trump card, but don't let yourself get distracted.

Work. Your biggest problem this month will be difficult relationships with partners, like-minded people, and friends, or someone highly placed in society.

This may be due to money, debts, and other material obligations. All month long, negotiations over this matter will be in the background, and things will not be resolved until September.

Your relationship with colleagues from other cities or abroad will develop with varying success. Things will go swimmingly with some partners, but in other cases, trouble is unavoidable.

This may involve colleagues with whom you have faced challenges in the past, in 2022. However, things are less critical now, and step by step, you will manage to resolve even the thorniest issues. Otherwise, your stubborn partners will be replaced, and the problem will solve itself.

Those with longstanding legal problems will see a new chapter in August. If the issue is money, you can expect to have to give some away this time.

Money. Financial problems are the theme of this month. Many Cancers will have to settle old debts, pay back loans, or resolve a tricky financial situation in their family.

You will have income, however, and you can expect the largest sums to come in on August 5-7, 15, 16, 25, and 26. This will allow you to avoid a default and resolve your financial troubles as they arise.

Love and family. Your personal life is full of financial conflicts, as well, this month. Couples who get along will resolve these difficult matters together, by leveraging wisdom and undying love. Divorced couples might yet again find themselves arguing over money.

Many families will experience trouble involving relatives, and close to the end of the month, you can expect a serious feud.

Alternatively, your relatives may fall ill or go through difficult times, and you will have to provide assistance in both words and deeds.

This is a difficult month for unmarried couples, as well. Your relationship may seem to cool off, or maybe you are reconsidering things altogether. In the worst-case scenario, you can expect financial claims against one another. It is a bad idea to mix love and money, and the stars recommend that you take a long, hard look at your relationship. It might not be what you need, and if that's the case, it's better to look at the truth head on.

Health. In August, you are feeling sluggish, so take care of yourself and take any necessary measures. All month long, be careful when traveling and driving.

Leo

In August, Venus will be in retrograde right in your sign. That means that you will need to be flexible as you maneuver around the many challenges that this beautiful summer month throws your way.

Work. In August, things at work may be heating up a bit.

Managers and business owners are likely to experience disagreements for various reasons – money or other material issues. You will have clashing viewpoints about business and each partner's role in its current and future development.

Employees may disagree with management, and regardless of where you stand, try to be more flexible and diplomatic. Conflicts will do you no good, right now. Your career has only just begun, you are charging ahead, and there is no need to ruin it over petty matters, which is what these problems are.

Money. August is full of ups and downs for your bank account. On one hand, you are making money, and you can expect the largest sums to come in on August 7-9, 17, 18, 27, and 28.

On the other hand, you will spend much of what you make. Old debts, paying off loans, and business investments, as well as family affairs will all make a significant dent.

There is hope, however, that your income will cover all these expenses, and closer to the end of the month, your balance will be back in the black.

Love and family. Your personal life is still turbulent. It seems that your long-term relationship is going through a rough patch, and you may be thinking about divorce or dividing up your belongings. If that is the decision you have made, let bygones be bygones. The future is a clean slate, and you can write it however you want.

Alternatively, your partner is going through a difficult period, and the entire family can feel it. This only applies to those who have experienced trouble in the past. If that is you, things will reach their logical conclusion.

Spouses who get along will work together to overcome August's hurdles.

Health. In August, you are feeling fairly energetic and the only thing you have to worry about is frayed nerves.

Virgo

This month, you will need to display both restraint and caution. August is not a particularly favorable time for you. Sometimes, we go through times like these, that is why the stars recommend that you ride it out rather than rushing into battle.

Work. This is not a good time for you at work. Those with connections to colleagues in other cities or abroad will face numerous challenges.

You may have to contend with the laws of another country, or legal hiccups on your road to success. A difficult relationship with a past partner may also come to a head. Conflict is likely all month long, but the second half will be particularly tense.

During this time, you might decide to react aggressively, but that will only exacerbate an already-difficult situation. Though delicate issues involving colleagues from faraway might be temporary, a challenging relationship with a colleague might become a longstanding, chronic issue. Keep that in mind and avoid beating your head against the wall – this time, it might turn out to be made of steel.

All month long, Venus will be in retrograde, and starting on August 23, Mercury will join it. These aspects mean that August is not a time for any permanent decision-making or hasty moves.

Make a point of being less active this month than usual, and watch your back, because you might also run into secret enemies and information that you'd rather keep quiet coming to the surface.

Money. With so many difficulties at work this month, you can expect money troubles to follow. However, On August 19-21, 28, and 29, you can count on receiving a decent sum.

Love and family . If your life path has taken you to a place where you are more focused on your personal life than work, here, you can expect to face some tough times. Your relationship with your spouse or partner might totally fall apart, and this will be partly your fault. Perhaps you will finally have to answer for mistakes made in the past.

The planets are aligned in such a way that even couples who get along might find themselves dealing with tensions.

Severe Saturn, which now rules your connections, suggests that by keeping a careful attitude toward one another, you will be able to avoid many problems.

Health. Those lucky enough to avoid unpleasant situations at home and at work may experience health issues in August. Be especially careful if you are elderly or suffer from chronic conditions. The stars recommend that you spend some time taking care of yourself and taking a step back from work. All month long, be careful driving and traveling. There is a rather high risk of road accidents this month.

Libra

The road to success is not always strewn with rose petals. But it is still there, and your job is to find it in the confusing labyrinth of life.

Work. You will spend much of August relaxing, somewhere with a warm, sunny beach. But if you absolutely cannot step away from work, the stars still recommend that you get your affairs in order, especially financial matters.

All month long, you may be bleeding money for various reasons. If you have debts, obligations to like-minded people, highly placed individuals, or friends, this is the time to settle them.

Another concern this month will be your relationship with your team at work, and you might expect conflicts with certain associates. This is nothing new to you, and certainly not the first time that these people have displayed such shortcomings. You should have made a change long ago, but nothing is stopping you from doing it right now.

Employees might see trouble brewing on their team, and the best thing you can do is show restraint and avoid any intrigue.

This month, beware of rumors, gossip, and unpleasant secrets, both yours and those around you. This may not be resolved until next month.

Money. August will leave your bank account in ruins. Your money will be burning a hole in your pocket, and this time, the culprit may be work, debts, or possibly your personal life, including recreation or your family's and children's needs.

You can be sure to count on support from a loved one who is experiencing a lucky streak at work.

Young people can count on their parents or older family members.

Love and family. Many Libras will be focused on relaxation during these dog days of summer. You can expect fun outings with friends, shopping, and the joy of forgetting about work and instead spending time with your loved ones and family – all you need in August.

Those planning any major construction or repairs might spend the lion's share of the family budget on these endeavors.

For lovers, the sky above you may be grey and cloudy in August. Your ruler, Venus, will be in retrograde all month long, so expect doubts and hesitations in your relationship, as well. If things remain cool, that may become dangerous. Keep that in mind, and if you want to save your relationship, be pure as a dove and wise as an owl.

Avoid gossip and intrigue.

Health. In August, be especially careful if you are elderly or suffer from chronic conditions. The stars recommend you be attentive to your body, especially during the last 10 days of the month.

Scorpio

August is a busy month, but also full of ups and downs. This is a nerve-wracking time for you, and you will need discipline, patience, and responsibility to get through it. But don't worry – you have these qualities in spades!

Work. Expect a very challenging month when it comes to anything work-related. You might face misunderstandings with partners, or conflicts and delays. Business owners might reconsider their current projects, and even shift course. Not everyone is likely to be happy with this, and your main task will be convincing partners that you have made the right choice. There may be trouble brewing at the top, and that will create tension on your team.

Your ties with colleagues in other cities or abroad are moving along nicely, though you will need to negotiate with them repeatedly. There is nothing here that can't be solved – you will manage to get things under control, and slowly but surely, everything will fall into place, both with business and your relationships.

Money. Despite the obvious problems at work, your financial situation is just fine. Expect the largest sums to come in on August 6, 7, 14-16, and 24-26.

Your expenses are low, and most of them are related to your children and loved ones.

Love and family. Many Scorpios are preoccupied with work in August, though your personal life will not entirely fade into the background.

In order to avoid emotional burnout, try to keep work out of your personal life as much as you can.

The stars recommend that you pay special attention to your children, as they may be experiencing tough times and need your moral and material support.

Many couples will reach a crossroads. Most likely, your relationship is coming to an end, or perhaps the time has come to take it to the next level. The time to make a decision will come soon, if it hasn't already.

Your relationship with relatives is improving, and you might travel to see those who live in another city or abroad.

Health. In August, you are healthy and active, but also a ball of anxiety. If you can, try to spend a few days focusing on yourself and those who love you. A bath with some relaxing oils or even some time surrounded by palm trees is the best medicine for you right now.

Sagittarius

The events of this month may seem like an obstacle course, but you are in no danger of failing. With your typical persistence and perseverance, you are able to overcome any hurdle.

Work. Sagittarians who are part of the working world can expect frayed nerves in August. Your connections to partners in other cities or abroad are experiencing a lot of ups and downs. Underhanded colleagues may throw a wrench in any decision-making, suddenly change the terms of cooperation, or simply waste your time.

At the same time, thanks to your own efforts, business will keep moving along, and slowly but surely, new projects will fall into place.

Closer to the end of the month, employees are likely to see changes at the top. Alternatively, there may be changes in your employer's goals and priorities.

These changes may be necessary, as it will be easier to see the task at hand and get rid of anything standing in your way. However, that will take time, and the real work will not start until sometime later.

Money. Despite the confusion at work, your bank account is in good shape. You may periodically receive large sums of money, especially on August 1, 7-9, 10, 18, 27, and 28.

Your expenses are low, and most of them are related to your family.

Love and family. Your personal life is seeing a continuation of trends that began earlier. Problems with parents or elderly family members may continue throughout August.

That may mean that someone is not yet over a recent quarrel, or perhaps, a family member is experiencing challenges that are felt by everyone else.

Couples are experiencing challenges in their relationship, and in order to extricate yourself from this maze of trouble, exercise the utmost self-control. Avoid any unnecessary outbursts, harsh words, and treat your partner with kid gloves – at least, this is what the stars recommend.

Alternatively, your loved one may simply disappear for a while, leaving you alone or, for various reasons, communication between you may become spotty.

Health. Be attentive when traveling or driving in August. There is a high probability of accidents all month long.

Capricorn

August might test your strength, but that's no reason to cry over spilled milk. Concrete actions are better for you than fanciful expectations that your problems will solve themselves.

Work. As often happens, you can expect to face a dilemma this summer – to relax in style or put your nose to the grindstone? The stars suggest that you will manage to do both but remain focused on all fronts and don't lose sight of the details.

Those with ties to colleagues in other cities or abroad may yet again face challenges in August. Perhaps there are financial demands or expenses that have been unaccounted for.

Negotiations in this area may go on all month long, and perhaps even into September. In some cases, you may even find yourself in legal proceedings. In time, things will resolve themselves, and that is most likely to happen in September or October. For now, do what you need to do and don't rush – the key to fixing anything right now is paying special attention to detail.

Money. Expect August to be a ruinous time for you. You will be spending constantly, perhaps due to work, or possibly vacations and y our personal life. Either way, control your spending and avoid any financial risks right now. That goes for both money and anything of material value.

Love and family. For many Capricorns, August is a time for resolving thorny issues in your personal life, too. Parents will support their children's education, development, and growth, which requires a lot of resources.

You can expect problems involving relatives to continue, and the cause depends on the past.

Couples will come to a major crossroads – will they remain together or separate forever?

All month long, Venus is in retrograde, and the last 10 days of August, Mercury will join it. That means that decision-making will be difficult, and maybe it's best to put things off until later. In time, the planets will calm down and you will see things in new light.

Alternatively, you may decide to separate for some time, and perhaps that is not such a bad idea, after all.

Health. This month, you are feeling tired, so take care of yourself and find some time to relax. You will have the opportunity to do just that. However, if you wish to go somewhere, select a place you have been several times before, and be mindful of other countries' laws.

All month long, take care when driving!

Aquarius

The celestial contradictions that are so abundant during this wonderful summer month will be reflected in your life, too. Keep your eyes on the prize and be patient if things don't immediately go your way.

Work. Relationships are the most important thing this month, whether with partners, opponents, or those who openly wish ill upon you. A disagreement with someone may become the backdrop of this entire month, and most likely, it will be over land, real estate, or other large property.

You may encounter financial or material claims. Negotiations in this area may drag on, as your adversaries will avoid any concrete answers, preferring trickery and obfuscation, instead. This goes for those who are busy expanding their business, as well as those who are trying to sell part of it.

Money. August is not the most sustainable time for your wallet. You may be spending constantly, and that could be due to challenges at work, or possibly in your home life.

All things considered, you will not find yourself in the red, as in mid-August, you can count on receiving a large sum of money.

Love and family. In many cases, the major events this month will take place in your personal life. Your relationship with your partner may grow insincere, turbulent, and occasionally a source of conflict.

That may be over various household issues, for example, different views on home improvement or purchasing a new residence. Alternatively, there may be clashes over real estate, which may involve various people for different reasons. Finally, the most unpleasant reason could be dividing up real estate between divorcing couples. All these issues may not be resolved this month, and things are likely to continue until they look clearer in mid-September or even October.

Any new people or romantic encounters in your life this month are unlikely to be lasting. Single people are advised to keep their feelings in check and not embark on any romantic flings.

Health. This month, you are feeling sluggish, so be sure to take the time to relax. The world will not come crashing to an end if you step away from work for a few days.

Pisces

This month, you might find yourself in a sticky situation – it will be impossible to move forward, but you certainly don't want to stay where you are. Don't make any sudden moves and stay right where you are.

Work. Your main problem during this wonderful summer month will be a shaky relationship with colleagues in other cities or abroad. Many managers, business owners, and anyone whose job involves travel, business trips, or even those just hoping to open their business in another city or abroad can expect much of the same. All month long, you will have to grapple with delicate work-related matters, no matter how many times you come back to the same issues.

You may face conflict with certain partners, and this time, it is worth being patient and flexible.

In all difficult situations, you can count on help from old friends or people who are highly placed in society. They will act as intermediaries, allies, and even your assistants. This is especially relevant when it comes to legal issues.

Employees may face gossip and various types of disagreements on their team. If this describes you, try to stay above the fray and avoid any intrigue.

All Pisces, regardless of their career path, should be especially careful when checking any information that comes their way, be conscientious with documents, and never rush things. That is the only way to see yourself through this month.

Money. Despite the hurdles at work, you will not face any money issues in August. Things are predictable and reasonable in this area of your life, and whatever you put in you will get back.

Love and family. If you are more focused on your personal life, here you will not be spared, either.

Those who have moved somewhere faraway may face obstacles including the laws of foreign countries and various domestic concerns.

If you are part of a turbulent couple, your relationship is still far from ideal, and it is likely that you are the culprit for the lion's share of this situation. Either harshness or excessive restraint – the qualities that your harsh Uncle Saturn gave you – may lead to alienation or outright conflict.

Your relationship with relatives looks complicated, but that is only temporary, especially if you don't sweat the small stuff and treat those around you with respect.

Health. In August, you are feeling rather tired, so it is worth letting your body take a break and perhaps visiting a spa. If you are unable to do that, try to spend more time in nature, which you are sure to find time to do in August.

September

New York Time		
Calendar Day	Lunar Day	Lunar Day Start Time
01/09/2023	18	8:28 PM
02/09/2023	19	8:59 PM
03/09/2023	20	9:32 PM
04/09/2023	21	10:07 PM
05/09/2023	22	10:46 PM
06/09/2023	23	11:30 PM
08/09/2023	24	12:19 AM
09/09/2023	25	1:13 AM
10/09/2023	26	2:09 AM
11/09/2023	27	3:08 AM
12/09/2023	28	4:07 AM
13/09/2023	29	5:05 AM
14/09/2023	30	6:04 AM
14/09/2023	1	9:40 PM
15/09/2023	2	7:03 AM
16/09/2023	3	8:02 AM
17/09/2023	4	9:02 AM
18/09/2023	5	10:03 AM
19/09/2023	6	11:06 AM
20/09/2023	7	12:10 PM
21/09/2023	8	1:13 PM
22/09/2023	9	2:13 PM
23/09/2023	10	3:09 PM
24/09/2023	11	3:58 PM
25/09/2023	12	4:41 PM
26/09/2023	13	5:18 PM
27/09/2023	14	5:52 PM
28/09/2023	15	6:24 PM
29/09/2023	16	6:55 PM
30/09/2023	17	7:27 PM

London Time		
Calendar Day	Lunar Day	Lunar Day Start Time
01/09/2023	17	8:24 PM
02/09/2023	18	8:46 PM
03/09/2023	19	9:09 PM
04/09/2023	20	9:34 PM
05/09/2023	21	10:05 PM
06/09/2023	22	10:43 PM
07/09/2023	23	11:28 PM
09/09/2023	24	12:21 AM
10/09/2023	25	1:21 AM
11/09/2023	26	2:25 AM
12/09/2023	27	3:31 AM
13/09/2023	28	4:38 AM
14/09/2023	29	5:45 AM
15/09/2023	1	2:40 AM
15/09/2023	2	6:52 AM
16/09/2023	3	7:59 AM
17/09/2023	4	9:07 AM
18/09/2023	5	10:16 AM
19/09/2023	6	11:27 AM
20/09/2023	7	12:39 PM
21/09/2023	8	1:48 PM
22/09/2023	9	2:52 PM
23/09/2023	10	3:48 PM
24/09/2023	11	4:33 PM
25/09/2023	12	5:09 PM
26/09/2023	13	5:38 PM
27/09/2023	14	6:03 PM
28/09/2023	15	6:25 PM
29/09/2023	16	6:46 PM
30/09/2023	17	7:08 PM

You can find the description of each lunar day in the chapter "A Guide to The Moon Cycle and Lunar Days"

Aries

You are an active, detail-oriented perfectionist, and it's hard for you to tolerate anything holding back your ideas. The most important thing is that you are on the right track, and in the end, everything will work out!

Work. September is a rush of activity, and you have a lot of work to do. You are striving toward your goals, but not everything is turning out the way you had imagined. Any events you plan will develop at a snail's pace, and you will constantly have to come back to the same issues and adjust your plans and activities.

Business owners and managers are advised to keep a closer eye on their subordinates, especially when it comes to financial matters. Remember that not everyone on your team might be responsible and honest, so keep your finger on the pulse of what's going on.

Employees may encounter disagreements, rumors, gossip, and arguments on their team. The stars recommend that you keep your head down and put your nose to the grindstone. Pay no mind to the pettiness around you, which might just be making mountains out of molehills, anyway. This situation will be over soon, anyway. By the second half of the month, everything will be back in order.

During the first half of September, the stars recommend meticulously checking any information and reading over any documents. Mercury will be in retrograde until September 15, and that often means misunderstandings and errors.

Money. Despite the problems at work, your pocketbook is just fine. You will have regular income, and somewhat more of it, too. Expect the largest sums to come in on September 4, 5, 13-15, 20, 23, 24, and 30.

Your expenses are low and most of them are related to your children or loved ones.

Love and family. Your personal life has been on the back burner, as most of the important events this month are taking place at work. But you can't totally ignore love or family, as they are the most important things in your life and taking care of your children involves spending money, too. This is probably not news to you.

September is a hard time for couples. Problems from the past have appeared once again, but this time, things look much simpler. Remember that even a tiny step toward compromise will go a long way to simmering down the tension. Closer to the end of the month, you will find your passion again, and everything will be harmonious.

Health. In September, you will feel a bit run-down if you are elderly or weakened. You are advised to take care of yourself and turn to your doctor for help whenever you need it.

Those who are young and strong should lead a healthy lifestyle.

September is a great time to end bad habits, visit a cosmetologist, and engage in some more intensive self-care routines.

Taurus

This month, things are looking up. That is good news in almost all areas of your life, whether political or personal.

Work. The best time for any professional events is the second half of September. During this time, you can count on work picking up significantly, and improvements to your finances.

You are busy talking with colleagues from other cities or abroad, and very soon, you can expect to make a very positive and impressive leap forward. Any trips planned after September 20 will be very successful.

At the beginning of September, things might be sluggish, and you can expect setbacks at work or to have trouble finding the people you need or grappling with red tape. In some cases, you will spend most of your time dealing with your personal problems, family, or even decide to take a little time off.

Money. The second half of September is also the best time for your finances. Expect to receive the largest sums on September 6, 7, 16, 17, and 25-27.

Your expenses are mostly related to your personal life and problems involving your home and family.

Love and family. Your personal life might be just as busy as work, right now. Taureans with families might be busy with their children, and that may require some financial or moral support.

Many will be concluding activities related to setting up their home, and this time, even the bothersome tasks promise to be very pleasant. You will be very pleased with the results.

Things are looking a bit confusing for couples. Some things left unanswered will demand a final answer. The stars are on the side of couples whose intentions are serious, honest, and aimed at a bright future. If that is you, you are sure to receive the go-ahead.

You may have an encounter with a former flame or old acquaintances who live in other cities or abroad.

Health. In September, you are healthy, energetic, and have no reason to fear falling ill.

Gemini

September is both hectic and intimate for you. Sometimes, you are impractical and absent-minded, but you won't be losing your grip on things, either.

Work. Many Geminis prefer to spend this month busy with their home and family. Those who remain focused on work, however, might be busy with administrative and organizational tasks.

Business owners and managers will get their office in order or work on another production space and might be acquiring real estate. A good opportunity to expand your business will appear, and it is worth taking advantage of that.

Employees might be distracted by personal matters, even in the workplace, so it is worth taking some time off in order to avoid sparking criticism and wagging tongues among your colleagues.

The stars recommend that all Geminis, regardless of their field, carefully read the fine print when signing any important documents during the first half of September. Mercury, your ruler, will be in retrograde until September 15, and the likelihood of errors is very high during this period.

During the second half of the month, things will be much more successful for you.

Your relationship with colleagues in other cities or abroad is developing with varying success. Some things will improve, while others will require more work. However, things are gradually moving toward something positive and that will continue into the future.

Money. September is a good time for your finances. Despite some setbacks, you will be able to count on support from a spouse, parents, or loved ones. You are likely to receive credit or profit from various real estate transactions, or possibly even receive an inheritance.

Love and family. In September, you may be most focused on your personal life. For a long time, you have dreamt of owning your own home, apartment, or summer house, and you are very close to making that happen. Many Geminis might be busy improving their home this month.

A difficult relationship with a relative has been troubling you, and things will be noticeably better. Despite some minor misunderstandings, slowly but surely, things are becoming stable again.

After some hesitation, couples will be deciding whether or not to live together.

If you are getting ready to move to a new home this month, it is best to wait until the second half of the month, when Mercury shifts from anger to mercy and begins moving on a straight path again. Any decisions you make while Mercury is in retrograde usually do not turn out well.

Health. This month, you are healthy, but you might have a tendency to gain weight, so be sure to eat a balanced diet and try to walk more.

Cancer

This month, you would do well to be cautious this month. You run the risk of getting caught up in fantastical ideas, making unrealistic commitments, or otherwise losing touch with reality. Remember that a bird in hand is worth two in the bush, and act accordingly.

Work. During the first half of September, things will be confusing and hectic. You are still dealing with some unfinished issues involving colleagues in other cities or abroad, and you might experience setbacks on a trip you planned.

Alternatively, you might continue to grapple with old legal trouble or visits from auditing agencies.

A relationship with like-minded people, friends, or someone highly placed in society might also become difficult. That may be over money, debts, or other material obligations. However, things will become clearer and calm down eventually.

The stars recommend all Cancers, regardless of their field, be very careful with paperwork during the first two weeks of the month. If you have to sign anything important, be very meticulous as you read the fine print. Mercury will be in retrograde until September 15, and during this time, there is a high probability of mistakes. If possible, plan any major activities or meetings for later in the month.

Money. In September, your finances are looking uneven. You will have your normal income, but you will be spending heavily. If you have any old debts, you may have to settle them this month. There is hope, however, that closer to the end of the month, you will be in the black.

Love and family. Severe Pluto is back in your sector of the sky related to long-term relationships, which means that you might be feeling pressure from the stars. Avoid any conflict and keep your emotions in check. Do not try to define any relationship unless absolutely necessary. This goes for both married and unmarried couples who have had problems in the past.

During the second half of the month, the stars recommend going on a trip. A week somewhere faraway will be restorative and help you understand your partner better.

Your relationship with relatives is still a challenge, but things are slowly becoming clearer and calming down. In time, you will reach peace and understanding.

Health. In September, you are the picture of health, but be careful when traveling or driving all month long.

Leo

All month, you will be busy with huge ideas and projects. The stars strongly urge you to keep your feet on the ground and busy yourself with practical, tangible tasks.

Work. September is a great time for anything work-related. It will become clear that the period of struggle and resistance is coming to an end, and your efforts have not been for naught. During the first half of the month, you might encounter some minor inconsistencies, but they will be resolved later in September.

This month, you might finally settle some issues from the past that have been causing you trouble and start a new project, too.

Employees might see positive changes in their career during the second half of September, such as a promotion with a corresponding raise, or perhaps a new job at a more promising organization. You might be negotiating a change like this during the first two weeks of September, but you will likely see the results a bit later.

Your relationship with colleagues from afar is improving, and you will notice this the most during the last 10 days of the month.

Money. Financially, September is one of the best months of the year for you. You will have regular income and significantly more of it, too. This means you will be able to pay your debts and face the future with confidence. Expect the largest sums on September 4, 5, 13-15, 23, and 24.

Love and family. Things are quieting down in your family and personal life. Divorcing spouses will be able to settle their mutual material claims in peace. Questions over who owes what will take place during the first half of the month, and later on, you will reach a compromise.

Your relationship with your spouse or partner will improve significantly, if you have gone through adversity and managed to hold onto your wisdom and love.

In late September or possibly October, you are likely to go on a trip, which will be very successful and strengthen your relationship further.

Close to the end of the month, you are likely to see your relationship improve with relatives, and you might visit family living in other cities or abroad.

Health. This month, your energy is high, and you have no reason to fear falling ill.

Virgo

Expect September to be overall positive for you. Your promising future looks more tangible every day, and it has a lot of good things in store for you! All you have to do is cut ties with the past.

Work. You will likely be able to divide September into two very different periods. During the first two weeks of the month, your ruler, Mercury, will be in retrograde, so you will see a lot of ups and downs, not to mention doubt when it comes to some matters. Most likely, this will involve a difficult relationship with a former business partner.

To summarize, things are about to reach a breaking point, and it's still unclear what your role is in all of this. It seems that the time has come to cut your losses and move on. You are about to embark on a new future, with new business and new partners. You will make a decision during the second half of the month, and the stars predict that it will be the right one. If you still have some material issues to deal with, they will be resolved in your favor.

This month, you will reach your goals when it comes to any planned move, work, or opening your business in another city or abroad. Closer to the end of September, you might take a trip or make a move. The second half of the month is a good time to start any studies, new ideas, or overhaul your life.

Money. The second half of September is a good time for your finances, and you can expect the largest sums to come in on September 25-27.

Love and family. Things in your personal life are still going well. Couples on the rocks might decide to divorce, and most likely, your spouse will have the last word.

During the first half of the month, you might be hoping to leave everything as it is, but that is unlikely to happen. There are many fish in the sea, however, and there is someone out there for you.

Couples who get along will be making plans for the future and working to make them a reality. If you want to move to another city or abroad, the next three months are the best time to make that happen.

Health. In September, you are feeling sluggish, and that is most noticeable during the first two weeks of the month. The stars advise you to spend less time getting upset over things and remember that Rome wasn't built in a day. If you keep your cool, you will have a lot less problems.

Libra

After a busy, hectic summer, the pendulum has swung to the other side. You might become slow and judicious, but that is the right path, right now – you will have far less errors to deal with.

Work. During the first two weeks of September, you can expect to run into some hiccups. You might have trouble at work, perhaps gossip involving competitors, and secret foes at play.

Managers and business owners are advised to keep an eye on their subordinates, as not everything is as it should be here. The planets predict that during the first half of the month, some of the people who should support you will display their shortcomings, which might make things significantly more difficult for you at work.

Alternatively, this might go beyond the matter of one forgetting his or her obligations, and into outright treachery. Look at all your options and take any measures you can.

Any events related to expanding your business, including major repairs or acquiring land or other real estate will turn out well. If you are purchasing something, it is best to wait until after September 15.

A difficult relationship with a friend or someone highly placed in society will be smoothed over. If the issue involves an argument over finances, you are sure to reach a compromise.

Money. When it comes to money, September is a positive month for you. You may have income from unofficial sources, including support from a loved one, parents, or instead receive credit or profit from a beneficial real estate transaction or an inheritance.

Love and family. In many cases, your personal life is more important than work right now. Your home is your castle, and most Libras are well aware of that. You might be busy with major repairs, buying a home, apartment, or summer home. In some cases, this began recently and is now reaching its logical conclusion.

Your relationship with your partner is looking wobbly, but there is a light at the end of the tunnel. Though things will be difficult and confusing as the month begins, after September 15, things will be much clearer. You might find a way to reconcile, or perhaps, in the most extreme cases, pressure from the stars will drive you to decide to end your relationship.

Health. The last month before your birthday is usually a time when one feels sluggish, and against that backdrop, you are likely to see old illnesses flare up again. Remember that and take care of yourself.

Scorpio

You are busy with big ideas, plans, and projects. In theory, everything is great, but in reality, you might be dealing with trouble. So don't lose touch with reality and think everything through!

Work. This month, it's all about networking. Thanks to your friends, like-minded people, and those who are highly placed in society, you are able to grapple with all the problems you faced last month, and possibly find common ground with your opponents.

That is likely to happen during the second half of the month, and during the first half, you can expect doubt, inconsistencies, and a lot of back and forth. You will not find a solution until the last 10 days of September.

You might be looking at a new job or a promotion right where you are, and you are going to need friendly support and a shoulder to lean on.

Your relationship with colleagues in other cities or abroad is moving along nicely, and closer to the end of the month, you are likely to go on a trip.

If your plans involve a move, working in another city, or abroad, that might happen during the months to come, while September serves as a bridge between the past and future.

Money. Financially, September is also a great time for you. You will have regular income and can expect the largest sums to come in on September 2, 3, 11-13, 21, 22, 29, and 30. Your expenses are low, and most of them are related to your children or a loved one.

Love and family. You still need a lot of clarity in your personal life. It seems that most of the month, your relationship will be a source of stress and confusion.

Long-term couples might feel a growing distance from one another, and you might spend some time apart. Alternatively, you may focus on other interests aside from him or her.

Spouses will have to deal with their children's problems, which will require a lot of money.

Health. For most of the month, you will be healthy, energetic, and popular. You may be at the very center of several different events, and this month will sure to be full of them. At the very end of September, however, you might start to feel fatigued from all of the communication at work and caring for people in your personal life. Try to plan some time off during the last few days of the month or in October. That will allow you to get everything in order and restore your body, mind, and soul.

Sagittarius

September will bring a lot of ups and downs. On one hand, you will be busy with work. On the other, bringing everything to life is not an overnight process. However, remember that the road is for those who walk it!

Work. The second half of September will be the most successful period for you. During this time, you will start major projects, which will bring you fame and fortune. Employees can count on a new job – possibly a promotion right where you are, or maybe something at an entirely new, more promising organization. That may happen during the second half of September or the beginning of October. You are likely to begin negotiations on this change in the first half of September.

It is not worth getting upset if things dragon a bit, as in the end, everything will turn out right.

Your relationship with colleagues in other cities or abroad is moving along nicely, a continuation of what happened in August. You can expect some misunderstandings, but in the end, things will fall into place.

Money. Financially, September is a great time. You will have a regular income, and it will be noticeably higher than usual. Expect the largest sums to come in September 4, 5, 13-15, 23, and 24.

Your expenses are low, and closer to the end of the month, your balance will be in the black.

Love and family. September will mean a lot of focus on work, and you may not have time left over for your personal life. What's more, the stars recommend that you pay attention to your family relationships. For various reasons, spouses might be spending time apart, and nothing good can come of it if that continues for too long.

Alternatively, you may have trouble with your parents or elderly family members, and this will lead to tension and stress for the entire family.

Your relationship with your partner is improving as September draws to a close, and you might travel somewhere together.

Health. In September, your anxious soul will turn out to be much stronger than your body. For now, you may not have to worry about any illnesses, but a little later – in late October or November, all of the stress you have been carrying will have an impact. Try to take some time away from work and remember that your health is number one.

Capricorn

September might seem quieter and more productive than the previous months. Good times are ahead!

Work. Things will be picking up again at work this month. Though you may have a lot of clouds on the horizon before September 15, during the second half of the month, the sky will clear.

You might be holding negotiations with colleagues in other cities or abroad during the first half of the month, and perhaps you are preparing for a trip. Mercury, the planet that rules connection and contacts will be in retrograde until September 15, so be prepared for the fact that things may not turn out as you hoped the first time around. You will have to reexamine some things, and perhaps even redo them.

However, during the second half of the month, everything will be complete, and you will be pleased with the results.

Your negotiations with colleagues from afar are on the right track, and closer to the end of September, you will get what you wanted.

During this time, Capricorns might suddenly become very popular within their own circles. You can expect visits and interesting, useful events – seminars, symposiums, and creative gatherings. You will show your best side and make new connections. Those who work in the creative fields will see the most success here – actors, artists, journalists, musicians, and of course, politicians. As your popularity grows, so will your income.

Money . The last 10 days of September is the best time for your finances. You can expect the largest sum to come in on September 25-27.

Your expenses are still high, and most of them are still related to your family's needs and those of your children and loved ones.

Love and family. Things will improve in your personal, romantic, and family life during the second half of September.

Couples will find a way to one another's hearts, and the stars urge you to go on a trip together. This will strengthen your relationship and allow you to see things from another perspective.

Spouses will improve their relationship with children, though that will still require a lot of money.

If you have any plans related to travel, be careful with your documents, and carefully study any maps before setting out. This month, try to choose places you have been a few times before. This is valid all month long, especially during the first half, and for any business travel.

Health. In September, you are feeling great about yourself, and any illness from last month will swiftly be but a bad memory.

Aquarius

This month, the anxiety that characterized August is fading away. You are able to calmly tackle most of your problems, and those remaining are no longer so pressing, after all.

Work. September is not the best time for anything work-related. You will see a continuation of the same issues you faced last month, but most of them are much less troublesome than before. Most likely, they are related to land or other real estate, and you might be involved in negotiations to resolve this all month long. The first half of the month is looking confusing, and you can expect these conversations to drag on, but after September 15, you can count on a favorable resolution.

Naturally, your opponents' main concern is financial or material in nature, and you will have to find a compromise that everyone can work with. The stars advise you to stand up to any pressure if you think that it is not fair, and only consent to an agreement if it respects all of your legal rights.

Your relationship with colleagues in other cities or abroad is moving along nicely, and during the last few days of the month, this will be especially clear.

Money. Your finances are looking tricky this month. You will be spending constantly, and that may be related to work, or possibly your personal life.

Love and family. In many cases, most of September's events will revolve around your personal life. Divorcing couples will continue to argue about property, mostly your home. During the first half of the month, you are unlikely to reach any agreement, but things will get much easier and your words will be less sharp later in September.

Couples who get along might resolve various problems together, especially those related to your home, perhaps repairs or purchasing a new apartment, house, or summer home. As usual, the details will add up and won't be cheap.

For most couples, you are neither experiencing peace or war. Most of the month, your relationship will feel unclear and incoherent. Your life together will become more complicated next month, but there is hope that you will make it through.

Health. In September, you are not feeling exactly vigorous, so take care of yourself. Closer to the end of September, you will have a chance to relax, and that may even take place somewhere faraway. September will probably wear you out, so take advantage of any chances you have to get away and remember that health is the best investment you can make.

Pisces

September will open your world a bit wider than you are used to. Try to appreciate the perspective of your opponents, partners, or simply people you frequently interact with. If you do, solving many of your problems will become much easier and faster.

Work. Your relationship with business partners will be the most important theme for you this month. Business owners and managers at every level will face the difficult task of smoothing over ties with colleagues in other cities or abroad and reining in an opponent who has proven him or herself to be a loose cannon. Try to be flexible and diplomatic, even patient. These qualities will get you through the first two weeks of September, which will be the most difficult period this month.

You may also experience misunderstandings with your subordinates, who might not be shouldering their responsibilities, for various reasons. In some cases, this may boil down to outright sabotage, and it is worth keeping this in mind if you are a business owner or manager.

Employees can expect competition and ill will on the part of their team this month. Do your job in good faith and avoid any gossip.

If you are planning any business travel, be attentive with any documents and don't skip over the details. That is very pertinent during the first half of September, when Mercury, the planet that rules connections, contacts, and any travel, will be in retrograde.

Money. Financially, you can count on September to be neutral. You will not see any major windfalls, but you will also not incur any losses. To summarize, it is what it is.

Love and family. It is hard to rewrite the rules of your relationship when you are right in the thick of it. So avoid that, especially if you feel like you do not have the upper hand right now. If you do not appreciate how your partner is conducting him or herself, it is worth waiting it out.

Those who are moving somewhere faraway or simply to a new home might be working with their partner to solve problems, and, fortunately, with each new day there are less problems to solve. Your relationship with relatives is also improving, and the stars give much of the credit for this to your spouse or partner.

If you plan to travel in September, select a place you have been before. That goes for the entire month, but especially during the first two weeks.

Health. In September, you are feeling rather sluggish, so don't overdo it, and try to strike a balance between work and play.

October

New York Time		
Calendar Day	Lunar Day	Lunar Day Start Time
01/10/2023	18	8:02 PM
02/10/2023	19	8:40 PM
03/10/2023	20	9:23 PM
04/10/2023	21	10:11 PM
05/10/2023	22	11:04 PM
07/10/2023	23	12:01 AM
08/10/2023	24	12:59 AM
09/10/2023	25	1:58 AM
10/10/2023	26	2:57 AM
11/10/2023	27	3:56 AM
12/10/2023	28	4:54 AM
13/10/2023	29	5:54 AM
14/10/2023	30	6:54 AM
14/10/2023	1	1:55 PM
15/10/2023	2	7:55 AM
16/10/2023	3	8:59 AM
17/10/2023	4	10:03 AM
18/10/2023	5	11:07 AM
19/10/2023	6	12:08 PM
20/10/2023	7	1:05 PM
21/10/2023	8	1:55 PM
22/10/2023	9	2:38 PM
23/10/2023	10	3:16 PM
24/10/2023	11	3:50 PM
25/10/2023	12	4:21 PM
26/10/2023	13	4:51 PM
27/10/2023	14	5:22 PM
28/10/2023	15	5:55 PM
29/10/2023	16	6:32 PM
30/10/2023	17	7:13 PM
31/10/2023	18	8:00 PM

London Time		
Calendar Day	Lunar Day	Lunar Day Start Time
01/10/2023	18	7:33 PM
02/10/2023	19	8:02 PM
03/10/2023	20	8:38 PM
04/10/2023	21	9:21 PM
05/10/2023	22	10:12 PM
06/10/2023	23	11:11 PM
08/10/2023	24	12:14 AM
09/10/2023	25	1:20 AM
10/10/2023	26	2:27 AM
11/10/2023	27	3:34 AM
12/10/2023	28	4:40 AM
13/10/2023	29	5:48 AM
14/10/2023	30	6:56 AM
14/10/2023	1	6:55 PM
15/10/2023	2	8:06 AM
16/10/2023	3	9:17 AM
17/10/2023	4	10:29 AM
18/10/2023	5	11:40 AM
19/10/2023	6	12:46 PM
20/10/2023	7	1:44 PM
21/10/2023	8	2:32 PM
22/10/2023	9	3:09 PM
23/10/2023	10	3:40 PM
24/10/2023	11	4:05 PM
25/10/2023	12	4:27 PM
26/10/2023	13	4:48 PM
27/10/2023	14	5:09 PM
28/10/2023	15	5:32 PM
29/10/2023	16	4:59 PM
30/10/2023	17	5:31 PM
31/10/2023	18	6:11 PM

You can find the description of each lunar day in the chapter "A Guide to The Moon Cycle and Lunar Days"

Aries

October's two eclipses will remind you of the importance of working together. Remember, no man is an island, and that is very valid advice for you right now.

Work. The most important thing this month is your relationship with business partners, and right now, your professional success depends on your ability to make that connection. There is no point in trying to have the last word right now, and flexibility and diplomacy are what you need.

The topic of the day is probably money or something of material value, and you will be immersed in discussions over this, whether you are a business owner or a manager of any level. The astrologist predicts that you will have the upper hand, which you should appreciate as you consider your partners' positions.

What's more, remember that bad peace is better than a good war, so avoid any arguments and do whatever needs to be done intentionally and diplomatically.

You can expect a lot of support from your colleagues and subordinates. Despite the minor inconsistencies at work, their efforts will be positive.

Employees will encounter some opposition from competitors, and the stars recommend watching your back. Your troubles will not be serious, however, and will be contained to gossip and minor intrigue.

Money. Financially, October is a great time for you. You will have regular income and much more of it than usual. Expect the largest sums to come in on October 1, 2, 11, 12, 20, 21, 29 and 30.

Your expenses are growing, however. The last 10 days of October are when you will spend the most, especially from October 28-30. That may be related to work, or perhaps your personal needs.

Love and family. If your personal life is most important to you, here, the stars recommend that you keep an eye on your loved ones.

Otherwise, you may end up hurting those around you and later come to regret it. You might expect an argument over the family budget, and here, your spouse's position may vary. You will win out in the end, so it is not worth piling too hard on your better half. Try to resolve delicate issues peacefully. Your loved ones will appreciate it, and a little later they will thank you.

In many families, you are going to need a lot of money to improve an old home, or perhaps buy a new one. As you know, that is a lot of work, and it doesn't come cheap.

Health. In October, you are not feeling particularly energetic, and that will be most noticeable during the last 10 days of the month. Take care of yourself during this time and try to avoid any fall colds or infections. Don't push yourself too hard. This is especially relevant during the eclipse on October 28-30.

Taurus

This month will be favorable but not particularly exciting for you. Hard work and patience will do the trick, and right now that advice was made just for you.

Work. October is a busy month for you, full of stress at work, which, at first glance, will not seem particularly efficient to you. But that is not the case, and the astrologist believes that you are gathering strength and laying the groundwork for what is to come. That is exactly what you need to be doing, as your opponents and those who envy you are vying for your position.

Business owners and managers will face this during the first and last 10 days of the month. You might experience serious opposition from colleagues in other cities and abroad during the first 10 days of the month, and you can expect the same from y our business partners and competitors after October 20.

You might also be subject to audits and face legal trouble.

Employees should diligently fulfill their duties without giving management any reason to complain about shortcomings. Remember, this month is a time to keep your head down and put your nose to the grindstone. All of these qualities will pay off in the future.

The stars remind you that Jupiter is on your side, which means that you are able to juggle many things at once, and in the end, you will write your own rules for the game.

Money. Financially, October is favorable. You will have your usual income, with low expenses. Expect the largest sums to come in on October 3, 4, 13, 14, 22, 23, and 31.

Love and family. This month's eclipse will force you to reconsider much in your personal life. Generally speaking, you are once again at a turning point, when your past relationships have become a burden, but you feel stuck and unable to make the next step forward right now. However, a serious conflict with your partner, which is likely during the last 10 days of October, will make you seriously think about whether you want to continue your relationship with him or her. You may already have a new love interest on the horizon. If there is already someone else in your life, he or she will be the nail in the coffin of your previous relationship. This of course applies to those who do not mind being part of a complicated love triangle.

Those with stable family lives will be able to tackle difficult issues together, especially those related to your children and home, and that will not always go smoothly.

Single people can count on a fateful encounter, which may end up in marriage.

Health. This month, you are not feeling particularly energetic, but you will not fall seriously ill if you stick to a schedule and make sure to move around in the mornings. These are simple rules to avoid a lot of trouble both now and later on.

will bring some trouble with it, as well. The problem may be unfulfilled promises from either end.

Health. In October, you are feeling energetic and have no reason to fear falling ill. You might feel a bit of fatigue during the last 10 days of the month, so take care of yourself during this time and avoid any fall infections or colds.

Virgo

This month, you will have an excellent opportunity to fix something you dealt with in the recent past. It seems that life is slowly improving!

Work. Things are palpably better for you at work. Your relationships with colleagues in other cities or abroad are better, and you might be involved in meetings, negotiations, or business travel. Despite the positive trend, however, there are still some problems on the horizon. They may show up at the very end of October and continue into November.

Another issue may be your relationship with a business partner. You are highly aware of the crux of the issue, as you have been here before. It may be worth separating, and in that case, resolving your financial issues in relative peace.

Those looking for a new job or to study in another city or abroad might count on doing just that this month.

Money. Financially, October is not bad at all. You will have regular income, and significantly more of it than usual. Expect the largest sums to come in on October 3, 4, 13, 14, 22, and 23. Your expenses are mostly related to your personal life and the demands of your children and loved ones, but they will still be relatively low.

Love and family. Your personal life is seeing a continuation of things that began in the recent past. Couples who are feuding or divorcing might confirm their position. Your partner will still be harsh and unbending, and there will be no way to get through to him or her. You still have your children together, but they will be unable to fully resolve this for you. Naturally, this only applies to those who have been warring for some time.

Alternatively, your spouse or loved one will continue to face challenges and you will have to provide them with moral and financial support. The third possibility is that you may have to spend some time apart.

Those moving somewhere faraway might deal with a series of issues this month.

Unmarried couples will have an easier time in October, and their relationship will not suffer.

Your relationship with your relatives is more complicated during the last 10 days of October, and you may experience conflict, which will continue into November.

Health. In October, you are feeling vigorous and have no reason to fear falling ill. However, after October 20, the stars recommend that you be careful when driving or traveling.

Libra

In October, you will prove yourself to be a tough boss and a total materialist. There is nothing you can do about that – it is the only way for you to solve a lot of problems. Since you are on the right path, the stars are sure to lend a hand!

Work. In October, many Libras will have a nice opportunity to resolve some of the difficulties that cropped up in September. Business owners are slowly but surely continuing to expand their business, and this month, you will be able to make several steps in that direction. You are still carrying out various transactions involving real estate, land, or other large property.

Not everything will go the way you had planned and hoped this month. Business owners and managers should be attentive with their subordinates, and employees should do the same with their colleagues. Right now, things are looking relatively easy, but disagreements are still likely. A mistake by someone who should be supporting you may end up costing you dearly.

This month, you would be wise to watch your back, as information you'd rather keep in the dark may surface.

Money. Financially, October is full of ups and downs. You will not end up bankrupt, but your expenses are high. The last 10 days of the month are especially acute here, when you can expect to be bleeding money. That may be related to work and expanding your business, or possibly with resolving issues at home and with your family.

Love and family. Things are not all rosy in your personal life. Couples who get along will be busy improving their home, and things will not go as planned. You may not agree on how you want your future home to look or how much to spend, and you may end up arguing, which will not end until you are done with the project.

You are likely to bicker over money, especially after October 20. Be careful and avoid pressuring your loved one. Mars is in your sign for almost the entire month, and it brings aggression and sudden moves. That might be a good quality at work, but it is less than ideal in your personal life.

All Libras should keep that in mind, whether they are married or not. Your sign's greatest skill is patience and an ability to be both diplomatic and delicate. Don't lose sight of that, and things will go much better for you.

Health. You are healthy, energetic, and busy this month, and no illness can keep you down.

Scorpio

October is not the best time for you. It is best to lay low this month, and if you can, get away from the office. Right now, the best investment you can make is in your family and your health.

Work. The best thing you can do at work this month is get things in order and work on your connections. October is not a bad time for reconnecting with people you lost touch with, regardless of why.

Your old friends or someone who is highly placed in society will help you out this month. Even if things are not turning out as you had hoped, any improvement is good news, right now.

The most difficult time for anything work-related is after October 20. During this time, you might have issues involving colleagues in other cities or abroad, or conflict involving a partner.

The eclipse on October 28 might lead to rash outbursts and harsh words, so think things through 100 times before acting.

Remember that your partners or opponents have the upper hand, and act accordingly, unless you are 100% sure you are in the right.

Money. Your finances are looking unclear in October. You might not have any major news here. But expect the largest sums to come in on October 3, 4, 8, 9, 18, 19, 27, and 28.

Love and family. In many cases, the main focus of October will be your personal life. If you have a chance to get away from work and focus on what you really like, be sure to take advantage of that. Your inner balance is the key to stability both at work and in your relationships this month.

October will be a challenging time for couples whether they are married or not, especially during the last 10 days of the month. You might need to make a change but feel unable to do it. You appear aggressive, and your partner is not ready for a compromise right now,

bodies, and employees will clash with management. Be careful with any of these problems, as they are likely to continue into November.

Business owners and managers would do well to get their documents in order, especially if there is a dispute over real estate. Employees should not forget about their main responsibilities.

Money. Things have been better for you financially. Be careful with your spending and managing your money. Severe Saturn, which is firmly entrenched in the financial sector of your sky for the next two years, is urging you to do just that. Money is not your forte, but the sooner you master this skill, the better.

Love and family. Things are quieter in your personal life. Warring couples might find common ground, and your conflict will gradually fade away. If you have been feuding over real estate or expenses related to it, in October, you will manage to resolve much of your troubles. That goes for anyone disputing over an inheritance.

Health. This month, you can expect a rush of strength and energy, which will allow you to tackle many things and get through this month.

Pisces

In October, you will have to strike a healthy balance between your desires and reality. Sometimes, the spirit is willing, but the flesh is weak.

Work. October is not a particularly successful month for you at work. Most likely, things are not as exciting as you would like.

The main task for any business owners or managers might be strengthening your relationship with colleagues from other cities or abroad. If you are thinking about doing business somewhere faraway from home, you will need to get a handle on who you will have to work with.

During the first 20 days of October, your relationship is progressing fairly well. You might be meeting, holding negotiations, or traveling to see colleagues from faraway. There may be some disagreements over financial issues. You may need to recognize that not all of your expectations will come true, and your expenses may be higher than you initially intended.

After October 20, you will be dealing with a different type of problem. One way or another, it will involve colleagues from somewhere faraway. You may see disagreements among the people who you need to work with, or possibly involving the laws of other countries, which you will need to overcome. There is hope that by December, this will be resolved.

Money. October is contradictory for your finances. You have a lot of expenses, and your income is low, and you can expect to spend the most during the first half of the month. There is hope that during the difficult days, a loved one or old friend will lend a hand.

Love and family. You are seeing a lot of ups and downs in your personal life. Those who are moving somewhere faraway will still be dealing with various tasks related to that difficult endeavor.

Couples may argue, and you will be the culprit. Lately, you have been rigid and unbending, and that may cause major problems in your relationships. Your partner seems a lot more flexible and diplomatic than you, and the stars confirm that he or she will have a lot to deal with. Keep that in mind and watch yourself.

Your relationship with relatives will be stable, constructive, and important until October 20. A family member may be useful in helping you solve a lot of problems. After that date, however, family members will bicker, and this time, you will end up acting as the referee capable of bringing your loved ones together again.

Health. In October, you are feeling sluggish, so take care of yourself. Be careful when driving and traveling, as the last 10 days of October will be the most difficult period for this.

November

New York Time		
Calendar Day	Lunar Day	Lunar Day Start Time
01/11/2023	19	8:52 PM
02/11/2023	20	9:49 PM
03/11/2023	21	10:47 PM
04/11/2023	22	11:47 PM
05/11/2023	23	11:46 PM
07/11/2023	24	12:45 AM
08/11/2023	25	1:43 AM
09/11/2023	26	2:42 AM
10/11/2023	27	3:42 AM
11/11/2023	28	4:43 AM
12/11/2023	29	5:46 AM
13/11/2023	1	4:27 AM
13/11/2023	2	6:51 AM
14/11/2023	3	7:57 AM
15/11/2023	4	9:01 AM
16/11/2023	5	10:00 AM
17/11/2023	6	10:53 AM
18/11/2023	7	11:39 AM
19/11/2023	8	12:18 PM
20/11/2023	9	12:52 PM
21/11/2023	10	1:23 PM
22/11/2023	11	1:52 PM
23/11/2023	12	2:22 PM
24/11/2023	13	2:53 PM
25/11/2023	14	3:27 PM
26/11/2023	15	4:05 PM
27/11/2023	16	4:49 PM
28/11/2023	17	5:39 PM
29/11/2023	18	6:35 PM
30/11/2023	19	7:33 PM

London Time		
Calendar Day	Lunar Day	Lunar Day Start Time
01/11/2023	19	7:00 PM
02/11/2023	20	7:57 PM
03/11/2023	21	9:00 PM
04/11/2023	22	10:06 PM
05/11/2023	23	11:13 PM
07/11/2023	24	12:20 AM
08/11/2023	25	1:26 AM
09/11/2023	26	2:33 AM
10/11/2023	27	3:41 AM
11/11/2023	28	4:50 AM
12/11/2023	29	6:02 AM
13/11/2023	30	7:15 AM
13/11/2023	1	9:27 AM
14/11/2023	2	8:28 AM
15/11/2023	3	9:38 AM
16/11/2023	4	10:40 AM
17/11/2023	5	11:31 AM
18/11/2023	6	12:12 PM
19/11/2023	7	12:44 PM
20/11/2023	8	1:10 PM
21/11/2023	9	1:32 PM
22/11/2023	10	1:52 PM
23/11/2023	11	2:12 PM
24/11/2023	12	2:34 PM
25/11/2023	13	2:58 PM
26/11/2023	14	3:27 PM
27/11/2023	15	4:03 PM
28/11/2023	16	4:48 PM
29/11/2023	17	5:42 PM
30/11/2023	18	6:43 PM

You can find the description of each lunar day in the chapter "A Guide to The Moon Cycle and Lunar Days"

Aries

This month will demand patience from you, as well as responsibility and organizational skills. Remember, if you're going to do something, do it right.

Work. You are still busy working on big ideas, plans, and projects. In theory, all is well, but in practice, you will face some difficulties here.

Business owners and managers will be discovering that major construction or large-scale projects are not just a physical undertaking, but also do not come cheap. Seeking additional funds and negotiations over this difficult issue will likely be the backdrop of all of November, though the stars predict that your efforts will pay off – you will find the funding to cover the budget.

Closer to the end of November, you will be speaking more frequently with colleagues in other cities or abroad, and you might take a trip. You will see two different trends at play here – your relationship with certain colleagues will be progressing nicely, while with others, you will still have several challenges to overcome. If these issues began in the recent past, you will be grappling with them for some time to come.

Employees will be busy with day-to-day problems all month long, so they would be wise to take a few days off and focus on yourself. The stars recommend that you avoid approaching management unless you absolutely must and try to solve your problems on your own.

Money. November will not be an easy time for your bank account. You will be spending nonstop all month long. That may be related to work, or possibly your personal life.

When things get critical, however, you will be able to rely on your business partner or support from a loved one.

In the most extreme cases, you will need to take out a loan.

Love and family. Your personal life is turbulent, as well. You might face conflicts over difficult household issues. That is especially the case

Health. This month, you are feeling energetic, but with the flurry of activity this month, you will start to feel fatigued during the last 10 days of the month. If that is your case, use a clear plan of action to find time to relax. An inner balance is your key to stability both at work and in your relationships this month.

Leo

This month, you will have to resolve many difficult, disparate tasks. If the going gets tough, remember that the road is made for those who walk it.

Work. November is not the best time for anything work-related. Both business owners and managers might tackle problems involving official bodies, and employees will have to tangle with management.

The stars recommend that you get all of your affairs in order, along with any red tape, and be ready for any type of claims at any moment.

Your relationship with colleagues in other cities or abroad is progressing well, and this might be the silver lining of November. You might even take a successful trip.

Many Leos will take a bit of time away from work and spend it with loved ones.

Money. The best time for anything financial is the first 10 days of the month. Expect the largest sums to come in on November 7, 8, 16, 17, 25, and 26. Your expenses will still be related to your children and loved ones.

Love and family. Many Leos will be more focused on home and family in November. You might be making small repairs at home, which will busy couples who get along as they lean on their wisdom and undying love. This time, these qualities will prove valuable, as everything will turn out just as you had originally hoped and planned.

Dysfunctional couples will tell an altogether different story, however –

they may once again find themselves fighting over property, particularly their home. Their children's influence might mitigate things somewhat but is unlikely to entirely resolve it.

The stars urge couples, whether married or not, to take a trip together. A new perspective will release the tension during a cold, grey month, and give you a more optimistic view of the future.

Health. This month, your energy levels are not particularly high, so try to keep your emotions in check and avoid any gossip. Remember that a week on a tropical island or a weekend out of town will give you the strength you need and help you better understand your loved ones.

Virgo

In order to leverage this month as best you can, you will need to be more precise as you react to the mood and initiative of those around you. Venus is on your side, which means that you will achieve a lot.

Work. This month, your interests are probably related to somewhere faraway. Not everything in this direction will go as you had planned, however. In mid-November, you will face unexpected obstacles, which may include the laws of another country, or possibly a difficult relationship with a colleague from afar.

Your relationships with former business partners, who caused you a lot of problems as 2023 draws to a close, has improved somewhat, but that does not mean that things are anywhere near resolved. Right now, though, you will have an opportunity to engage in peaceful negotiations and constructively work to fix things from the past.

This month will be action-packed, which is both good and bad. It will cause you a lot more work, but that's just life!

Money. After November 10, your financial situation will be looking up. Expect to receive the largest sums on November 1, 2,10, 11, 18-20, 27, and 28. Your expenses are low, and all of them are both predictable and reasonable.

Love and family. In your personal life, you will have to overcome difficult issues involving those around you. That is likely your relationships with close relatives. Someone in your family member has probably had a serious argument and you will need to help those close to you find common ground.

Those who are moving somewhere faraway will deal with various hurdles – the laws of another country, or various logistical challenges.

Most of these problems will occur during the middle of the month, but thanks to your efforts, they will eventually fade away.

Divorcing couples or those who are on the rocks will still have a difficult relationship, but things are likely to improve. Your children might help you achieve that, or perhaps your desire to smooth the rough edges will be motivation enough.

Your partner may be unwilling to meet you halfway, but there is reason to remember that if the mountain will not come to Mohammed, then Mohammed must go to the mountain, and act accordingly. You may be pleasantly surprised by the reaction.

Health. This month, you are energetic and active, but stressed and anxious. If that sounds like you, then remember that the best way to relax is by getting enough sleep. Be careful when driving and traveling – the second 10 days of the month will be the most dangerous time.

Libra

All month long, you will need to stand up for your views and defend your values. They may be either moral or material in nature.

Work. November is a busy, active, and very productive month for you at work. Those who are busy expanding their business might make a lot of headway in this direction this month.

You are likely to face large expenses related to the scale of this kind of event, and that may lead to disagreements with your partners. The most challenging conversations about this will take place during the second 10 days of the month, if they happen at all. A compromise is possible, but you will have to be the one making an effort in this direction.

Your relationship with colleagues in other cities or abroad is moving along with varying success, and the biggest problems will rear their heads after November 20, when clashing views on your cooperation together might spill over into a serious conflict.

All month long, managers would do well to keep an eye on their subordinates, and employees should do the same with their colleagues. You have needed to monitor this part of your job for some time now, and you need to take steps now, before it is too late.

Money. Your financial outlook is unstable this month. You will be spending constantly, perhaps due to your business development, or alternatively, your personal life. In any case, be careful during the second ten days of the month, when you may experience financial loss in addition to all of your spending.

Love and family. Your personal life is no less busy than work in November. You are still seeing the continuation of events related to improving your home, and this time, they will cost a pretty penny. In some cases, spouses may have a serious disagreement, with the worst likely to take place between November 10 and 20. You are making mountains out of molehills, however – the family budget is able to comfortably cover any of these growing expenses.

Health. This month, you are feeling sluggish, and this will be most noticeable during the New Moon from November 12 to 14. Be attentive during the second 10 days of the month, as the likelihood of injury and accident is rather high.

items for your interior décor.

Petty disagreements over household issues may be in the background all month long, but the middle and end of November will be the most difficult time for this.

For couples, this is a challenging time, as disagreements may pop up during the New Moon from November 12-14. You might see some secrets, whether yours or your partner's, come to light unexpectedly, and that will complicate your relationship. Guard your reputation and try to be diplomatic and delicate, even though these qualities are rather foreign to you.

You value being frank and open, but tact would be more advisable right now.

Health. Those who manage to evade any professional or personal strife may be facing setbacks with their health, instead. In November, your energy levels are lower than usual, and you are likely to get a cold or infection.

Capricorn

This month, you are opening yet another door to the future. It is just what you dreamt of, but there are some clear shortcomings here. You will need November to fix them.

Work. For anything work-related, November is a great month. Your ties with colleagues in other cities and abroad are stable and moving along. You might engage in constructive negotiations, or perhaps go on a successful trip.

Your positive experiences with managers or auditing bodies help to smooth over some difficulties which will reveal themselves during the second 10 days of the month. That may involve claims from certain people, possibly financial or ideological in nature. However, there is nothing that can't be resolved, and this time, there is nothing stopping you from doing that this month.

Minor misunderstandings with a colleague from afar can certainly be fixed, your will, perseverance, and a bit of luck will be all you need, this time.

Money. Financially speaking, November is stable for you. Expect the largest sums to come in on November 1, 10-11, 18, 19, 27, and 28. Your expenses are still related to your children or loved ones.

Love and family. You might see squabbling in your personal life that occasionally breaks into a full-on argument. That is especially the case for unmarried couples, who will not be able to define how their relationship should look in the future. With characteristic caution, you are constantly going over everything in your mind. Did you do everything right? How will your relationship look? It doesn't really matter. Just let things be as they may, and don't pressure your partner. Just be glad he or she is there.

You may also have to put out some fires over the New Moon period from November 12-14.

Parents might have to solve problems involving their children. That may mean facing difficult tasks involving adult children's demands or spending more energy taking care of those who are still small.

After November 20, you might also face challenges related to your relatives. You are well-acquainted with these issues already, and there is nothing new here.

Health. Much of November will see you as healthy, energetic, and able to tackle anything that this month throws your way. You may feel a bit less vigorous during the last 10 days of the month, so try to stick to a schedule and remember to get enough sleep. Be careful when traveling and driving, too. This is especially pertinent during the last 10 days of the month.

Aquarius

November is a positive month that promises to keep you busy. The only downside is being able to divide your time between work and many family obligations. But you are probably used to this, aren't you?

Work. November is a promising month for anything work-related. Your goal is clear, and you know what you need to do to get there. That is the path to success, and you can make it happen. But alas, the world isn't as perfect as you'd like it to be. It is very important that you steel yourself for any problems that you may encounter along the way in mid-November.

Business owners and managers will deal with difficult official bodies, and possibly competitors, as well. However, things are not all bad – any arguments that you present will be effective. Everything will be resolved by New Years, with some things already back on track this month!

Your relationship with colleagues in other cities or abroad is progressing well, and if you are planning on expanding your business to a new location, you can count on a positive result.

Money. November is a great time for your bank account. You will have regular income and much more of it than usual. Expect the largest sums to come in on November 2, 3, 12, 13, 21-23, and 29-30.

Love and family. Your personal life might be on the back burner in November, with so much going on at work. In some cases, that may leave your partner feeling neglected, and potentially lead to family arguments. If that sounds like you, the stars recommend that you keep your partner up to speed with the goings-on at work in order to avoid any issues.

Any events related to improving your home will continue favorably. Your partner may end up shouldering much of the day-to-day tasks related to this.

If you are dealing with a real estate dispute, things will resolve in your favor, but you may have to spend some time talking it all over, first.

Health. In November, you have energy to spare! You might even say that thanks to being so active, you are able to solve all your own problems along with those of your loved ones!

Pisces

Multitasking is your forte, and here, you are able to show that ability off to those around you. The obstacle course continues!

Work. In November, you are hardly ever seen at home. Travel, meetings, and negotiations are your backdrop all month.

Your links to colleagues in other cities and abroad are the most important issue in your professional life right now, but in mid-November, you might experience some hiccups here. Your colleagues might act in poor faith, and your efforts alone will make it possible to restore balance to this relationship. Friends and like-minded people will have your back, so your foes will eventually have to give in.

Employees should be careful during the last 10 days of the month. During this time, there is a high likelihood of disagreements with managers, who may grow excessively demanding, among other things. It is also likely that you have a hand in some of this, yourself. Seek out any weak links in your work and do what you can to fix them while you can.

Money. Your finances are stable, but that's all. You will not see any surprises, whether pleasant or not.

Love and family. November is a relatively peaceful time in your personal life. Couples might go on a trip together, but the stars do urge you to avoid doing that between November 10 and 20, when aggressive Mars will be in conflict with unpredictable Uranus, which means there is a likelihood of incidents on the road.

During the same period, you might see conflicts among your close relatives. This situation is nothing new to you, and its roots began in the recent past.

Those who are moving to another city or abroad will face a variety of difficulties, so consider other options and take any necessary measures. You're only as strong as your weakest link during this difficult time!

Health. You are active, energetic, and the picture of health this month. The stars urge you to be careful when traveling and driving. From November 10 to 20, there is a very high chance of road accidents.

If you are elderly or weakened, take any preventive measures you can when it comes to chronic illnesses, in order to avoid any serious complications.

The most difficult period is the New Moon, from November 12 to 14.

December

New York Time				London Time		
Calendar Day	Lunar Day	Lunar Day Start Time		Calendar Day	Lunar Day	Lunar Day Start Time
01/12/2023	20	8:33 PM		01/12/2023	19	7:49 PM
02/12/2023	21	9:34 PM		02/12/2023	20	8:57 PM
03/12/2023	22	10:33 PM		03/12/2023	21	10:04 PM
04/12/2023	23	11:31 PM		04/12/2023	22	11:11 PM
06/12/2023	24	12:29 AM		06/12/2023	23	12:17 AM
07/12/2023	25	1:28 AM		07/12/2023	24	1:24 AM
08/12/2023	26	2:28 AM		08/12/2023	25	2:32 AM
09/12/2023	27	3:30 AM		09/12/2023	26	3:42 AM
10/12/2023	28	4:34 AM		10/12/2023	27	4:54 AM
11/12/2023	29	5:40 AM		11/12/2023	28	6:08 AM
12/12/2023	30	6:46 AM		12/12/2023	29	7:21 AM
12/12/2023	1	6:32 PM		12/12/2023	1	11:32 PM
13/12/2023	2	7:49 AM		13/12/2023	2	8:28 AM
14/12/2023	3	8:46 AM		14/12/2023	3	9:25 AM
15/12/2023	4	9:36 AM		15/12/2023	4	10:11 AM
16/12/2023	5	10:18 AM		16/12/2023	5	10:47 AM
17/12/2023	6	10:55 AM		17/12/2023	6	11:15 AM
18/12/2023	7	11:27 AM		18/12/2023	7	11:38 AM
19/12/2023	8	11:56 AM		19/12/2023	8	11:59 AM
20/12/2023	9	12:25 PM		20/12/2023	9	12:19 PM
21/12/2023	10	12:55 PM		21/12/2023	10	12:39 PM
22/12/2023	11	1:27 PM		22/12/2023	11	1:02 PM
23/12/2023	12	2:02 PM		23/12/2023	12	1:28 PM
24/12/2023	13	2:43 PM		24/12/2023	13	2:00 PM
25/12/2023	14	3:30 PM		25/12/2023	14	2:41 PM
26/12/2023	15	4:23 PM		26/12/2023	15	3:30 PM
27/12/2023	16	5:20 PM		27/12/2023	16	4:28 PM
28/12/2023	17	6:20 PM		28/12/2023	17	5:33 PM
29/12/2023	18	7:21 PM		29/12/2023	18	6:40 PM
30/12/2023	19	8:21 PM		30/12/2023	19	7:48 PM
31/12/2023	20	9:20 PM		31/12/2023	20	8:56 PM

You can find the description of each lunar day in the chapter "A Guide to The Moon Cycle and Lunar Days"

Aries

The last month of the year will have no shortage of emotional intensity for you. And though you can expect an obstacle course, you are sure to come out on top!

Work. You are still focused on big ideas, plans, and projects. In theory, things are still going well for you, but in practice, you might see some challenges in making all of that come to life. Some problems might pop up involving your colleagues in other cities or abroad, who may say one thing and then do another, but still imply something totally different altogether. Any administrative tasks will turn out to be complicated and are likely to require a lot more resources than you had initially planned.

From December 13 to January 2, Mercury will be in retrograde. This is the planet responsible for connections, and that means that a lot of setbacks are to be expected. During this time, be careful with the details, as well as with any financial documents, since any oversights here may lead to serious trouble down the road. That is relevant for both business owners and employees.

Regardless of how things look here, your business is moving ahead, and close to the end of the year, there will be no doubts of that.

Money. Your financial outlook is stable in December. You will have regular income and can expect the largest sums to come in at the end of the month, and on December 4-6, 8, 14, 15, 18, 22, 23, and 31.

Your expenses are also normal and may be related to business or possibly your personal life.

You might be negotiating over bonuses, financial benefits, or sponsorship. This is highly likely during the second half of the month, and things should work out your way.

Love and family. Your personal life is looking more peaceful and gentler this month. You might expect some arguments over money. However, they will gradually work themselves out, as the situation becomes less acute and pressing. If this involves home improvements, you might see clashing views over how to reach your goals and differing tastes.

Couples should avoid jealousy and gossip in December. Try to avoid saying something unless you are completely sure. Things are better that way.

Any travel planned for December should be carefully planned, especially during the second half of the month.

Health. This month, you are feeling energetic and have no reason to fear falling ill. However, all month long, the stars urge you to be careful when driving or traveling.

Taurus

You are looking at an active, but also a rather difficult month. If you have any trouble, listen to your inner voice, which will only give you correct advice.

Work. December is not the most auspicious time for anything work-related. You will have to deal with various administrative matters, which is not always easy. You might disagree with like-minded people, friends, or people who are highly placed in society. Once again, this may be over money or something of material value.

After December 15, you will step up communications with colleagues in other cities or abroad, and you are likely to take a trip. You may come back to a former business partner and renew a partnership that you had long-since buried. However, new colleagues who appear during this period will not be particularly useful, and your relationship with them may soon fizzle out, leaving behind nothing but unpleasant memories.

Mercury, the planet of connections, will be in retrograde from December 13 to January 2, which is a better time to renew old connections than try to make any new ones.

Your relationship with certain business partners will be uneven, and it boils down to the fact that you do not want to cooperate or reach a compromise.

Money. This is not the best time for your bank account. You have high expenses, but you are not earning much. Closer to the end of the month, your budget will have some serious gaps. That may be due to work or paying off old debts, or possibly resolving issues with your family and home.

Love and family. Expect trouble in paradise this month. You may have to decide what you really want and what you do not. In some cases, a new partner will force you to cut off ties with an old one, and that may be painful, both for you and for those who fate sent your way for a time. Conflicts are likely, even among spouses with a stable marriage, and here, the problem is you and your unwillingness to listen to your partner. Lately, you have been ambitious, and you want to do everything your way and have the last word, which will certainly lead to a response. The stars predict that your partner's demands will be much less than yours.

Health. This month, you are feeling sluggish, and that will be most palpable during the New Moon from December 11-13. During this period, try to lay low and spend time on yourself. If you plan on taking a trip in late December, choose a place you have been before. Otherwise, you may be disappointed.

Gemini

All month long, you will have to deal with other peoples' opinions. They may be in conflict with your own, but sometimes, that is the way the cookie crumbles. They say that the truth is born in an argument, and that just may be the case for you.

Work. All month long, you will have to be very careful and cautious with your usual business. Business owners and managers will have to fend off their foes, who are proving themselves to be unusually tenacious, if not outright hostile. You may experience disagreements over shared business, and in the most extreme cases, you may find yourself in court.

Alternatively, you will continue to experience misunderstandings on your team, as well as difficulties with certain associates and subordinates.

Employees can expect competition and intrigue from certain colleagues.

During the second half of the month, from December 12 to January 2, 2024, your ruler, Mercury, will be in retrograde, and during this time, you might experience anxiety, worry, and stress. Try to avoid any mistakes and focus on what you think is most important.

Those who are busy expanding or organizing their business would do well to be attentive with documents and prepare for an audit or inspection.

Money. Financially, December is not particularly promising for you. You have a lot of expenses, perhaps related to work, or maybe taking care of your family and home. There is hope, however, that your loved ones will show up for you when the going gets tough. You might also receive a small bonus, a favorable loan, or receive credit.

Love and family. Your personal life might be just as busy as your work life in December.

Any events related to a new home are not making you happy just yet. You may have to go back to the same issue time and again, and this will take a toll even on the strongest relationships. You be the judge – on one hand, you are anxious and frazzled, on the other, your partner is acting unyielding and aggressive. That potent cocktail of emotions will explode into conflicts, and your other family members may be dragged into the mess.

You have a good sense of humor, so try to keep a smile on as you deal with these problems, which will help you resolve them much faster, until they simply fade away.

likely, any red lines were crossed long ago and there is no way back.

Alternatively, your spouse will suffer a major illness or problems at work, which will make life difficult for the entire family.

Health. This month, you are feeling sluggish, but you have no reason to fear falling seriously ill as long as you lead a healthy lifestyle and get some exercise in the mornings.

Libra

Some work that you recently completed will bear its fruit this month. You will get what you want, if not this year, in 2024. Your prize awaits!

Work. Your main task this month will be improving your relationship with colleagues in other cities or abroad. Here, you will once again deal with problems that require your attention and efforts. This will be the underlying issue of a conflict that breaks out in December. But remember, it's not as bad as it looks, so you will manage to overcome this before the month ends, and you can tie up any loose ends later.

Those who are busy expanding their business are advised to be careful with any documents, especially if they have anything to do with money.

From December 13 to January 2, Mercury, the planet that rules connections and contacts, will be in retrograde, so you will have to come back to the same issues time and again, and reconsider and implement corrections to your current projects.

Managers and business owners are still advised to keep a close eye on their subordinates, and consider changing up your team, if you can. This is a thorny issue that has been bothering you for some time, so take the stars' advice more seriously. It is not worth trying to build something with people when you just don't trust each other.

Employees might be thinking about a new job and taking steps in that direction. However, it is not quite time for that right now, so just look at your options and don't be afraid to walk away from what you have now.

Money. Financially, December is full of ups and downs. On one hand, you will not end up bankrupt, on the other, you are spending a lot. The main reason for this is expanding your business or working on your home. Here, every heart knows its own bitterness.

Love and family. Your personal life is not less active than work, this month. You are still busy setting up or improving your home, and this means your expenses are continuing along with these difficult obstacles.

However, some of those issues may already be resolved, which means lower expenses for you. A conflict in your family is not particularly likely, but there may be periodic outbursts.

Those planning on purchasing real estate in another country will deal with serious issues this month. They include foreign laws and organizational tasks.

Your relationship with relatives is still rocky, and in many cases, this may involve your in-laws. You may be able to solve this, or perhaps you will once again be taking your gloves off for a fight.

Health. In December, you are feeling energetic and have no reason to fear falling ill. However, all month long, the stars advise you to be more careful when traveling and driving.

Scorpio

As is often the case, the last month of the year has you as busy as ever. Time to roll up your sleeves and get to work!

Work. When it comes to work, you can divide December into two very different periods. During the first 10 days of the month, things will be going well for you, as planned, and without any setbacks.

From December 12 to January 2, however, Mercury will be in retrograde, which means that you will need to reconsider and redo many things. Business owners and managers whose work involves other regions should pay close attention to their partners and keep an eye on any financial documents.

Any trips planned for the second half of December or into January of 2024 should be carefully planned out, as things may not turn out as you initially expected.

Money. December is an important month for tying up financial loose ends. On one hand, you will not find yourself totally broke, and in some cases, your income will even rise. On the other, however, you have a lot of expenses. In many cases, you are spending the most on your children's and loved ones' needs.

It is worth paying close attention to your money, regardless of the field you work in. Any mistakes here could lead to serious losses.

Love and family. Your personal situation is quieting down, mostly thanks to you. The stars recommend that you avoid reacting to any stubbornness on the part of your partner trying to insist that you do what he or she thinks is right. Exercise diplomacy, calm, and if there were any mistakes in November, now is the time to fix them. That goes whether you are married or not.

Your relationship with your children is still demanding a lot of your attention, efforts, and money. Your children may in fact be your largest expense this month. Regardless of how the situation may look, you will have to solve a lot of their problems for them.

Your relationship with your partner is far from ideal, as well, and in the most difficult cases, you may decide to separate. Even if that doesn't happen now, there is reason to give it some consideration, along with what you really need, and what you could easily walk away from. The alarm bells are starting to sound, and the stars recommend you keep a close eye on them.

Health . In December, you are not feeling particularly energetic, so take care of yourself and find the time to relax. Your strategic goal is to stay healthy, which is the most important thing, and everything else will follow, one way or another.

Sagittarius

You are on full alert as you begin the month of your birth. You are decisive, thanks to Mars, which helps you overcome any obstacle you face as 2023 draws to a close.

Work. You will have a lot of work this month, and gradually, the challenges you faced in November will start to improve.

Business owners and managers will be handling legal troubles and getting things in order on their team. Not everything will work out the first time, but eventually, you will overcome most of your problems.

Things are looking up for employees, too. You will manage to handle hostile colleagues as well as challenging relationships on your team. Even if there might still be some hiccups, things are working out the way you need them to, and this will continue.

From December 13 to January 2, Mercury, the planet in charge of connections and contacts, will be in retrograde. That means you can expect setbacks at work, red tape, and problems with your contacts. Be especially cautious with financial documents and be sure to read them in detail.

Money. You will have to spend a lot of time dealing with financial matters this month, and with good reason! Here, things will be looking significantly better, and that will continue into 2024. Expect the largest sums to come in on December 4-6, 14, 15, 22, 23, and 31.

If you face any delays, don't worry – next year, things are sure to look up for you.

Love and family. You will need to be patient and delicate when it comes to your personal life. Some aggression is a good thing at work, but that is not the case when it comes to your loved ones. Avoid acting like a bull in a China shop and keep the last word to yourself. The stars advise you to be careful with your parents and loved ones and remember that a smile and a kind word will be more effective than arguing or making demands. If you take this to heart, you will avoid a lot of trouble.

Health. This month, you are supported by Mars, a powerful source of energy. The stars urge you to use these powers for peaceful purposes only.

Capricorn

The last month of 2023 will not be an easy time for you. You will have to focus on your home, work, and various organizational tasks, as well. The stars advise you to keep a schedule and concentrate on what's most important.

Work. December is a time for you to get serious about administrative tasks, as well as certain relationships with people in your circle.

Your connection to colleagues in other cities or abroad is still something that requires a special approach, adaptability, and diplomacy on your part. Here, not everything will be going as planned, but you will be sure to see improvements compared to the past.

In order to resolve these problems, you may have to turn to an old friend, but you're the one who's going to have to do the heavy lifting. Fortunately, you're strong enough for it. This has happened before, so it won't be very difficult for you to handle.

Try to deal with any difficult tasks during the first half of December, because from the 13th to January 2, 2024, Mercury will be in retrograde and in your sign, too. You may tend to change your mind constantly and feel agitated and anxious.

Remember that it is not a good time to make any important decisions, sign any major documents, or start new projects! Remember that slow and steady is the way ahead right now and keep that in mind as you gradually resolve whatever comes your way. You will be able to avoid any problems and once again get back to the straight and narrow path toward success and prosperity in no time.

Money. December is fairly modest for your finances. You will not run into any unexpected gifts from fate, but whatever you earned with an honest day's work is not going anywhere, either. Your main expenses are related to your children and loved ones.

Love and family. This month, your personal life may keep you busier than work. You are doing everything you can to repair your relationship with your children, and you will make a lot of progress here. Most likely, things will quiet down, but you can expect some disagreements here and there.

In many families, you will continue to see difficulties involving relatives, but here, there is nothing new. There may be an old quarrel at play, or possibly a family member who is facing hard times.

Most couples are restoring balance to their relationships. There is no doubt about what your trump card is, here – you will make the first step to reconcile with your partner, and he or she will respond in kind.

Health. In December, you are not feeling as energetic as in the past, and that will be most noticeable during the New Moon from December 11-13. During this time, take care of yourself and avoid excessive eating or drinking. Stay away from any winter infections or colds, or a reappearance of old, chronic illnesses. Spend the holidays with your loved ones.

Aquarius

This month, you are at the center of it all, and among the people you hold dear. You are ending the year on a high note. You have done everything you can, and you will finish up the rest next year.

Work. December is not a bad time at all for you at work. Your relationship with management and official bodies is much better these days, than it was in November. Your relationship with a friend or someone highly placed in society is not looking so auspicious, however. You might argue over money or material matters.

Alternatively, you might have to settle up old debts or take on responsibilities to start the new year with a clean slate.

If you are planning on expanding your business, repairs, or construction, these cumbersome tasks will not be over just yet.

The first half of December is smooth sailing and predictable, but the second may bring delays and difficulties. They are unlikely to put the brakes on your projects entirely, but you can expect some minor misunderstandings. That might involve red tape, a lack of necessary information, or the people you need simply not being there when you need them. Expect at least some of this after December 15.

Money. December is a good time for your bank account. You will have regular income, and significantly more of it than usual. You might also count on help from a loved one or receiving an inheritance.

Your expenses are also likely to rise. That may be due to your friends, debts, or taking on additional responsibilities, or possibly various events related to the holidays.

Love and family. Your personal life continues to see you working on improving your home. You may have to do a lot of work on this right before the most festive season of the year in order to have things set before bringing in the new year.

Your relationship with family members is predictable and calm, and spouses might have found common ground, which will allow them to resolve many household tasks together. You may have to spend some time apart and reconsider your relationships and what you need to do moving forward.

Couples might decide about living together, and if that is your case, the best time to do it is during the first half of December. From December 12 to January 2, Mercury will be in retrograde, and that is not the best time for new beginnings.

Health. In December, you have enough energy that you have no reason to fear falling ill. You might feel a bit fatigued during the last week of the month, so take care of yourself and try to celebrate the holidays in good health and happiness.

Pisces

Your decisive attitude toward work is paying off – you have accomplished a lot and are celebrating the holidays with the satisfaction of a job well done. You took the bull by the horns!

Work. You have a lot of work this month, and you are able to handle most of it with flying colors.

Your relationship with colleagues from other cities or abroad will be smooth and predictable. You may get some help here from old friends or someone highly placed in society. Thanks to your shared success, you are able to handle it all with aplomb and be very productive.

Your relationship with management or representatives from official bodies may also take some work this month. The former mostly concerns employees, while the latter will impact business owners. Here, you will see some clouds gather, but be flexible and diplomatic, and you will be able to shelter yourself from the storm.

Overall, however, you will make progress and cover a lot of ground.

The stars recommend being more attentive with your contacts and documents during the second half of the month. From December 12 to January 3, Mercury, the planet responsible for connections and contacts will be in retrograde, which means you may see some quarreling with like-minded people. There is no hostility, but you may find yourself coming back to the same issues over and over again.

Money. Your finances are looking good in December, and you will have regular income, which will increase significantly. Your expenses are low and mostly pleasant in nature.

Love and family. Your personal life may be looking uncertain. In some cases, you are pouring all of your efforts into work, and in others, after a difficult autumn, there is neither peace nor war in your relationships.

Pisces moving somewhere faraway might successfully overcome various problems, which will fade a bit more with each passing day.

Your relationship with relatives will also soften. Your problems will be surmountable, and you will tie up loose ends either this month or a little later on.

Travel is likely in December, and it is a good idea to prepare carefully, if that is going to take place during the second half of the month. It is also best to select a place you have been to several times in the past.

Health. In December, you are healthy, energetic, and ready to move mountains. You may not have to, though – the mountains may simply move to make way for you.

Description of Zodiac Signs

ARIES DESCRIPTION

Sign. Masculine, fire, cardinal.

Rulers. Mars and Pluto in retrograde.

Exaltation. Sun.

Temperament. Choleric, impulsive, aggressive.

Positive traits. Logical, self-confident, decisive, determined, vigorous, persistence, proactive, entrepreneurial, ambitious, optimistic, dynamic.

Negative traits. Irritable, excitable, impulsive, intolerant, stubborn, grumpy, reckless, a tendency to exaggerate and sensationalize, unchecked passion, aggressive, despotic, tyrannical.

Weaknesses in the body. Head, brain, central nervous system, face, eyes, ears, teeth, tongue, nose, mouth, upper jaw, chin.

Metal. Iron.

Minerals. For a talisman, red jasper. Generally: rubies, carnet, diamond, Indian carnelian.

Numbers. 5, 7, 9.

Day. Tuesday.

Color. Red. **Aries's Energy**

Aries opens the Zodiac and is first in the circle of signs. This is reflected in life, as Aries always tries to be first with everything – and he manages to do it, too! Aries is a fire sign, which symbolizes the material embodiment of the spirit, power, and transformation. In the trigon of fire signs, it is the first manifestation of cosmic fire – a fire of life that erupted, giving way to obsession and the desire to unleash one's natural potential.

Aries is ruled by Mars, which gives its children incredible energy reserves and enviable creativity. This planet is named for the mythological hero associated with victory and incredible powers; in ancient times, he was depicted as an angel with a magic sword cutting through the darkness. The energy of both Mars and Fire makes Aries the most active and powerful sign of the zodiac, with the greatest chances of conquering the highest mountains.

Astrological portrait of Aries

Anyone born under this sign believes in self-affirmation: "I am." He takes initiative and is a sure leader and moves forward, and doesn't worry about the consequences (those who follow will do that for you), guided by ideas that inspire and encourage – this is Aries' highest cosmic task.

Aries is symbolized by a ram, an animal that is direct and courageous as it tackles the challenges thrown at it by Fate. Aries are no different. They conquer the world with strength, assertiveness, and aggression. They are courageous and fearless. They cut straight to the chase, pushing any obstacles out of the way. Aries are never discouraged, they are always moving ahead as they dive into work with a passion, making waves, learn from the school of hard knocks, and in the end, are victorious.

To an Aries, life is a battlefield, and he is ready for anything, has no fear of insults or humiliation, and will not stop in the face of failure or difficulties. Fearlessness often drives an Aries to risk, and for the right cause, an Aries might even risk his or her life. But once in a crisis,

Aries has strong intuition, and therefore can rule and cope without any outside assistance.

All of Aries' excess fire makes him or her active, always striving to be the first and the best in everything, with a thirst for fame and recognition. Aries lights up at the sight of a new business and begins to radiate joy and electrify those around him. He is capable of leading large crowds with almost magical influence; this is why he is always in a position of power – either physical or psychological.

Aries is self-absorbed and views the world around him as an extension of himself. The feelings and interests of others are of little interest, and he does not know how to tap into the secrets of the human soul. It is not worth blaming him for that. Aries is able to succeed precisely because of this individualism. However, Aries has something that the other signs do not have – he is honest, noble, and absolutely sincere in every way. Lies and deceit are unknown to an Aries, which softens some of his selfishness. Another valuable quality is Aries' ability to always come to the rescue in times of suffering and need. He is a strong shoulder to lean on during tough times. Once Aries has lent a hand in a difficult time, he will do it again and again, though he may feel hurt if his own worries and concerns go unnoticed.

For all of Aries' bravery, assertiveness, and aggression, he is a very sensitive and defenseless child underneath. It is easy to insult or offend him. However, he quickly gets over any such attacks, as long as you provide him with praise and affection. Despite having a short fuse (Aries can descend into boorishness, scandal, and even fights), Aries will quickly walk away, and he will not waste much sulking before forgiving the offender, especially if he or she has a kind word to say about him.

But don't hold your breath waiting for an Aries to discover tact and the ability to smooth over disagreements and avoid outbursts. These qualities are not on his list of virtues. To an Aries, diplomacy means directness, ingenuity, and honesty. Thanks to their incredible work ethic, Aries tend to be wealthy, though they are never stingy and are willing to share it with others. After all, despite their selfishness, one of Aries' most fundamental needs is to bring joy to others. What's the point of wealth if there's no one to share it with?

How to recognize an Aries by appearances

There are two types of Aries: strong and muscular, or weak and sickly, which is what happens to them if they do not live in harmony with their sign, which requires a healthy diet and constant physical activity. Aries is lively in appearance, speaking quickly and in imperative tones, moving around decisively.

Aries is distinguished by a ruddy complexion. Mars, the red planet, bestows this on its children. Aries' face has a certain roughness, stiffness, and a pronounced nose. Aries women are somewhat masculine in their appearance, with a strong torso, broad shoulders, a narrow waist and hips, and a low, often hoarse voice.

Charting Aries' Fate

Generally speaking, Aries' fate is positive, though his path in life is unlikely to be called "smooth". There will be many changes, crises, and acute situations. Usually, Aries have had a restless youth and later settle down as adults. They always achieve anything they set their mind to, and their dreams and plans come true. But their success is theirs alone – Aries are workaholics, unafraid to take a risk, take great chances in life, and never fixate on past failures. They take Fate by the horns, and will not surrender, no matter what is thrown their way. They simply know no fear and ignore their failures. This, along with their self-confidence are Aries' trump cards.

Aries' impulsivity and scatterbrained nature may become obstacles to success. Aries is inspired by many ideas and perpetually rushing around and has a difficult time focusing on just one thing. They want to do it all, and right now. Therefore, they often do not see things through. The root cause of this is a lack of inner grounding and discipline; Aries is stubborn though and will replace them with stubbornness. He simply keeps charging forward, sometimes without even looking where he is going, until he is running into serious obstacles. In order to overcome this problem, he must:

• Find the right way to channel this energy into something inspiring.

• Create a set of behavioral rules for himself. He needs to be educated, have high standards for himself, but not be too strict, as being too hard one himself will be counterproductive), that is, to show both love and high standards at once, while occasionally indulging himself;

• learn to think first and have a clear behavioral standard. He can start small – count to 10 before saying or doing anything;

• Do away with black and white thinking – mine-yours, friend-enemy, good-bad) and expand his mind;

• Occasionally look within and reflect on his spiritual impulses and do a "debriefing". Aries is the only sign that does not fall into depression triggered by self-discovery.

TAURUS DESCRIPTION

Sign. Feminine, Earth, fixed.,

Ruler. Venus.

Exaltation. Moon.

Temperament. Melancholic, slow.

Positive traits. Persistent, patient, restrained, diligent, thorough, careful, a good judge, consistent, honest, a good temperament.

Negative traits. Stubborn, willful, overly sensitive, pessimistic, lazy, apathetic, sluggish, conservative.

Weaknesses in the body. Neck and internal organs. Thyroid gland, tonsils, frontal sinuses, vocal cords, trachea. The esophagus. Occipital and cerebellum.

Metal. Copper.

Minerals. For talisman – carnelian orange. For general wearing – hyacinth, coral, pink quartz.

Number. 6.

Day. Friday.

Color. Yellow-orange and bright green.

It is great fortune to be born under the sign of Taurus, and receive the energy of Venus, the ruler of beauty, harmony, love, and prosperity. Taurus is made to flourish and prosper in everything – in love, with money, friends, knowledge, and spiritual values.

The Earth element means that people born under Taurus are practical, incredibly patient, strong, and tenacious. These are their trump cards. Taureans know exactly what they want, and they are determined as they work toward their goals, and these efforts are not in vain! Often, Taureans manage to become wealthy and well-known, with few exceptions.

Astrological portrait of Taurus

Taurus's motto is "acquire, accumulate, possess". They are extremely practical, and their goal is to take ideas in the spiritual phase and make them take shape by creating, building, and strengthening. In everything Taureans do, they are guided by common sense. They are materialists and pragmatists who place great importance on comfort, satisfaction, and prosperity. They are ready to overcome any obstacles on the way to financial stability – but they are not driven by greed or a passion for hoarding wealth, but rather a need to feel comfortable in this world. This is the only way a Taurus can be effective in life, when she feels the ground beneath her feet. The best support you can give a Taurus is material possessions or monetary savings. Taurus is distinguished by her poise and emotional stability – it is hard to get him/her to lose control, and even harder to prove something to her.

Taureans will hold onto certain beliefs until they have been disappointed. They are stubborn, though they would not agree with that description. Taureans are willing to gain strength, experience, and knowledge over a long time in hopes of achieving their goals and then make an overnight breakthrough to see unprecedented results.

Taurus is patient, reliable, responsible, and consistent in everything. As long as this determination lasts, she can withstand just about anything. She is loyal to friends, business partners, and loved ones, so long as they are honest with her.

Taurus still has some shortcomings. First of all, she is conservative. On the other hand, however, conservatism can be necessary and even a virtue in serious matters. That is why if Taurus shows a healthy level of conservatism, that is only an advantage. Taurus's desire to follow the established order also means she is capable of achieving great success.

Taurus also has some unusual qualities. She is hypersensitive. At her highest level of spiritual development, she will literally achieve the state of being a medium, perceiving objects in her world at the most subtle levels of energy. Many Taureans are often soothsayers, psychics, and healers who are capable of accumulating natural energy. J.R.R. Tolkien describes the highest level of Taurus in Lord of the Rings. Hobbits are true Taureans, capable of having fun, living an earthly life, and also guarding eternal values. Other Taureans should strive for the same.

How to recognize Taurus by appearances

A typical Taurus is calm, charming, and friendly, with a harmonious build, though she may tend to gain weight. Men tend to be large and robust. Taureans inspire confidence and authority. One might describe them as "well-cut and well-stitched". Women are extremely attractive, with big, beautiful eyes to lose oneself in, curved eyelashes, a flirtatious, upturned nose, and irresistible dimples. They have a dense build and a rounded shape and are always surrounded by admirers.

Charting Taurus's Fate

A young Taurus is restless, and usually needy, deprived, and her own worst enemy. But during the second half of life, she will see a period of prosperity. Taureans are business-minded, practical people who plan life several years in advance. They are methodical as they move toward their goals, and in the end, their persistence pays off, as they get everything they have been striving for. Everything that Taurus dreamt of is sure to come true. It might not be right away, but gradually, with enormous effort, they will soar to new heights!

Generally speaking, Taurus is healthy, with enviable strength.

GEMINI DESCRIPTION

Sign. Masculine, air, mutable.

Ruler. Mercury.

Exaltation. Mercury, Ascendant Lunar node.

Temperament. Sanguine, nervous, easygoing, volatile.

Positive traits. Intelligent and intuitive, very perceptive, quick to react, agile, observant, very imaginative, curious, honest, full of good will.

Negative traits. Superficial, unreliable, immodest, talkative, scattered, cold, reckless.

Weaknesses in the body. Hands. Respiratory organs. Tongue. Nervous system. Grey matter of the brain. The psyche.

Metal. Mercury.

Minerals. For a talisman – gold topaz, yellow beryl. Generally: topaz, tiger's eye, chrysoprase, carnelian.

Numbers. 5, 12.

Days. Wednesday.

Color. Orange-yellow and yellow green.

Gemini's energy

Gemini's personality is formed by the energy of Mercury, the closest planet to the Sun. It rotates far more quickly than the other planets. One side of Mercury is constantly facing the Sun, while the other side faces away from it with temperatures far below zero. This speed and duality are also a good description of Gemini. Geminis rush through life at the speed of light, constantly afraid of not having time to do something, and are reminiscent of Julius Caesar, who was known for being a master multitasker. Gemini is an air sign, which means that he has the gift of communication, along with inconsistency and a bit of a tendency toward the superficial. It is very difficult for a Gemini to focus on one thing at a time and see things through to the end. However, that is not too much of an obstacle in their lives.

Astrological portrait of Gemini

Geminis are cute, attractive, and a pleasure to spend time with. Their best qualities are their energy, mental alertness, intuition, and insight. They are observant, capable of easily and quickly grasping information, and process it just as quickly. Mercury rules the mental processes, among other things, meaning that Gemini is the sign of intellectuals. People born under this sign achieve great success and have incredible public speaking skills. Coming from them, just about anything can seem true, and they are able to convince anyone of anything. Gemini's duty to himself is to not waste these qualities, and channel them in the right direction instead.

Gemini is restless, temperamental, and inconsistent. He rushes around from one extreme to the other, is in constant motion, and always looking to meet new friends and make new connections at every level. He eats breakfast, lunch, and dinner at the same time, has office romances at work, talks about work issues with their spouse, especially at night, when it is time to go to bed. A Gemini's mood changes from one second to the next. He might be prone to acting irrationally when he is in a bad mood, only to later regret it.

Geminis have a double nature. They can be both happy and sad at the same time. Everything in their lives exists in a duplicate – apartments, families, friends, girlfriends or boyfriends, lovers, and work. Things change with astonishing speed. You might say that to a Gemini, the purpose of life is trying it all.

One of Gemini's more troublesome qualities is inconsistency. If astrologers could rename Gemini, they might refer to this sign as a chameleon, which changes colors in order to camouflage and protect itself. We might add sensitivity to that inconsistency, as Geminis have a tendency to exaggerate the most minute details. They are known for emotional restraint, but this is not out of callousness, but rather a defense mechanism against other peoples' criticisms.

All Gemini tend to hide their true intentions. You will never know what a Gemini is really thinking deep down, even after living with him for decades. They are prone to fantasizing, have rich imaginations, and are inclined to embellish everything. But even in a lie, Gemini is harmless. He is not seeking revenge or to humiliate anyone in order to raise himself up in his own eyes. He is simply protecting his personal space and secrets. He is always interested in those he communicates with, reaching out and easily making a connection. With Gemini, you can always reach an understanding.

How to recognize Gemini by appearance

A typical Gemini is of average height, slim, agile, sociable, and charming. He has thin, pointed facial features.

Charting Gemini's Fate

Gemini's Fate reflects his nature. His life is an endless series of ups and downs. It is very difficult for Geminis to focus on just one thing, even if it is very important. Failing to address this can feed into Gemini's fatalism-they often let things float away from them.

Gemini tends to have an unstable family life, due to his overwhelming desire for new experiences. This sign is not exactly adapted to marriage, at least in the traditional sense.

Nature has bestowed Gemini with many talents. If he manages to harness at least a modicum of perseverance, he will achieve incredible success. He should avoid throwing himself into things or making hasty decisions.

CANCER DESCRIPTION

Sign. Feminine, water, cardinal.

Ruler. Moon.

Exaltation. Jupiter and Neptune in retrograde.

Temperament. Melancholic, with a tendency toward phlegmatic.

Positive traits. Adaptable, sensitive, romantic, intuitive, emotional, purposeful, patient, persistent, responsible, thrifty, caring, soft, restrained, imaginative, has a good memory.

Negative traits. Irritable, violently reactive, a tendency toward exaggeration, fearful, hysterical, cowardly, resentful, capricious, volatile, lazy, moody, passive, arrogant.

Weaknesses in the body. Stomach, digestive organs, pleura, mucous membranes, breasts, mammary glands, lymph.

Metal. Silver

Minerals. For a talisman – chrysoprase and emerald. In general: pearls, moonstone (selenite), opal.

Number. 5.

Day. Monday

Color. Bright green and purple.

Cancer energy

The volatile Moon changes phases four times in a month, making its children sensitive, easily influenced by their emotions, and mood swings. When Cancers are in a good mood, they are friendly and benevolent, but when their mood shifts to bad, it is best to avoid them. Cancers are forgiven for any mistake. What else would they do? After all, they are surprisingly cute and charming.

Despite the fact that Cancers are confident in themselves, they reach out to others. They have an undeniable talent for attracting others, because they need support and emotional energy from others. This is no surprise, given the fact that they are ruled by the Moon, which reflects the light of the Sun.

Cancer is a water sign, giving her an astuteness and intuition bordering on clairvoyance, as well as real skills at making money. Few others on the Zodiac are as adept at handling people and leveraging the energy of money. Cancers have turned this into an art form.

Astrological portrait of Cancer

Those born under Cancer are the most sensitive and emotional signs of the entire Zodiac. They have a rich spiritual life, which is always changing, just like the Moon, which is born, grows, climaxes, diminishes, and dies in order to do it all over again. Frequent mood swings are one of Cancer's traits. When Cancer is in a good mood, she is sweet, charming, and friendly. When she is in a bad mood, she has a tendency to slip into a long depression.

Cancer's motto is "I feel, therefore, I am". However, this does not mean we should assume that Cancer's heart is inherently warm or that she tends to feel sympathy for others. Cancers take much more than they give, and mainly have empathy for themselves. They will come to the rescue only when they can be convinced that there is no other option. Cancer seeks to be loved and cared for. However, she remains a bit of a mystery and will never fully reveal herself.

Cancers are vulnerable and sensitive to criticism and will react sharply to ridicule and sarcasm. Cancer is easily offended by a "wrong" look or tone. However, she is capable of defending herself. Cancer's self-defense mechanisms are very strong. A typical response is to lurk silently. Do not think for a second that she will forget or ignore what has happened, however. Cancer rarely forgives insults but believes that revenge is a dish best served cold. She might take a long time to come up with a plan for retaliation, and then leverage a convenient situation. It is best to stay neutral with a person like this.

Cancers tend to be successful people. They are not given to impulsivity or haste, but rather are cautious and risk-averse. Before doing anything, Cancer weighs the pros and cons. Only rarely will she listen to anyone else's advice. She prefers to resolve everything on her own and is not afraid of responsibility. Cancers do what they say and succeed at it. Mistakes are a rarity, thanks in large part to their outstanding intellectual abilities. Cancers perceive all nuances of what is happening around them. All of this is the influence of the Moon, which perceives and reflects the light of the Sun. Much like the Moon, Cancer perceives the outside world and immediately reflects it back.

Cancer's intuition is more developed than most other signs, meaning that she is excellent at understanding how other people are feeling and anticipating how situations will play out. Cancer is able to build a strong cause and effect relationship and find the root causes of certain problems, facts, and phenomena.

It is almost impossible to deceive a Cancer, and they should be treated with kindness. Pressuring them is useless – Cancer has developed a multi-stage defense mechanism, and the only way you can influence a Cancer is to pique her interest.

Cancers are persistent and assertive. If they have decided to do something, nothing will stop them. But in setting a goal, Cancer will never get straight to the point. Rather, she will bide her time, circle around the target, and keep an eye on it until she manages to reach it.

Despite Cancer's love of changes, novelty, and travel, they are strongly drawn to the home and their loved ones, especially their mother and children. To a Cancer, children are the world's greatest gift. Cancer is a home-bound and family sign, the keeper of family traditions. She adores her home and does not feel as relaxed and comfortable anywhere else.

If a Cancer is unable to achieve normal intellectual development, she might develop negative traits such as stinginess, childishness, or become conniving.

Cancers are often spilling over with emotions: it is normal for them to speak in loud tones, argue, or experience bouts of melancholy and even depression. This heightened sensitivity and vulnerability can eventually develop into complexes or neuroses. Cancer tries very hard to fulfill the ideal and be a strong person but continues to feel vulnerable.

Cancer is capable of seeing the true nature of the world around her and its essence, and carries higher ideas, and is a great zealot and creator. She passes all of the dirtiness in the world through her soul but holds onto her own pure soul. This is why it is wise to pay attention not only to a Cancer's outward appearance, but also her essence when dealing with her. If you manage to lure her out of her shell, you will be repaid in the highest form. After all, Cancer is not always on her best behavior, and not because she harbors any ill will. At her core, she is kind and selfless, due to her heightened sensitivity. Her soul cannot withstand the cruelty of the outside world. This might break Cancer, so she is forced to defend herself. If you cannot get her to open up, you will have to deal with her as though she were a child.

How to recognize Cancer by appearances

Cancer does not like to draw attention to herself, though she is very sociable by nature. She behaves modestly and exercises restraint. Cancers are rarely tall, and tend to be obese, though they often look more overweight than they really are, due to the roundness of their figure. They tend to have a round face, like the Moon, which may look childlike due to its puffiness.

Their eyes are framed by long, thick eyelashes. They tend to gaze around themselves, often with a slightly sad look. Their thick eyebrows often meet over their nose, and their nose tends to be slightly upturned. Their lips are not distinctive, though often a bit smudged, puffy, and "sensual". Their hair is usually dark and curly, with pale skin and small hands.

Charting Cancer's Fate

Up until about 30-35 years of age, Cancer is fickle, full of worries, disappointments, and conflicts. They do not always succeed in marriage – divorce and separation are possible. Cancers are sensitive, vulnerable people, who depend on the opinions of others. They are characterized by volatile emotional outbursts. All of this may be a red flag to potential partners. This is why Cancers should be taught to reign in their temper from early childhood.

In adulthood, Fate rewards Cancers for all of the challenges they have faced. They will reach a decent position in society and earn a sizeable fortune.

It is important for Cancers to remember that in order to move forward, they need to always be looking backward, that is, to come back to their roots and build on the past. Roots are our first home and family. Build your own nest, and the rest will fall into place. Without a strong home, Cancers lack the support they need to succeed in society.

Excessive caution and suspiciousness can throw a wrench in Cancer's ability to succeed. Cancers are often prone to building safety nets where there is no threat.

LEO DESCRIPTION

Sign. Masculine, fire, fixed.

Ruler. Sun.

Exaltation. Pluto

Temperament. Slightly choleric, with a strong sense of self-esteem.

Positive traits. Proud, self-confident, noble, indulgent, ambitious, determined, passionate, bold, loyal, honest, efficient, eloquent.

Negative traits. Arrogant, insolent, vain, conceited, nervous, cruel, treacherous, demands attention, in love with luxury.

Weaknesses in the body. Left eye in women, right eye in men, upper back, heart, aorta, cardiovascular system, back, spine, spinal cord, ribs, spleen, diaphragm, arterial circulation.

Metal. Gold.

Minerals. For a talisman- rock crystal. Generally- diamond, ruby, chrysoberyl, gold quartz, beryl, jasper, hyacinth, chrysolite.

Numbers. 1, 4, 9.

Day. Sunday.

Color. Purple-red and yellow green.

Leo energy

The Sun is Leo's celestial ruler. It bestows Leo with qualities such as endurance, powerful creative potential, and an incredible range of both soul and generosity. Leo can also be rather vain, however. His ambition means he will not simply stop and rest on his laurels. Leo has a truly regal gaze and is always looking ahead. He has enough innate qualities to satisfy himself. Leo is the sign of winners and rulers. Figuratively speaking, Leos have a special mission, specifically to light the spark of God in themselves to ignite a divine cosmic fire and lead others to the height of spiritual evolution and develop their best qualities. They must understand that the power given to them carries great responsibility.

Astrological portrait of Leo

Leos are born leaders. They aspire to exert control over everything and everyone. Leos like to wear the purple mantle and laurel wreath of a victorious leader in society, and to share this generosity with their neighbors. There are some Leos who do not wish to rule over anyone. These people are individualists who rule themselves and their own destiny. They do not impose their will on anyone, but will not allow anyone to command them, either. No Leo will tolerate orders from someone else. Even if he may occasionally make a concession, he will gradually gain the upper hand by any means necessary.

Usually, Leos do not actively try to take power. Rather, they have been given this job from the very beginning. They are never climbers, and do not push others around. They are totally convinced of their own uniqueness, and subconsciously try to stand out and show others what makes them special. They radiate sunshine and tend to act through intermediaries or assistance. People are drawn to Leo, as they are drawn to the sunlight.

Leos stand out for their great physical and spiritual strength. They are capable of great achievements, and constantly seek to do more. However, they do not openly reveal this, and almost seem embarrassed of their own drive. As far as a Leo is concerned, for the right cause, he is capable of putting it all on the line and going for broke. Fortune is always smiling on him. When it seems that there is no way out, Leo will suddenly find that his supporters and allies open the door to new horizons, seemingly out of thin air.

The most important thing in a Leo's life is his career. He is ready to give it his very all. Family is also very important. Often, Leo views his home as another office. Most Leos have extraordinary talent, and great creative potential. These qualities are on display when Leo manages to fully realize himself. Leo is sincere, trusting, and honest, but also easily influenced by others and prone to ending up in a sticky situation. Leo does not tolerate betrayal in others and is intensely loyal himself.

They are intensely self-sufficient and will never ask anyone else for help, though they are happy to lend a hand to others. They reject anyone's advice, and might make a mistake, but will never regret the experience. Leo simply continues his climb to the top and will eventually conquer his goals. Leo loves the good life, expensive, high-quality things, pleasures, and sports. Physical activity helps him get rid of negative emotions and tension while increasing his energy.

Those born under Leo tend to be friendly and polite, with deep, sincere feelings. They are capable of being very chivalrous, and will never finish off a defeated enemy, just because they can.

Leo's greatest shortcoming is his vanity and pride, which make it difficult to capitalize on all of his virtues. Leo is constant in everything, even his delusions; pressuring him only makes him grow more stubborn, and he has zero humility. As far as Leo is concerned, there are only two opinions – mine and the wrong one. If Leo were to start acting more democratic toward others and treat them with just a little more patience, they would automatically do his bidding. Developing that humility is Leo's great challenge, though he is equipped with the intelligence and drive to win this battle with himself.

Leo feeds off of attention from others. He suffers when no one noticed him. He is easily swayed by flattery, meaning that it may not be difficult to deceive him. If for some reason, Leo is unable to realize his rich potential, he might fall into a real depression and become locked in a vicious cycle.

For this reason, from an early age, Leo needs to be taught to manage his emotions and get used to the idea of rolling up his sleeves and getting to work. Do not encourage him if he is trying to humiliate his peers or tries to prove his point through tantrums and physical violence.

How to recognize Leo by appearances

A typical Leo has prominent, bright features, and a large figure. Their incredible energy is palpable. They are always being noticed, even if discreetly dressed. Generally, they are medium height or tall, with beautiful, almond-shaped eyes, a straight, aristocratic nose, and long, graceful arms. They often have light hair, and men might tend to experience male pattern baldness from a young age. Their body is well-developed, muscular, and usually top-heavy. They have a direct gaze, and a habit of looking right into the eyes of anyone talking to them.

Charting Leo's Fate

Overall, Leo has a good chance of achieving success. When Leo was born, there was a feast in heaven, and God, who was feeling generous, showered Leo with many blessings. Leos may be known as the favorites of Fortune, but that does not always mean they go through life laughing. They pay a high price for their success, and only gain the strength and opportunities they need after making it through several taxing trials. Even if a Leo does not have any particular talent, he will eventually reach the summit thanks to incredible perseverance. Leo is the sign of victory! He should remember that nature has been very kind to him, and he needs to use his gifts.

VIRGO DESCRIPTION

Sign. Feminine, earth, mutable.

Ruler. Mercury.

Exaltation. Mercury.

Temperament. Melancholic, restrained, cold yet anxious.

Positive traits. Hard-working, business-minded, intelligent and with a great memory, teachable, methodical, punctual, pragmatic, neat, dignified.

Negative traits. Formal, petty, thoughtless, anxious, indecisive, self-centered, self-interested, cunning, prone to flattery, resentful, capricious, greedy, vain.

Weaknesses in the body. Gastro-intestinal tract, solar plexus, pylorus, duodenum, cecum, pancreas, spleen, liver, gallbladder, autonomic nervous system, abdominal cavity.

Metal. Brass.

Minerals. For a talisman- yellow agate and jasper. Generally- yellow sapphire, amber, citrine, chrysolite.

Numbers. 5, 10.

Day. Wednesday.

Colors. Bright green and yellow brown.

Virgo energy

Virgo's personality is colored by the energy of two planets – Mercury and Proserpina. Mercury impacts Virgos differently than it does Geminis, creating a calmer, less independent character. One might say that Proserpina's unhurried effect "slows down" Mercury's influence in Virgo. Virgo and Gemini share a brilliant intellect, but Proserpina is a powerful planet that unleashes the swirl of time. She endows her children with a sense of duty, punctuality, clarity, analytical abilities, a tendency to study the root cause of any problem, grow, and transition to a higher state. In order to that to happen, though, the conscious must work, which is what Virgo has been doing her entire life. Virgo is an Earth sign, making her a practical materialist guided by logic and common sense.

Astrological portrait of Virgo

Virgo is a sign associated with work, service, and duty. It is a sign that is capable of overcoming difficulties. This is why Virgo is always concerned with her health and does not hesitate to seek medical attention. Virgos are willing to work tirelessly for a good cause. Their goals are clear and real rather than simply theoretical ideals. Virgos do not build pies in the sky, and their work is what gives life meaning. Virgos cannot tolerate laziness in others and will not aid those who refuse to work.

Virgos analyze. They are rational, with perfectly developed logic. They have a clear mind, with few illusions about life or other people. Even in love, they are capable of seeing their partner's shortcomings and turn to various methods to correct them. This does not mean that Virgos are devoid of emotions or purely driven by logic, however. Virgo's feelings are there, but she will only rarely reveal them. Even love is first and foremost a duty to Virgo. If someone is truly in need, she will happily step up and do whatever is necessary. Virgo is an intellectual sign, and people born under it constantly strive for new knowledge. They are skilled at absorbing information and memorizing facts. This is why many Virgos are known to their friends as a walking encyclopedia. They seem to know everything and give intelligent, practical advice on any topic. When asked about anything, it is as if they had a file in their head storing complete information on whatever topic is at hand, and they will not be satisfied until they have informed you of all of it. Virgo seeks knowledge to subdue matters with their mind – this is their great, cosmic task.

Virgos are thorough critics. But they are also extremely ambitious and painfully sensitive to any comments. If you start criticizing a Virgo, she will refute all of your arguments, and you will come to regret ever starting the discussion. Virgos are pedantic, judgmental, and calculated, and their ability to impose their opinion on others mean they are impervious to criticism.

Virgos may lack intuition and creativity. They have a need to touch and see everything with their own eyes, and it is difficult for them to grasp the abstract. They subject the entire world to excellent analysis but are less gifted at synthesizing what they perceive. This means that Virgos might have a tendency to miss the forest for the trees. Virgo's home is usually in perfect order. Less pleasant traits may be her coldness and emotional rigidity.

At her highest level, a Virgo is an erudite person full of information, but her greatest battle will be her own pedantry.

How to recognize a Virgo by appearance

A typical Virgo is a slender person with a somewhat disproportional figure. In adulthood, Virgo women may tend to lose more weight than they gain, and will stay in good physical shape, even in old age. Virgos have wide bones, and their facial expressions are serious and stern. They tend to be tall but are rarely excessively so. Their faces tend to be long, as is their nose, which thickens into the shape of a water droplet. Their features are thin and well-defined. They have small eyes. Virgos are modest and often shy, and do not seek to draw attention to themselves, even if they are famous.

Charting Virgo's Fate

In childhood and adolescence, Virgos will face great difficulties. Later, they will manage to reach stability and security. Virgo builds her own happiness through decades of hard work and trial and error. Virgos tend to suffer a crisis in their personal life between the ages of about 18 to 29. They may experience marriage followed by divorce. Perhaps it finding a suitable partner seems impossible. Virgos reach personal harmony rather late in life, after the age of 36, and in some cases, as late as 42.

LIBRA DESCRIPTION

Sign. Masculine, air, cardinal.

Ruler. Venus.

Exaltation. Saturn, Uranus.

Temperament. Sanguine.

Positive traits. Diplomatic, intuitive, loves harmony, idealist, romantic, friendly, tender, fair, noble, light, refined, drawn to beauty, needs a partner.

Negative traits. Lacks self-confidence, volatile, unbalanced, sensitive, weak-willed, detached from reality.

Weaknesses in the body. Groin, uterus, bladder, kidneys, thighs, skin, veins.

Metal. Copper.

Minerals. For a talisman- orange topaz. Generally- hyacinth, orange corundum, diamond, rock crystal, coral.

Numbers. 6, 8, 12.

Day. Friday.

Color. Red-orange and green blue.

Libra energy

Libra is ruled by two planets – Venus (the planet of love, beauty, and prosperity) and Chiron (the symbol of balance and justice). Venus is known to astrologists as "small happiness" (Jupiter is known as "big happiness"). Venus's energy brings Libras good luck, but behind the scenes, Libras need to work hard. They achieve much thanks to their talents, charms, persuasiveness, and ability to smooth over any contradictions. Chiron gives them the key to all kinds of information. Libras can combine that which seems incompatible – they manage to work two jobs, bring enemies and friends together, and maintain a balance, all the while.

The element of air starts off active, before getting carried away. It brings Libra the ability to keep a cool head, remain calm, and seek compromises while getting along with others and avoiding causing a conflict.

Astrological portrait of Libra

Libras are connoisseurs of beauty, aesthetics, and they strive to find the golden mean in everything. Their contradictory natures make it difficult to achieve complete harmony. Libras love people but hate crowds. They are kind and sociable while also experiencing long bouts of depression. They can be intelligent but naïve. Restless and mobile, but never in a hurry. They do not tolerate rudeness but are capable of saying a harsh word in their hearts. It is worth noting that this kind of behavior is just a mask to hide their insecurities. In fact, Libras are good-natured, and any rudeness is contrived rather than their nature. Libra's character is

Negative traits. Irritable, excitable, willful, critical, deceptive, rude, vindictive, insidious, passion is unbridled, excessively sexual.

Weaknesses in the body. Lower abdomen, groin, reproductive system. Organs of secretion. Bladder and renal pelvis. Gallbladder, veins.

Metal. Iron and bronze.

Minerals. For a talisman – sarder. Generally – ruby, red carnelian.

Numbers. 4, 9, 14.

Day. Tuesday.

Color. Bright red and black.

Scorpio Energy

Scorpio is a water sign ruled by Mars and Pluto. The energy of these two planets is related, and both give off sexuality, fearlessness, determination, and the ability to make decisions in extreme situations. Scorpio is capable of withstanding any battle, making the necessary changes within and rising from the ashes to a new life. Scorpio's main driving force is her incredible sexual appetite, which she gets from both Mars and Pluto. This is reflected in self-expression, love, and creativity. One's sexual energy tends to be expressed outwardly, but the water element holds it back in Scorpio, meaning that her passions live within and rarely splash out.

Astrological portrait of Scorpio

Scorpio is the most complex, mysterious, and sexiest of the Zodiac signs. It is also the strongest sign psychologically – Scorpios are considered to be innate magicians. They possess incredible intuition, and have a real talent for guessing others' thoughts, along with an ability to get those around them to speak frankly and openly. Scorpio is a sign of transformation, perfection, and rebirth. Scorpio's entire life consists of ups and downs, and the lower she falls, the higher she will climb.

Scorpio is mocking and snide, and to her, there are no secrets in human nature. Scorpio's loved ones are open books that she can easily read. Generally speaking, they strive for self-improvement, with a strong will and emotions. Few notice these emotions, however, as they burn inside, given that Scorpios are actually secretive and reserved by nature.

Scorpios are fearless and can tolerate the toughest conditions and recover from any crisis. They despise any weakness in themselves or others, and this is a constant struggle for them. By nature, Scorpios are loners and sometimes, they find it difficult to connect with others. Their personalities are very attractive and charismatic – social, active, and diplomatic, capable of controlling the powerful energy that nature has given them since birth and unwinding the collective energy to subordinate their will onto others. Scorpios are capable of achieving great things in life.

Scorpios are always consistent – in their views, in love, affection, and what they dislike. They can tend toward being overbearing or even authoritarian, but occasionally allow themselves to be manipulated. Scorpio's hardest task is coping with her passions and inner contradictions.

On one hand, Scorpios are strict (both with themselves and others), suspicious, and secretive. On the other, however, they are seeking spiritual transformation and knowledge, and are persistent, determined, fearless, and soft-hearted. This is probably why Scorpios are so attractive, too. They are capable of making a real impression and drawing everyone's attention. They are witty, but that wit can be sharp and even wound. Keep that in mind when communicating with a Scorpio.

Despite Scorpio's secrecy and distrustfulness, she can often be sincere and frank with those close to her. That trust is not easy to earn, however. This is why Scorpios tend to have a very small circle of friends they have known since childhood.

Scorpios must learn how to restrain their passions and angry outbursts. It is very difficult for them to control themselves and their temper. They need to channel that energy into something constructive, preferably creative.

How to recognize Scorpio by appearances

Outwardly, Scorpio does not appear to be particularly strong. Her strength is, after all, spiritual, rather than physical. She may appear to be rather ordinary, but there is something fascinating about her, and it not related to her external beauty.

Scorpios always look right into their partners' eyes. This is a serious, burning, and penetrating gaze. They tend to be ironic and mocking, and over time, develop characteristic crows' eyes.

Female Scorpios are easy to spot by their clothes. They love red and black (they also dye their hair these colors). Often, they prefer tight, revealing clothing, however you will rarely find a Scorpio woman who looks vulgar or tacky.

Charting Scorpio's Fate

A Scorpio's youth is a time of excitement and fateful changes. They reach success slightly later in life – after 30. Marriage is beneficial to them. This is a very sensual sign. When alone, Scorpio becomes an ascetic, channeling her sexual energy into professional endeavors.

The quality of a Scorpio's life depends on how she uses her energy. She can channel it into one of three ways.

The first path is the "Scorpian path". Scorpios here have a hard time finding their place in society. In time, they become aggressive and even dangerous. Their worst qualities take over – insidious, treacherous, a lack of empathy, unclear moral principles. They become vulnerable to many vices and dangerous addictions and get into self-destruct mode.

The second path is that of the "eagle". A Scorpio who takes this journey is aware of her power and authority. "I am so strong that I don't need to attack anyone!" is her attitude to life. Such a Scorpio becomes wise, powerful, and fair, and her energy drives her creativity. She is sociable and gifted, great company, an advocate and a fighter against injustice.

The third way is the path of the "grey lizard", or the path of least resistance. Here, Scorpio's energy does not find a worthy channel. She is dissatisfied with herself and others but does nothing to change things, becomes pessimistic, and loses her vitality.

SAGITTARIUS DESCRIPTION

Sign. Masculine, Fire, Mutable.

Ruler. Jupiter, Neptune.

Exaltation. Descending lunar node.

Temperament. Choleric, impulsive.

Positive traits. Strives for freedom and independence. Honest, fair. Persistent, and has good will. Intuitive, a good judge, and has ambitious goals. Optimist, reasonable, compassionate, generous. Is able to manage skills, brave, energetic, enthusiastic, ambitious, and lacks prejudice.

Negative traits. Craves power, fame, and respect in society. Always wants more. Impatient with any restrictions, oppressive, violent, coercive. Tends to exaggerate, charm, seduce, and build a good opinion and impression of themselves. Loves pleasures, entertainment, and joyful feasts. Tends to be a risk taker, seeking romance and adventure. Excessively polite, sociable, makes rash decisions, direct, abrupt, adventurist.

Weaknesses in the body. Hips, pelvis, back muscles, tendons, and ligaments. Autonomic nervous system.

Metal. Tin.

Minerals. For a talisman – chalcedony. Other good minerals are turquoise, topaz, heliotrope, lapis lazuli, emerald, hyacinth, chrysolite.

Numbers. 3,4, 15.

Day. Thursday.

Color. Indigo.

Sagittarius energy

Jupiter is the planet of luck. Astrologists refer to it as "big happiness". It bestows its children with a special charisma and good luck. Success comes easily to Sagittarians, and they are admired people of honor. But before Sagittarius receives these gifts, Jupiter will put him to the test, and he will have to cross the seven seas in order to find his ideal, which, in the end, will turn out to be within himself. And yet, Sagittarius is incredibly lucky. Jupiter is generous, and Sagittarius always manages to be in the right place at the right time. The fire element gives Sagittarius his organizational skills, energy, and zest for life. Naturally, life reciprocates.

Astrological portrait of Sagittarius

Sagittarians are reckless, life-loving, and open-minded people. They are always positive no matter what the circumstances are, and manage to keep their chin up, so Fate is on their side. Many people envy Sagittarius's success – often people cannot understand how life can be so kind to him. What they do not know is that Sagittarius carefully plans his future success, and always knows his next move in advance. He may give off the impression of flying by the seat of his pants, but in fact, he has a rigid structure and clear life plan. What's more, Sagittarius is highly principled and slightly conservative. He is used to acting intelligently. Yet, he can at times be impulsive and rash. Sagittarius would be wise to learn to wait and analyze his own behavior.

Most Sagittarians are sociable and open. They are characterized by independence and seek to throw off any restrictions they may face – whether internal or external. Sagittarius is incapable of engaging in deception. Intrigue and trickery are not for him, and he is straightforward and open, which those dealing with him need to understand. Sagittarius is not known for being tactful or delicate, though in his mind, he is a model of politeness and diplomacy. He is well-meaning and generous, though he is also capable of standing up for himself. He does not allow anyone to infringe on his rights or property.

Sagittarius is always charming, and that is usually not due to his appearance. Sagittarius's smile lights up a room. His natural charm is an aid as he gains authority and climbs to high positions, which are his main aspirations in life.

Sagittarius is in need of recognition, and it is important for him to be admired by those around him and that they listen to what he has to say. Sagittarians are very good at this, as being in charge and running things is their calling.

Sagittarians travel a lot. They crave new experiences, have a thirst for learning, and want to try everything before their earthly journey is over. It is difficult for them to sit still. They tend to accumulate large libraries, learn on their own, and are excellent teachers, lecturers, and religious leaders. Spiritually, they are open and want to share their ideas with everyone and teach others. At their best, Sagittarians become highly spiritual and might devote themselves to religious activities, missionary work, or simply preach spiritual knowledge.

If Sagittarius does not receive a normal spiritual and intellectual development, he may tend to become authoritarian and arrogant, with a weakness for awards and accolades. He will not tolerate defeat or the slightest criticism.

Sagittarius's most difficult task is to fight his own weaknesses and shortcomings. The most important thing is that his human nature wins, rather than animal nature. After all, Sagittarius is a centaur – half animal (horse) and half human.

How to recognize Sagittarius by appearances

Sagittarians are medium height to tall, with a dense figure and broad bones. They tend to be obese, and so they need to keep an eye on their physical shape from a young age. They have a certain robustness to them. If you see someone who seems like he would be a great boss,

Color. Green-blue, grey.

Number. 2.

Aquarius energy

Aquarius is ruled by Uranus, which does not behave like other planets in the solar system. Its axis is deflected from the plane of orbit by 98 degrees, as though the planet were laying on its side. When the Sun is opposite to the North Pole, the southern half of Uranus sinks into the shadows for 20 years. These features of Uranus are a perfect metaphor for those born under its energy. Aquarians are known for their unconventional views and rebelliousness. They see a world thirsty for radical changes, but when push comes to shove, they tread carefully and tend not to get their own hands dirty, preferring instead to inspire others to act.

Astrological portrait of Aquarius

Uranus was revered in ancient times as the god of heaven, thunder, and lightening. Aquarius is not afraid of making changes to his life and is quick to make a decision and act. Uranus is the planet of freedom, spontaneity, and providence, after all. Aquarius is known for his originality, friendship, camaraderie with everyone, eccentricity, and stubbornness. He feels misunderstood, can be defiant, and is often offended. He is not entirely wrong on this count. Aquarius is the Zodiac's most obscure sign, and his behavior often raises eyebrows. He is always unpredictable, marches to the beat of his own drum, and lives based on his own lived experience. He does not always feel it necessary to share his motivations with others.

Aquarius's driving force is absolute justice, which he will defend, no matter whose rights have been trampled. He loves to express his opinions but never imposes them on others. He has respect for individual thought. He has no patience for flattery, hypocrisy, and lies, though he engages in all three. He will not follow the crowd or adjust his ways.

Despite all of this, Aquarius is not a loner or recluse. He loves his circle of friends and needs communication and human contact. These ties are shallow, though, and Aquarius does not let anyone into his soul, no matter how close they are. He is somewhat aloof, with a stiff upper lip and focused on practicality. Inside, however, Aquarius feels isolated and prefers to watch from a distance. He is not a fighter or aggressive in any way, though he will not give up his positions in the face of pressure.

Aquarius sometimes has spontaneous moments of revelation, bordering on prophecy. He can guess others' thoughts and is ahead of his time in his ideas. Aquarius is the sign with the most geniuses. But Aquarius can easily shift his own views and adopt those of his foes. He may not have a lack of clear principles, and a relatively lax attitude toward morality and public opinion, but thanks to his charm, he can be forgiven for many sins.

How to recognize Aquarius by appearances

Aquarius is original and unpredictable in everything, even outward appearances. There is always something extraordinary about him, and he manages to catch everyone's eye. He may be tall with long limbs, and be the picture of contrasts – for example, dark hair with light skin and light-colored eyes. His movements are impulsive and jerky. He is verbose, speaks quickly, and talks with his hands.

Charting Aquarius's Fate

Aquarius's life is full of changes. In his youth, he might spend a lot of time trying to find his path. In adulthood, however, this change becomes internal and therefore more manageable. Aquarians love to travel, especially overseas for long trips, and they bring good luck with them.

PISCES DESCRIPTION

Sign. Feminine, water, mutable.

Ruler. Neptune, Pluto.

Exaltation. Venus.

Positive traits. Highly imaginative, kind, adaptable, tranquil, peaceful, receptive, impressive, modest, compassionate, caring, delicate, gentle, idealistic, religious, deep.

Negative traits. Passive, shy, fanatical, impractical, fantastical, slovenly, volatile, unreliable, self-indulgent, overly sensual, malleable, submissive, dependent, moody, lazy, apathetic.

Weaknesses in the body. Legs – ankles, toe joints, toes. Tendons and ligaments. Digestive, lymphatic, and endocrine systems, heart and circulatory system.

Metal. Platinum and tin.

Minerals. For a talisman – amethyst and chrysolite. Opal, jasper, and coral are compatible.

Numbers. 3, 11, 19.

Day. Thursday.

Color. Purple and indigo.

Pisces energy

Pisces is influenced by the energies of both Neptune and Jupiter. In ancient cultures, Neptune was revered as the ruler of the seas. He represents the primal ocean and chaos where all opportunities lie, but nothing ever comes to life on its own. Neptune is the highest faith, psychic phenomena, hypersensitivity, deep and intuitive understanding of things and capacity for unearthly love. All of these traits are inherent to Pisces, and generous Jupiter bestows them with confidence in their own importance, a happy life, and great vitality.

Astrological portrait of Pisces

Pisces closes the Zodiac. This sign is a mirror of all the others, with a focus on their strengths and weaknesses. Pisces is a self-redeemer who is able to purify others by taking on the negativity. That is Pisces's greatest mission. Empathy, compassion, and the ability to reflect the qualities of any other sign with detachment are her main traits. "I feel, therefore I am" is Pisces's motto. However, in their negative manifestations, Pisces are ambivalent, unreliable, and prone to betrayal at any time. They make big promises and hardly ever follow through. They seek their own benefits and are very dishonest. Pisces always reflect their environment, which will determine their behavior. They are easily influenced by others, though this is usually unconscious. Without even realizing it, they take on the feelings and thoughts of whomever they are talking to. They can get carried away and simply go with the flow like water, not trying to change their own destiny. Pisces lack willpower and the ability to stand on their own two feet or have the inner core they need to resist the influence of others. Pisces is symbolized by two fish swimming in opposite directions. One fish is living, while the other is depicted as dead. This is Pisces – the living fish is in harmony with God and one with the cosmos. The dead Pisces is illusions, speculation of one's own weakness, opportunism, and chaos. At their worst, Pisces are capable of showing the vile human traits, only to be tormented by remorse afterward.

Pisces is a wise sign, with an understanding of others' suffering. They are capable of sacrificing themselves to help others. They are humane, merciful, and optimistic. But they are also overly sensitive and feel others' pain as their own. Pisces make good psychologists, and they are drawn to that which is hidden. They like to wrap their lives in mystery and express themselves symbolically. They tend to fantasize a lot. Others may not always understand Pisces, which causes her to suffer. She hates arguments and scandal but would rather tolerate evil and injustice than actually fight them. She has a good sense of humor, is friendly, humble, and calm. This draws many people in and opens doors. Pisces wants financial well-being but is rarely able to gain it on her own. As Pisces ages, she is eventually able to achieve peace and prosperity.

Pisces's great task is to carry divine love into the world, have compassion for her neighbors, and help them in their spiritual development. Nearly all Pisces are creative – many are musicians, artists, writers, performers, psychologist, or mystics.

How to recognize Pisces by appearances

Pisces is a sign that is constantly changing. Their appearance is a reflection of their inner state. Pisces tend to have large, deep, and alluring eyes, with an inward or wandering gaze that makes them look mysterious and almost absent. Pisces hardly ever look others in the eye. Their eyelids often appear red and irritated. Their skin is soft, pale, and almost transparent. Their hair is thin rather than thick, and their hands are small and soft, even in men. Pisces tend to gain weight, but they keep an eye on their figure.

Charting Pisces's Fate

Pisces's life path is often difficult and full of ups and downs. If she is not guided by someone else's strong hand, she may not achieve success. Pisces needs something or someone to stimulate and inspire her, especially among men. Female Pisces are often strong-minded, strong-willed individuals who forge their own path in life and are very successful in all of their endeavors.

A Guide to The Moon Cycle and Lunar Days

Since Ancient times, people have noticed that the moon has a strong influence on nature. Our Earth and everything living on it is a single living being, which is why the phases of the moon have such an effect on our health and mental state, and therefore, our lives. Remember Shakespeare and his description of Othello's jealousy in his famous tragedy:

"It is the very error of the moon, She comes more nearer Earth than she was wont And makes men mad."

If our inner rhythm is in harmony with that of the cosmos, we are able to achieve much more. People were aware of this a thousand years ago. The lunar calendar is ancient. We can find it among the ancient Sumerians (4000-3000 BC), the inhabitants of Mesopotamia, Native Americans, Hindus, and ancient Slavs. There is evidence that the Siberian Yakuts had a lunar calendar, as did the Malaysians.

Primitive tribes saw the moon as a source of fertility. Long before Christianity, the waxing moon was seen as favorable for planting new crops and starting a new business, for success and making money, while the waning moon was a sign that business would end.

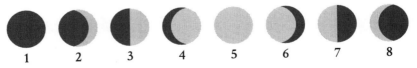

1   2   3   4   5   6   7   8

What are the phases of the moon?

- Phase 1 – new moon
- Phase 2 – waxing crescent moon
- Phase 3 – first quarter moon
- Phase 4 – waxing gibbous moon
- Phase 5 – full moon
- Phase 6 – waning gibbous moon
- Phase 7 – third quarter moon
- Phase 8 – waning crescent moon

To simplify things, we can divide the month into two phases:
Waxing crescent moon - before the full moon
Waning crescent moon - after the full moon

New Moon

We cannot see the new moon, as it is hidden. People might complain about feeling weak, mental imbalance, and fatigue. During this time, we want to avoid taking on too much or overdoing things. Generally, people are not very responsive and react poorly to requests, which is why it is best to look out for yourself, while not keeping your plate too full.

The new moon is a bad time for advertising – it will go unnoticed. It is not worth preparing any presentations, parties, or loud gatherings. People are feeling constrained, not very social, and sluggish.

This is also a less than ideal time for surgery, as your recovery will be slow, and the likelihood of medical error is high.

It is also difficult to get an accurate diagnosis during the new moon – diseases might seem to be hidden, and doctors might not see the real underlying cause of what ails you.

The new moon is also a bad time for dates, and sexual encounters may be dissatisfying and leave you feeling disappointed. Ancient astrologers did not advise planning a wedding night during the new moon.

Waxing Crescent Moon

It is easy to identify a waxing crescent moon. If you draw an imaginary line between the two "horns", you should see the letter P. The waxing moon is then divided into one and two quarters.

During the first quarter moon, we need to focus on planning – setting goals and thinking of how we will set about achieving them. However, it is still a good idea to hold back a bit and not overdo things. Energy levels are still low, though they are growing along with the moon. It is still a good idea to avoid any medical procedures during this time.

The second quarter is a time for bold, decisive action. Things will come easy, and there is a greater chance of a lucky break. This is a good time for weddings, especially if the moon will be in Libra, Cancer, or Taurus. Nevertheless, it is a good idea to put off any advertising activities and public speaking until closer to the full moon, if you can.

Full Moon

During the full moon, the Earth is located between the sun and the moon. During this time, the moon is round and fully illuminated. This takes place during days 14-16 of the lunar cycle.

During the full moon, many people feel more vigorous than usual. They are emotional, sociable, and actively seeking more contact, so this may be a good time for any celebrations.

However, be careful not to drink too much – you can relax to the point that you lose control, and the consequences of that can be very unpleasant. If you are able to stick to moderation, there is no better time for a party!

The full moon is also the best time for advertising, as not only will your campaign be widely seen, people will be apt to remember it.

The full moon is also a favorable time for dates, and during this time, people are at their most open, romantic, and willing to tell each other something important that might take their relationship to the next level of trust and understanding.

Moreover, during the full moon, people feel a surge of energy, which may lead to hyperactivity, restlessness, and insomnia.

It will be harder to keep your emotions in check. You might face conflicts with friends, disasters, and accidents. During the full moon, any surgeries are **not a good idea**, as the risk of complications and bleeding is on the rise. Plastic surgery is also a bad idea, as swelling and bruises might be much worse than in another lunar phase. At the same time, the full moon is a good time to get an accurate diagnosis.

During this time, try to limit your calories and liquid intake (especially if you deal with bloating and excess weight), as your body is absorbing both calories and liquids faster during the full moon, and it can be very difficult to get rid of the weight later on.

Waning Crescent Moon

The full moon is over, and a new phase is beginning – the waning moon. This is a quieter time, when all of the jobs you started earlier are being partly or entirely completed (it all depends on the speed and scale).

Surgery will turn out much better if it is performed during the waning moon. Your recovery will be faster, and the likelihood of complications is much lower. If you have any plans to lose weight, the waning moon is the best time to do that. This is also a good time for quitting bad habits, such as smoking or cursing.

The waning moon can also be divided into the third and fourth quarters.

Third quarter - this is a favorable period, and you are able to resolve a lot of problems without conflict. People are calming down and ready to listen and take in information, while still being active. However, this is not the best time to begin any major projects, especially if you are unsure if you will be able to complete them by the start of the new lunar month.

The third quarter is a good time to get married, especially if the moon is in Cancer, Taurus, or Libra.

Fourth quarter – This is the most passive period of the lunar cycle. You are not as strong as usual. Your energy is lagging. You will be tired until reaching a new beginning. The best thing you can do as the lunar cycle comes to an end is to get things in order, and avoid anything that might get in your way at work or in personal relationships. Examine your successes and failures.

Now, let's discuss the lunar days in greater detail. For centuries, people around the world have described the influence of lunar days, and modern astrologers only add to this work, as they compare old texts to modern life.

The 1ˢᵗ lunar day

The first lunar day is extremely important for the rest of the lunar month. This is a much-needed day to carefully plan your activities and lay the groundwork for the rest of the lunar month. Remember that the first lunar day is not a good day for major activities, but rather for sitting down and planning things.

Avoid conflicts on this day, unless you want them to overshadow the rest of the month. Try to see the positive side of things and imagine that the lunar month will bring you good things both at work and in love. The more vividly you can imagine this, the sooner your desires will come to fruition. Perhaps it would be a good idea to jot down plans that will bring you closer to achieving your dreams. This is the best time for both manifesting and making wishes!

This is also a favorable day when it comes to seeking a new job or starting an academic program.

It is fine to go out on a date on the first lunar day, but limit any sexual contact, as your energy levels are low, and you are likely to end up disappointed.

Getting married on the first lunar day is not recommended.

Avoid getting a haircut – there are many indications that cutting your hair on the first lunar day will have a negative effect on your health and life expectancy.

Under no circumstances should you undergo any major cosmetic procedures, including plastic surgery. Energy levels are low, your skin is dull and almost stagnant. The results will not live up to your expectations, and in the worst-case scenario, you will end up looking worse than before. It is common for cosmetic procedures performed on this day to be disappointing or even useless. Even the best surgeons are less capable.

Your good dreams on the first lunar day foretell happiness and joy. Bad ones usually do not come true.

The 2nd lunar day

This is considered a lucky day, and is symbolized by a cornucopia. It is not an exaggeration to say that the second lunar day is a favorable time for both work and love. It is a time for action, and a great period to work on yourself, look for a new job, start something new, or complete any financial transaction, whether a sale or purchase. This is also a great time for creative and scientific insights, and a good time for any meeting – whether political or romantic.

Any romantic dates or sexual encounters during the second lunar day are unlikely to disappoint. This is also a good day for weddings or taking a trip with someone special.

During the second lunar day, the moon is beginning its waxing phase, which is a good time for anything you might to do nourish and restore your skin. This is a great time for any cosmetic procedures aimed at preservation, though it is best to put off any plastic surgery until the waning moon. If that is not possible, then the second lunar day is acceptable, if not ideal, and you will not run into any complications.

Folklore tells us that this is not a good day for a haircut, as that may lead to arguments with a loved one.

This is the best time for exercise – your body is in good shape, and you are able to handle new exercise regimens. If the moon happens to be in Scorpio, though, be careful.

This is a good day for anything positive, but avoid any conflicts, discussions about the status of your relationship, or litigation.

Dreams of the second lunar day are usually not prophetic.

The 3rd lunar day

On this day, we are usually able to make out a thin sliver of the lunar crescent. It is a longstanding tradition to show money during the new month – it is believed that as the moon grows, so will your savings.

However, astrological systems around the world consider this an unlucky, unfavorable day. It is not a good idea to travel, begin any new business, or give into your bad mood.

You might run into many a lot of problems at work on this day, which will cause you a lot of anxiety. However, it is a good day to take a step back and identify and set about fixing any flaws and shortcomings. Remember that everything tends to look worse on this day than it actually is.

It is not the time to ask management for anything – you are likely to walk away disappointed, and end up unfairly reprimanded rather than receiving a promotion or raise. Instead, focus on areas of work that need to be smoothed over or studied further. It will be clear what problems you are facing, and you will easily be able to find a remedy.

Do not rush to criticize your loved ones – things may not be as they appear. "Measure twice and cut once" is your motto on this day.

This is not a good day to get married, as the couple is likely to have a turbulent, short-lived marriage.

You can schedule a cosmetic procedure for this day, but only if it is relatively minor. Plastic surgery should wait.

Do exercises as usual, without overdoing it or adding any new routines.

Dreams on this day do not mean anything.

The 4th lunar day

These are relatively neutral days, in that they are unlikely to bring anything bad, but they also will not bring you any windfalls. The fourth lunar day is symbolized by a tree of paradise, the tree of knowledge, and the choice between good and evil. Things ultimately depend on us and our final decisions.

This is a great day for anything money-related – signing contracts, agreements, or even taking on credit. There are also a lot of contradictions on this day – on one hand, we are likely to receive money, which is a good thing, but on the other, we will have to give some of it away, which is never particularly fun or pleasant. There is good reason to consider all of your opportunities and possibilities before acting.

It is not a good day to get married, as the wedding will not be as fun as you had hoped. However, the fourth lunar day is, in fact, a good day for sex and conceiving a healthy child.

Be careful on this day if you happen to engage in any physical exercise, as it is not a good idea to overeat or abuse alcohol. Take care of yourself. Any illnesses which began on this day may be extremely dangerous, if they are not dealt with immediately.

Cosmetic procedures are not contraindicated, as long as they are to preserve your appearance. Plastic surgery can be performed if you truly feel it is necessary.

However, avoid getting a haircut, as it is unlikely to grow back healthily, and will become brittle and dull. However, if the moon is in Leo, you can disregard this advice.

Dreams may turn out to be real.

The 5th lunar day

Traditionally, the fifth lunar day is one of the worst of the lunar month. It is symbolized by a unicorn. Unicorns need to be tamed, but only a virgin is capable of doing so. Many people will feel drained on this day, or frustrated with themselves, those around them, and life in general.

Try to avoid arguments- any conflicts are likely to drag out for a long time, and then you may be overcome with guilt. This advice is relevant for both work and love.

Sexual encounters may be pleasant, but this is not a good day to plan a wedding, as it is likely to lead to a marriage full of unpleasant incidents.

Do not start any new businesses, or ask those around you for favors- you may be misunderstood and rejected.

It is fine to engage in physical exercise, but if you overdo it on this day, you may injure yourself.

Your energy levels are low. Cosmetic procedures may not be effective, and avoid any plastic surgeries.

It is good if you dream something connected with the road, trips or with movement in general. A bad dream might be a sign of a health problem which should be addressed.

The 6th lunar day

The symbol of the sixth lunar day is a cloud and a crane. This is a philosophical combination that suggests that it is not worth rushing things on these days. This is a very positive, lucky day for both work and love. Creative work will be especially successful, as will any attempts at opening a new business in your field.

The sixth lunar day is a good time for resolving any financial matters. There is one limitation, however – do not give anyone a loan, as they may not pay it back. But you can certainly sponsor and support those who are more vulnerable than you.

This day is a good time to go on a trip, whether close to home or far away.

This is also a good day for dates, weddings, and marriage proposals. Remember that energy is more romantic than sexual, so it is better to give the gift of roses and a bottle of champagne than hot, passionate sex.

It is a good idea to get some exercise, but do not overdo things, though you will probably not want to, either.

Cosmetic procedures will be successful, and you can even have plastic surgery performed, so long as the moon is not in Scorpio.

It is still a good idea to avoid getting your hair cut, as you might "cut off" something good in addition to your hair.

It is better to not discuss dreams as they are usually true. Your dreams of this day can remind you of something that needs to be completed as soon as possible.

The 7th lunar day

This is also a favorable lunar day, and it is symbolized by a fighting cock, which is an Avestan deity. Avoid any aggression on this day, and instead work on yourself, spend time at home or in nature. Avoid discussing the status of your relationship with anyone, arguing, or wishing bad things on anyone. Everything will come back to haunt you, remember, silence is golden.

Business negotiations and contracts will be successful. You can find support, sponsors, and people ready to help you in both words and deeds.

Lighten up with your colleagues and subordinates. Pay attention not only to their shortcomings, but also to their skills. This is a good day for reconciliation and creating both political and romantic unions.

The seventh lunar day is good for traveling, no matter how near or far from home.

It is also a favorable time for love and marriage.

Exercise moderately, and any plastic surgeries will go very smoothly, as long as the moon is not in Scorpio.

Dreams of this day may become a reality.

The 8th lunar day

The symbol for this day is a Phoenix, which symbolizes eternal rebirth and renewal, because this day is a great time for changes in all areas of your life. Your energy is likely to be high, and you want to do something new and unusual. This is a good time to look for a new job or begin studying something. Any out-of-the-box thinking is welcome, along with shaking things up a bit in order to improve your life.

However, avoid any financial transactions, as you may incur losses.

Avoid aggression. You can share your opinion by presenting well-founded arguments and facts, instead.

The phoenix rises from the ashes, so this is a good time to be careful with electrical appliances and fire in general. The risk of housefires is high.

Avoid any major financial transactions on the eighth day, as you may end up facing a series of complications. You can pay people their salaries, as this is unlikely to be a large sum.

This is a good day for weddings, but only if you and your future spouse are restless, creative souls and hope to achieve personal development through your marriage.

Any cosmetic procedures and plastic surgeries will go well today, as they are related to rebirth and renewal. Surgeons may find that they are true artists on this day!

You can try to change your hairstyle and get a fashionable haircut on this day.

You can trust your dreams seen on this day.

The 9th lunar day

The ninth lunar day is not particularly auspicious, and is even referred to as "Satan's" day. You may be overcome with doubt, suspicions, even depression and conflicts.

Your self-esteem will suffer, so don't overdo things physically, and avoid overeating or abusing alcohol.

This is a negative day for any business deals, travel, or financial transactions.

This is a particularly bad day for any events, so keep your head down at work and avoid any new initiatives.

It is better to avoid getting married on "Satan's" day, as the marriage will not last very long. Avoid sex, as well, but you can take care of your partner, listen them, and support them however they need.

Any cosmetic procedures will not have a lasting effect, and avoid any plastic surgery. A haircut will not turn out as you hoped.

Dreams of this day are usually prophetic.

The 10th lunar day

This is one of the luckiest days of the lunar month. It is symbolized by a spring, mushroom, or phallus. This is a time for starting a new business, learning new things, and creating.

The 10th lunar day is particularly lucky for business. Networking and financial transactions will be a success and bring hope. This is an ideal time for changing jobs, shifting your business tactics, and other renewals.

This is a perfect time for people in creative fields and those working in science, who may come up with incredible ideas that will bring many successful returns.

This is a very successful day for building a family and proposing marriage. This is a good time for celebrations and communication, so plan parties, meet with friends, and plan a romantic date.

One of the symbols for this day is a phallus, so sexual encounters are likely to be particularly satisfying.

The 10th lunar day is the best time to begin repairs, buying furniture, and items for home improvement.

You can exercise vigorously, and cosmetic procedures and plastic surgery will be very effective.

Dreams of this day will not come true.

The 11th lunar day

This is one of the best lunar days, and seen as the pinnacle of the lunar cycle. People are likely to be energetic, enthusiastic, and ready to move forward toward their goals.

The 11th lunar day is very successful for any financial transactions or business deals and meetings.

You might actively make yourself known, approach management to discuss a promotion, or look for a new job. This is an auspicious time for advertising campaigns, performances, and holding meetings.

Any trips planned will be a great success, whether near or far from home.

Romantic relationships are improving, sex is harmonious, and very desired.

Weddings held on this day will be fun, and the marriage will be a source of joy and happiness.

Exercise is a great idea, and you might even beat your own personal record.

This is an ideal time for any cosmetic procedures, but any more serious plastic surgeries might lead to a lot of bruising and swelling.

A haircut will turn out as you had hoped, and you can experiment a bit with your appearance.

You can ignore dreams of this day – usually they do not mean anything.

The 12th lunar day

This day is symbolized by the Grail and a heart. As we move closer to the full moon, our emotions are at their most open. During this time, if you ask someone for something, your request will be heeded. This is a day of faith, goodness, and divine revelations.

For business and financial transactions, this is not the most promising day. However, if you help others on this day, your good deeds are sure to come back to you.

This is a day for reconciliation, so do not try to explain your relationships, as no one is at fault, and it is better to focus on yourself, anyway.

Avoid weddings and sex on this day, but if you want to do what your partner asks, there is no better time.

Many may feel less than confident and cheerful during this day, so take it easy when working out. Avoid overeating, stay hydrated, and avoid alcohol.

The 12th lunar day is not the best for getting married or having sex, but the stars would welcome affection and a kind word.

Avoid getting a haircut, or any plastic surgeries. This is a neutral day for minor cosmetic procedures.

Nearly all dreams will come true.

The 13th lunar day

This day is symbolized by Samsara, the wheel of fate, which is very erratic and capable of moving in any direction. This is why the 13th lunar day is full of contradictions. In Indian traditions, this day is compared to a snake eating its own tail. This is a day for paying off old debts and returning to unfinished business.

Avoid beginning any new business on this day. It is preferable to finish old tasks and proofread your work. Information you receive on this day may not be reliable and must be verified.

Avoid getting your hair cut, though this is a relatively neutral day for a haircut, which might turn out well, and though it will not exceed your expectations, it will also not leave you upset. Avoid any plastic surgeries.

Dreams on this day will come true.

The 19th lunar day

This is a very difficult day and it is represented by a spider. The energy is complicated, if not outright dangerous. Don't panic or get depressed, though – this is a test of your strength, and if you are able to hold onto all you have achieved. This is relevant for both work and love. On the 19th day, you should avoid taking any trips.

The energy of the 19th lunar day is very unfavorable for beginning any major projects, and business in general. Work on what you started earlier, get your affairs in order, think over your ideas and emotions, and check to make sure that everything you have done hitherto is living up to your expectations. Do not carry out any financial transactions or take out any loans – do not loan anyone else money, either. Do not ask your managers for anything as they are unlikely to listen to what you have to say, and make judgments instead.

This is a day when you might face outright deception, so do not take any risks and ignore rumors. Do not work on anything related to real estate or legal matters.

This is a very hard time for people with an unbalanced psyche, as they may experience sudden exacerbations or even suicidal ideations.

This is a very unlucky day to get married. Sexual encounters might be disappointing and significantly worsen your relationship.

Avoid any haircuts or cosmetic procedures or surgeries.

Your dreams of this day will come true.

The 20th lunar day

This is also a difficult day, though less so than the 19th. It is represented by an eagle. This is a good time to work on your own development and spiritual growth, by speaking to a psychologist or astrologer.

Avoid pride, anger, arrogance, and envy.

The 20th lunar day is a good time for people who are active and decisive. They will be able to easily overcome any obstacles, flying over them just like an eagle. If you have to overcome your own fears, you will be able to do so – don't limit yourself, and you will see that there is nothing to be afraid of. It is a good day for any financial transactions, signing contracts, and reaching agreements, as well as networking.

The 20th lunar day is a favorable time for those who work in the creative fields, as they will be able to dream up the idea that will open up a whole host of new possibilities. Avoid conflicts – they may ruin your relationship with a lot of people, and it will not be easy to come back from that.

This is a lucky day for getting married, but only if you have been with your partner for several years, now. Sexual encounters will not be particularly joyful, but they also will not cause you any problems.

Avoid getting your hair cut, but you can certainly get it styled. The 20th lunar day is a good day for those who are looking to lose weight. You will be able to do so quickly, and it will be easy for you to follow a diet.

Cosmetic procedures will be a success, as will any plastic surgeries.

Pay attention to dreams of this day as they are likely to come true.

The 21st lunar day

This is one of the most successful days of the lunar month, and it is symbolized by a herd of horses – imagine energy, strength, speed, and bravery. Everything you think up will happen quickly, and you will be able to easily overcome obstacles. A mare is not only brave but also an honest animal, so you will only experience this luck if you remember that honesty is always the best policy.

This is also a favorable day for business. Reaching new agreements and signing contracts, or dealing with foreign partners – it is all likely to be a success. Any financial issues will be resolved successfully.

Those in the creative world will be able to show off their talent and be recognized for their work. Anyone involved in the performing arts can expect success, luck, and recognition. A galloping herd of horses moves quickly, so you might transition to a new job, move to a new apartment, or go on a business trip or travel with your better half.

The 21st lunar day is one of the best to get married or have a sexual encounter.

This is a great time for athletes, hunters, and anyone who likes adventurous activities.

But for criminals and thieves, this is not a lucky or happy day – they will quickly be brought to justice.

Any haircuts or cosmetic procedures are likely to be a huge success and bring both beauty and happiness. You will recover quickly after any surgeries, perhaps without any swelling or bruising at all.

Dreams tend to not be reliable.

The 22nd lunar day

This day will be strange and contradictory. It is symbolized by the elephant Ganesha. According to Indian mythology, Ganesha is the patron saint of hidden knowledge. so this is a favorable day for anyone who is trying to learn more about the world and ready to find the truth, though this is often seen as a hopeless endeavor. This is a day for philosophers and wisemen and women. However, it is an inauspicious day for business, and unlikely to lead to resolving financial issues, signing contracts, agreements, or beginning new projects. You can expect trouble at work.

For creative people, and new employees, this is a successful day.

This is a good day for apologies and reconciliation.

Avoid getting married, though you can feel free to engage in sexual encounters.

For haircuts and cosmetic procedures, this is a fantastic day. Surgeries will also turn out, as long as the moon is not in Scorpio.

Dreams will come true.

The 23rd lunar day

This is a challenging day represented by a crocodile, which is a very aggressive animal. This is a day of strong energy, but it is also adventurous and tough. Your main task is to focus your energy in the right direction. There may be accidents, arguments, conflicts, fights, and violence, which is why it is important to strive for balance and calm.

Keep a close eye on your surroundings – there may be traitors or people who do not wish you well, so be careful.

However, this is still a favorable day for business – many problems will be resolved successfully. You are able to sign contracts and receive credit successfully, as long as you remain active and decisive in what you do.

This is not a day for changing jobs or working on real estate transactions or legal proceedings. This is not a favorable day for traveling, no matter how near or far you plan on going.

This is not a promising day to get married – things may end in conflict, if not an all-out brawl.

Sexual relations are not off the table, as long as the couple trusts one another.

Haircuts or cosmetic procedures will not turn out as you had hoped, so avoid them.

Dreams during this lunar day usually mean something opposite of what awaits you, so you can disregard them.

The 24th lunar day

This is a neutral, calm day that is symbolized by a bear. It is favorable for forgiveness and reconciliation.

This is also a good day for learning new things, reading, self-development, and taking time to relax in nature.

This is a great day for any type of financial activity, conferences, academic meetings, and faraway travel.

The 24th lunar day is a good time for love and getting married, as any marriage will be strong and lasting.

Cosmetic procedures and plastic surgery will be a success, and you can expect a speedy recovery.

Avoid getting a haircut on this day, however, as your hair will likely thin and grow back slowly.

Dreams of this lunar day are usually connected with your personal life.

The 25th lunar day

This is still another quiet day, symbolized by a turtle.

Just like a turtle, this is not a day to rush, and it is best to sit down and take stock of your life. This is a good time for resolving any personal problems, as the moon's energy makes it possible for you to calm down and find the right path.

This is also not a bad day for business. It is believed that any business you begin on this day is sure to be a success. This is especially the case for trade and any monetary activities.

The 25th lunar day is not a good day to get married, especially if the couple is very young.

This is a neutral day for sexual encounters, as the moon is waning, energy is low, so the decision is yours.

Avoid any cosmetic procedures, except those for cleansing your skin. This is not a favorable day for haircuts or plastic surgery – unless the moon is in Libra or Leo.

You can have a prophetic dream on this day.

The 26th lunar day

The 26th lunar day is full of contradictions and complicated. It is represented by a toad.

It is not time to start or take on something new, as nothing good will come of it. Avoid any major purchases, as you will later come to see that your money was wasted. The best thing you can do on this day is stay at home and watch a good movie or read a good book.

Avoid traveling on this day, as it may not turn out well.

The 26th lunar day is a negative day for any business negotiations and starting new businesses. Do not complete any business deals or financial transactions. Your colleagues may be arguing, and your managers may be dissatisfied. But if you have decided to leave your job, there is no better time to do so.

This is not a good day to get married, as both partners' expectations may fall flat, and they will soon be disappointed.

The waning moon carries a negative charge, so avoid any haircuts and surgeries, though you can get cosmetic procedures if they are relatively minor.

Your dreams will come true.

The 27th lunar day

The 27th lunar day is one of the best days of the month, and it is represented by a ship. You can boldly start any new business, which is sure to be promising. This is a great day for students, teachers, and learning new things. Any information that comes to you on this day may be extremely valuable and useful to you.

The 27th day is good for communication and travel, whether near or far from home, and no matter whether it is for work or pleasure.

This is also a good day for any professional activities or financial transactions. If there are people around you who need help, you must support them, as your good deeds will come back 100-fold.

Romantic dates will go well, though any weddings should be quiet and subdued. This is a particularly good day for older couples or second marriages.

The waning moon means that hair will grow back very slowly, but in general, you can expect a haircut to turn out well. This is a great day for plastic surgery or cosmetic procedures, as the results will be pleasing, and you will have a speedy recovery, without any bruising or swelling, most of the time.

However, beware if the moon is in Scorpio on this day – that is not a good omen for any plastic surgery.

Do not pay any attention to dreams on this day.

The 28ᵗʰ lunar day

This is another favorable day in the waning moon cycle, and it is represented by a lotus. This is a day of wisdom and spiritual awakening. If possible, spend part of the day in nature. It is important to take stock of the last month and decide what you need to do during its two remaining days.

This is a good time for any career development, changing jobs, conducting business, decision-making, and signing agreements, as well as going on a trip. You might conclude any business deal, hold negotiations, work with money and securities.

This is also a good day for any repairs or improvements around your home or apartment.

Anyweddingstodayshouldbesubduedandmodest,andrestrictedtofamily members only. A loud, raucous wedding might not turn out very well.

Your hair will grow slowly, but any haircuts will turn out very elegant and stylish. Cosmetic procedures and surgeries are not contraindicated. You will recover quickly with little bruising and swelling.

Do not take any dreams too seriously.

The 29ᵗʰ lunar day

This is one of the most difficult days of the lunar month, and it is considered a Satanic day, unlucky for everyone and everything. It is symbolized by an octopus.

This is a dark day, and many will feel melancholy, depression, and a desire to simply be left alone. This is a day full of conflict and injuries, so be careful everywhere and with everyone. If you can, avoid any travel, and be particularly careful when handling any sharp objects. Do not engage in any business negotiations, sign any contracts, or take part in any networking.

Astrologers believe that anything you start on this day will completely fall apart. For once and for all, get rid of things that are impeding you from living your life. This is a good time to avoid people who you do find unpleasant.

This is also a time for fasting and limitations for everyone. Do not hold any celebrations, weddings, or have sexual relations – these events may not turn out as you hoped, and instead bring you nothing but suffering and strife.

Avoid getting a haircut, as well, as it will not make you look more beautiful and your hair will come back lifeless and dull. Cosmetic procedures can go ahead, but avoid any surgeries.

Dreams are likely to be true.

The 30th lunar day

There is not always a 30th lunar day, as some lunar months have only 29 days. This day is represented by a swan. The 30th lunar day is usually very short, and sometimes, it lasts less than an hour. This is a time for forgiveness and calm.

You might take stock of the last month, while also avoiding anything you do not need around you. Pay back loans, make donations, reconcile with those who recently offended you, and stop speaking to people who cause you suffering.

This is a good time for tying up loose ends, and many astrologers believe that it is also a good day to start new business.

However, avoid celebrations or weddings on this day. Spouses will either not live long, or they will quickly grow apart.

Do not get a haircut on this day, though cosmetic procedures are possible, as long as you avoid any surgeries.

Dreams promise happiness and should come true.

A Guide to Zodiac Compatibility

Often, when we meet a person, we get a feeling that they are good and we take an instant liking to them. Another person, however, gives us immediate feelings of distrust, fear and hostility. Is there an astrological reason why people say that 'the first impression is the most accurate'? How can we detect those who will bring us nothing but trouble and unhappiness?

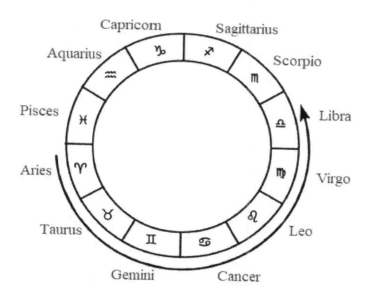

Without going too deeply into astrological subtleties unfamiliar to some readers, it is possible to determine the traits according to which friendship, love or business relationships will develop.

Let's begin with problematic relationships - our most difficult are with our **8th sign**. For example, for Aries the 8th sign is Scorpio, for Taurus it is Sagittarius and so on. Finding your 8th sign is easy; assume your own sign to be first (see above Figure) and then move eight signs counter clockwise around the Zodiac circle. This is also how the other signs (fourth, ninth and so on) that we mention are to be found.

Ancient astrologers variously referred to the 8th sign as the symbol of death, of destruction, of fated love or unfathomable attraction. In astrological terms, this pair is called 'master and slave' or 'boa constrictor and rabbit', with the role of 'master' or 'boa constrictor' being played by our 8th sign.

This relationship is especially difficult for politicians and business people.

We can take the example of a recent political confrontation in the USA. Hilary Clinton is a Scorpio while Donald Trump is a Gemini - her 8th sign. Even though many were certain that Clinton would be elected President, she lost.

To take another example, Hitler was a Taurus and his opponents – Stalin and Churchill - were both of his 8th sign, Sagittarius. The result of their confrontation is well known. Interestingly, the Russian Marshals who dealt crushing military blows to Hitler and so helped end the Third Reich - Konstantin Rokossovsky and Georgy Zhukov - were also Sagittarian, Hitler's 8th sign.

In another historical illustration, Lenin was also a Taurus. Stalin was of Lenin's 8th sign and was ultimately responsible for the downfall and possibly death of his one-time comrade-in-arms.

Business ties with those of our 8th sign are hazardous as they ultimately lead to stress and loss; both financial and moral. So, do not tangle with your 8th sign and never fight with it - your chances of winning are remote!

Such relationships are very interesting in terms of love and romance, however. We are magnetically attracted to our 8th sign and even though it may be very intense physically, it is very difficult for family life;

'Feeling bad when together, feeling worse when apart'.

As an example, let us take the famous lovers - George Sand who was Cancer and Alfred de Musset who was Sagittarius. Cancer is the 8th sign for Sagittarius, and the story of their crazy two-year love affair was the subject of much attention throughout France. Critics and writers were divided into 'Mussulist' and 'Sandist' camps; they debated fiercely about who was to blame for the sad ending to their love story - him or her. It's hard to imagine the energy needed to captivate the public for so long, but that energy was destructive for the couple. Passion raged in their hearts, but neither of them was able to comprehend their situation.

Georges Sand wrote to Musset, "*I on't love you anymore, an I will always a ore you. I on't want you anymore, an I can't o without you. It seems that nothing but a heavenly lightning strike can heal me by estroying me. Goo - bye! Stay or go, but on't say that I am not suffering. This is the only thing that can make me suffer even more, my love, my life, my bloo ! Go away, but kill me, leaving.*" Musset replied only in brief, but its power surpassed Sand's tirade, "*When you embrace me, I felt something that is still bothering me, making it impossible for me to approach another woman.*" These two people loved each other passionately and for two years lived together in a powder keg of passion, hatred and treachery.

When someone enters into a romantic liaison with their 8th sign, there will be no peace; indeed, these relationships are very attractive to those who enjoy the edgy, the borderline and, in the Dostoevsky style, the melodramatic. The first to lose interest in the relationship is, as a rule, the 8th sign.

If, by turn of fate, our child is born under our 8th sign, they will be very different from us and, in some ways, not live up to our expectations. It may be best to let them choose their own path.

In business and political relationships, the combination with our **12th sign** is also a complicated one.

We can take two political examples. Angela Merkel is a Cancer while Donald Trump is a Gemini - her 12th sign. This is why their relations are strained and complicated and we can even perhaps assume that the American president will achieve his political goals at her expense. Boris Yeltsin (Aquarius) was the 12th sign to Mikhail Gorbachev (Pisces) and it was Yeltsin who managed to dethrone the champion of Perestroika.

Even ancient astrologers noticed that our relationships with our 12th signs can never develop evenly; it is one of the most curious and problematic combinations. They are our hidden enemies and they seem to be digging a hole for us; they ingratiate themselves with us, discover our innermost secrets. As a result, we become bewildered and make mistakes when we deal with them. Among the Roman emperors murdered by members of their entourage, there was an interesting pattern - all the murderers were the 12th sign of the murdered.

We can also see this pernicious effect in Russian history: the German princess Alexandra (Gemini) married the last Russian Tsar Nicholas II (Taurus) - he was her 12th sign and brought her a tragic death. The wicked genius Grigory Rasputin (Cancer) made friends with Tsarina Alexandra, who was his 12th sign, and was murdered as a result of their odd friendship. The weakness of Nicholas II was exposed, and his authority reduced after the death of the economic and social reformer Pyotr Stolypin, who was his 12th sign. Thus, we see a chain of people whose downfall was brought about by their 12th sign.

So, it makes sense to be cautious of your 12th sign, especially if you have business ties. Usually, these people know much more about us than we want them to and they will often reveal our secrets for personal gain if it suits them. However, the outset of these relationships is, as a rule, quite normal - sometimes the two people will be friends, but sooner or later one will betray the other one or divulge a secret; inadvertently or not.

In terms of romantic relationships, our 12th sign is gentle, they take care of us and are tender towards us. They know our weaknesses well but accept them with understanding. It is they who guide us, although sometimes almost imperceptibly. Sexual attraction is usually strong.

For example, Meghan Markle is a Leo, the 12th sign for Prince Harry, who is a Virgo. Despite Queen Elizabeth II being lukewarm about the match, Harry's love was so strong that they did marry.

If a child is our 12th sign, it later becomes clear that they know all our secrets, even those that they are not supposed to know. It is very difficult to control them as they do everything in their own way.

Relations with our 7th **sign** are also interesting. They are like our opposite; they have something to learn from us while we, in turn, have something to learn from them. This combination, in business and personal relationships, can be very positive and stimulating provided that both partners are quite intelligent and have high moral standards but if not, constant misunderstandings and challenges follow. Marriage or co-operation with the 7th sign can only exist as the union of two fully-fledged individuals and in this case love, significant business achievements and social success are possible.

However, the combination can be not only interesting, but also quite complicated.

An example is Angelina Jolie, a Gemini, and Brad Pitt, a Sagittarius. This is a typical bond with a 7th sign - it's lively and interesting, but rather stressful. Although such a couple may quarrel and even part from time to time, never do they lose interest in each other.

This may be why this combination is more stable in middle-age when there is an understanding of the true nature of marriage and partnership. In global, political terms, this suggests a state of eternal tension - a cold war - for example between Yeltsin (Aquarius) and Bill Clinton (Leo).

Relations with our 9th **sign** are very good; they are our teacher and advisor - one who reveals things we are unaware of and our relationships with them very often involve travel or re-location. The combination can lead to spiritual growth and can be beneficial in terms of business.

Although, for example, Trump and Putin are political opponents, they can come to an understanding and even feel a certain sympathy for each other because Putin is a Libra while Trump is a Gemini, his 9th sign.

This union is also quite harmonious for conjugal and romantic relationships.

We treat our 3rd **sign** somewhat condescendingly. They are like our younger siblings; we teach them and expect them to listen attentively. Our younger brothers and sisters are more often than not born under this sign. In terms of personal and sexual relationships, the union is not very inspiring and can end quickly, although this is not always the case. In terms of business, it is fairly average as it often connects partners from different cities or countries.

We treat our 5th **sign** as a child and we must take care of them accordingly. The combination is not very good for business, however, since our 5th sign triumphs over us in terms of connections and finances, and thereby gives us very little in return save for love or sympathy. However, they are very good for family and romantic relationships, especially if the 5th sign is female. If a child is born as a 5th sign to their parents, their relationship will be a mutually smooth, loving and understanding one that lasts a lifetime.

Our 10th **sign** is a born leader. Depending on the spiritual level of those involved, both pleasant and tense relations are possible; the relationship is often mutually beneficial in the good times but mutually disruptive in the bad times. In family relations, our 10th sign always tries to lead and will do so according to their intelligence and upbringing.

Our 4th **sign** protects our home and can act as a sponsor to strengthen our financial or moral positions. Their advice should be heeded in all cases as it can be very effective, albeit very unobtrusive. If a woman takes this role, the relationship can be long and romantic, since all the spouse's wishes are usually met one way or another. Sometimes, such couples achieve great social success; for instance, Hilary Clinton, a Scorpio is the 4th sign to Bill Clinton, a Leo. On the other hand, if the husband is the 4th sign for his wife, he tends to be henpecked. There is often a strong sexual attraction. Our 4th sign can improve our living conditions and care for us in a parental way. If a child is our 4th sign, they are close to us and support us affectionately.

Relations with our **11th sign** are often either friendly or patronizing; we treat them reverently, while they treat us with friendly condescension. Sometimes, these relationships develop in an 'older brother' or 'high-ranking friend' sense; indeed, older brothers and sisters are often our 11th sign. In terms of personal and sexual relationships, our 11th sign is always inclined to enslave us. This tendency is most clearly manifested in such alliances as Capricorn and Pisces or Leo and Libra. A child who is the 11th sign to their parents will achieve greater success than their parents, but this will only make the parents proud.

Our **2nd sign** should bring us financial or other benefits; we receive a lot from them in both our business and our family life. In married couples, the 2nd sign usually looks after the financial situation for the benefit of the family. Sexual attraction is strong.

Our **6th sign** is our 'slave'; we always benefit from working with them and it's very difficult for them to escape our influence. In the event of hostility, especially if they have provoked the conflict, they receive a powerful retaliatory strike. In personal relations, we can almost destroy them by making them dance to our tune. For example, if a husband doesn't allow his wife to work or there are other adverse family circumstances, she gradually becomes lost as an individual despite being surrounded by care. This is the best-case scenario; worse outcomes are possible. Our 6th sign has a strong sexual attraction to us because we are the fatal 8th sign for them; we cool down quickly, however, and often make all kinds of demands. If the relationship with our 6th sign is a long one, there is a danger that routine, boredom and stagnation will ultimately destroy the relationship. A child born under our 6th sign needs particularly careful handling as they can feel fear or embarrassment when communicating with us. Their health often needs increased attention and we should also remember that they are very different from us emotionally.

Finally, we turn to relations with **our own sign**. Scorpio with Scorpio and Cancer with Cancer get along well, but in most other cases, however, our own sign is of little interest to us as it has a similar energy. Sometimes, this relationship can develop as a rivalry, either in business or in love.

There is another interesting detail - we are often attracted to one particular sign. For example, a man's wife and mistress often have the same sign. If there is confrontation between the two, the stronger character displaces the weaker one. As an example, Prince Charles is a Scorpio, while both Princess Diana and Camilla Parker Bowles were born under the sign of Cancer. Camilla was the more assertive and became dominant.

Of course, in order to draw any definitive conclusions, we need an individually prepared horoscope, but the above always, one way or another, manifests itself.

Love Description of Zodiac Signs

We know that human sexual behavior has been studied at length. Entire libraries have been written about it, with the aim of helping us understand ourselves and our partners. But is that even possible? It may not be; no matter how smart we are, when it comes to love and sex, there is always an infinite amount to learn. But we have to strive for perfection, and astrology, with its millennia of research, twelve astrological types, and twelve zodiac signs, may hold the key. Below, you will find a brief and accurate description of each zodiac sign's characteristics in love, for both men and women.

Men

ARIES

Aries men are not particularly deep or wise, but they make up for it in sincerity and loyalty. They are active, even aggressive lovers, but a hopeless romantic may be lurking just below the surface. Aries are often monogamous and chivalrous men, for whom there is only one woman (of course, in her absence, they can sleep around with no remorse). If the object of your affection is an Aries, be sure to give him a lot of sex, and remember that for an Aries, when it comes to sex, anything goes. Aries cannot stand women who are negative or disheveled. They need someone energetic, lively, and to feel exciting feelings of romance.

The best partner for an Aries is Cancer, Sagittarius, or Leo. Aquarius can also be a good match, but the relationship will be rather friendly in nature. Partnering with a Scorpio or Taurus will be difficult, but they can be stimulating lovers for an Aries. Virgos are good business contacts, but a poor match as lovers or spouses.

TAURUS

A typical Taurean man is warm, friendly, gentle, and passionate, even if he doesn't always show it. He is utterly captivated by the beauty of the female body, and can find inspiration in any woman. A Taurus has such excess physical and sexual prowess, that to him, sex is a way to relax and calm down. He is the most passionate and emotional lover of the Zodiac, but he expects his partner to take the initiative, and if she doesn't, he will easily find someone else. Taureans rarely divorce, and are true to the end – if not sexually, at least spiritually. They are secretive, keep their cards close, and may have secret lovers. If a Taurus does not feel a deep emotional connection with someone, he won't be shy to ask her friends for their number. He prefers a voluptuous figure over an athletic or skinny woman.

The best partners for a Taurus are Cancer, Virgo, Pisces, or Scorpio. Sagittarius can show a Taurus real delights in both body and spirit, but they are unlikely to make it down the aisle. They can have an interesting relationship with an Aquarius – these signs are very different, but sometimes can spend their lives together. They might initially feel attracted to an Aries, before rejecting her.

GEMINI

The typical Gemini man is easygoing and polite. He is calm, collected, and analytical. For a Gemini, passion is closely linked to intellect, to the point that they will try to find an explanation for their actions before carrying them out. But passion cannot be explained, which scares a Gemini, and they begin jumping from one extreme to the other. This is why you will find more bigamists among Geminis than any other sign of the Zodiac. Sometimes, Gemini men even have two families, or divorce and marry several times throughout the course of their lives. This may be because they simply can't let new and interesting experiences pass them by. A Gemini's wife or lover needs to be smart, quick, and always looking ahead. If she isn't, he will find a new object for his affection.

Aquarians, Libras, and Aries make good partners for a Gemini. A Sagittarius can be fascinating for him, but they will not marry before he reaches middle age, as both partners will be fickle while they are younger. A Gemini and Scorpio are likely to be a difficult match, and the Gemini will try to wriggle out of the Scorpio's tight embrace. A Taurus will be an exciting sex partner, but their partnership won't be for long, and the Taurus is often at fault.

CANCER

Cancers tend to be deep, emotional individuals, who are both sensitive and highly sexual. Their charm is almost mystical, and they know how to use it. Cancers may be the most promiscuous sign of the Zodiac, and open to absolutely anything in bed. Younger Cancers look for women who are more mature, as they are skilled lovers. As they age, they look for someone young enough to be their own daughter, and delight in taking on the role of a teacher. Cancers are devoted to building a family and an inviting home, but once they achieve that goal, they are likely to have a wandering eye. They will not seek moral justification, as they sincerely believe it is simply something everyone does. Their charm works in such a way that women are deeply convinced they are the most important love in a Cancer's life, and that circumstances are the only thing preventing them from being together. Remember that a Cancer man is a master manipulator, and will not be yours unless he is sure you have throngs of admirers. He loves feminine curves, and is turned on by exquisite fragrances. Cancers don't end things with old lovers, and often go back for a visit after a breakup. Another type of Cancer is rarer – a faithful friend, and up for anything in order to provide for his wife and children. He is patriotic and a responsible worker.

Scorpios, Pisces, and other Cancers are a good match. A Taurus can make for a lasting relationship, as both signs place great value on family and are able to get along with one another. A Sagittarius will result in fights and blowouts from the very beginning, followed by conflicts and breakups. The Sagittarius will suffer the most. Marriage to an Aries isn't off the table, but it won't last very long.

LEO

A typical Leo is handsome, proud, and vain, with a need to be the center of attention at all times. They often pretend to be virtuous, until they are able to actually master it. They crave flattery, and prefer women who comply and cater to them. Leos demand unconditional obedience, and constant approval. When a Leo is in love, he is fairly sexual, and capable of being devoted and faithful. Cheap love affairs are not his thing, and Leos are highly aware of how expensive it is to divorce. They make excellent fathers. A Leo's partner needs to look polished and well-dressed, and he will not tolerate either frumpiness or nerds.

Aries, Sagittarius, and Gemini make for good matches. Leos are often very beguiling to Libras; this is the most infamous astrological "master-slave" pairing. Leos are also inexplicably drawn to Pisces – this is the only sign capable of taming them. A Leo and Virgo will face a host of problems sooner or later, and they might be material in nature. The Virgo will attempt to conquer him, and if she does, a breakup is inevitable.

VIRGO

Virgo is a highly intellectual sign, who likes to take a step back and spend his time studying the big picture. But love inherently does not lend itself to analysis, and this can leave Virgos feeling perplexed. While Virgo is taking his time, studying the object of his affection, someone else will swoop in and take her away, leaving him bitterly disappointed. Perhaps for that reason, Virgos tend to marry late, but once they are married, they remain true, and hardly ever initiate divorce. In bed, they are modest and reserved, as they see sex as some sort of quirk of nature, designed solely for procreation. Most Virgos have a gifted sense of taste, hearing, and smell. They cannot tolerate pungent odors and can be squeamish; they believe their partners should always take pains to be very clean. Virgos usually hate over-the-top expressions of love, and are immune to sex as a mean s of control. Many Virgos are stingy and more appropriate as husbands than lovers. Male Virgos tend to be monogamous, though if they are unhappy or disappointed with their partner, they may begin to look for comfort elsewhere and often give in to drunkenness.

Taurus, Capricorn, and Scorpio make the best partners for a Virgo. They may feel inexplicable attraction for Aquarians. They will form friendships with Aries, but rarely will this couple make it down the aisle. With Leos, be careful – this sign is best as a lover, not a spouse.

LIBRA

Libra is a very complex, wishy-washy sign. They are constantly seeking perfection, which often leaves them in discord with the reality around them. Libra men are elegant and refined, and expect no less from their partner. Many Libras treat their partners like a beautiful work of art, and have trouble holding onto the object of their affection. They view love itself as a very abstract concept, and can get tired of the physical aspect of their relationship. They are much more drawn to intrigue and the chase- dreams, candlelit evenings, and other symbols of romance. A high percentage of Libra men are gay, and they view sex with other men as the more elite option. Even when Libras are unhappy in their marriages, they never divorce willingly. Their wives might leave them, however, or they might be taken away by a more decisive partner.

Aquarius and Gemini make the best matches for Libras. Libra can also easily control an independent Sagittarius, and can easily fall under the influence of a powerful and determined Leo, before putting all his strength and effort into breaking free. Relationships with Scorpios are difficult; they may become lovers, but will rarely marry.

SCORPIO

Though it is common to perceive Scorpios as incredibly sexual, they are, in fact, very unassuming, and never brag about their exploits. They will, however, be faithful and devoted to the right woman. The Scorpio man is taciturn, and you can't expect any tender words from him, but he will defend those he loves to the very end. Despite his outward control, Scorpio is very emotional; he needs and craves love, and is willing to fight for it. Scorpios are incredible lovers, and rather than leaving them tired, sex leaves them feeling energized. They are always sexy, even if they aren't particularly handsome. They are unconcerned with the ceremony of wooing you, and more focused on the act of love itself.

Expressive Cancers and gentle, amenable Pisces make the best partners. A Scorpio might also fall under the spell of a Virgo, who is adept at taking the lead. Sparks might fly between two Scorpios, or with a Taurus, who is perfect for a Scorpio in bed. Relationships with Libras, Sagittarians, and Aries are difficult.

SAGITTARIUS

Sagittarian men are lucky, curious, and gregarious. Younger Sagittarians are romantic, passionate, and burning with desire to experience every type of love. Sagittarius is a very idealistic sign, and in that search for perfection, they tend to flit from one partner to another, eventually forgetting what they were even looking for in the first place. A negative Sagittarius might have two or three relationships going on at once, assigning each partner a different day of the week. On the other hand, a positive Sagittarius will channel his powerful sexual energy into creativity, and take his career to new heights. Generally speaking, after multiple relationships and divorces, the Sagittarian man will conclude that his ideal marriage is one where his partner is willing to look the other way.

Aries and Leo make the best matches for a Sagittarius. He might fall under the spell of a Cancer, but would not be happy being married to her. Gemini can be very intriguing, but will only make for a happy marriage after middle age, when both partners are older and wiser. Younger Sagittarians often marry Aquarian women, but things quickly fall apart. Scorpios can make for an interesting relationship, but if the

Sagittarius fails to comply, divorce is inevitable.

CAPRICORN

Practical, reserved Capricorn is one of the least sexual signs of the Zodiac. He views sex as an idle way to pass the time, and something he can live without, until he wants to start a family. He tends to marry late, and almost never divorces. Young Capricorns are prone to suppressing their sexual desires, and only discover them later in life, when they have already achieved everything a real man needs – a career and money. We'll be frank – Capricorn is not the best lover, but he can compensate by being caring, attentive, and showering you with valuable gifts. Ever cautious, Capricorn loves to schedule his sexual relationships, and this is something partners will just have to accept. Women should understand that Capricorn needs some help relaxing – perhaps with alcohol. They prefer inconspicuous, unassuming women, and run away from a fashion plate.

The best partners for a Capricorn are Virgo, Taurus, or Scorpio. Cancers might catch his attention, and if they marry, it is likely to be for life. Capricorn is able to easily dominate Pisces, and Pisces-Capricorn is a well-known "slave and master" combination. Relationships with Leos tend to be erratic, and they are unlikely to wed. Aries might make for a cozy family at first, but things will cool off quickly, and often, the marriage only lasts as long as Capricorn is unwilling to make a change in his life.

AQUARIUS

Aquarian men are mercurial, and often come off as peculiar, unusual, or aloof, and detached. Aquarians are turned on by anything novel or strange, and they are constantly looking for new and interesting people. They are stimulated by having a variety of sexual partners, but they consider this to simply be normal life, rather than sexually immoral. Aquarians are unique – they are more abstract than realistic, and can be cold and incomprehensible, even in close relationships.

Once an Aquarius gets married, he will try to remain within the realm of decency, but often fails. An Aquarian's partners need uncommon patience, as nothing they do can restrain him. Occasionally, one might encounter another kind of Aquarius – a responsible, hard worker, and exemplary family man.

The best matches for an Aquarius are female fellow Aquarians, Libras, and Sagittarians. When Aquarius seeks out yet another affair, he is not choosy, and will be happy with anyone.

PISCES

Pisces is the most eccentric sign of the Zodiac. This is reflected in his romantic tendencies and sex life. Pisces men become very dependent on those with whom they have a close relationship. Paradoxically, they are simultaneously crafty and childlike when it comes to playing games, and they are easily deceived. As a double bodied sign, Pisces rarely marry just once, as they are very sexual, easily fall in love, and are constantly seeking their ideal. Pisces are very warm people, who love to take care of others and are inclined toward "slave-master" relationships, in which they are the submissive partner. But after catering to so many lovers, Pisces will remain elusive. They are impossible to figure out ahead of time – today, they might be declaring their love for you, but tomorrow, they may disappear – possibly forever! To a Pisces, love is a fantasy, illusion, and dream, and they might spend their whole lives in pursuit of it. Pisces who are unhappy in love are vulnerable to alcoholism or drug addiction.

Cancer and Scorpio make the best partners for a Pisces. He is also easily dominated by Capricorn and Libra, but in turn will conquer even a queen-like Leo. Often, they are fascinated by Geminis – if they marry, it will last a long time, but likely not forever. Relationships with Aries and Sagittarians are erratic, though initially, things can seem almost perfect.

Women

ARIES

Aries women are leaders. They are decisive, bold, and very protective. An Aries can take initiative and is not afraid to make the first move. Her ideal man is strong, and someone she can admire. But remember, at the slightest whiff of weakness, she will knock him off his pedestal. She does not like dull, whiny men, and thinks that there is always a way out of any situation. If she loves someone, she will be faithful. Aries women are too honest to try leading a double life. They are possessive, jealous, and not only will they not forgive those who are unfaithful, their revenge may be brutal; they know no limits. If you can handle an Aries, don't try to put her in a cage; it is best to give her a long leash. Periodically give her some space – then she will seek you out herself. She is sexual, and believe that anything goes in bed.

Her best partners are a Sagittarius or Leo. A Libra can make a good match after middle age, once both partners have grown wiser and settled down a bit. Gemini and Aquarius are only good partners during the initial phase, when everything is still new, but soon enough, they will lose interest in each other. Scorpios are good matches in bed, but only suitable as lovers.

TAURUS

Taurean women possess qualities that men often dream about, but rarely find in the flesh – they are soft, charming, practical, and reliable – they are very caring and will support their partner in every way. A Taurus is highly sexual, affectionate, and can show a man how to take pleasure to new heights. She is also strong and intense. If she is in love, she will be faithful. But when love fades away, she might find someone else on the side, though she will still fight to save her marriage, particularly if her husband earns good money. A Taurus will not tolerate a man who is disheveled or disorganized, and anyone dating her needs to always be on his toes. She will expect gifts, and likes being taken to expensive restaurants, concerts, and other events. If you argue, try to make the first peace offering, because a Taurus finds it very hard to do so – she might withdraw and ruminate for a long time. Never air your dirty laundry; solve all your problems one-on-one.

Scorpio, Virgo, Capricorn, and Cancer make the best matches. A relationship with an Aries or Sagittarius would be difficult. There is little attraction between a Taurus and a Leo, and initially Libras can make for a good partner in bed, but things will quickly cool off and fall apart. A Taurus and Aquarius make an interesting match – despite the difference in signs, their relationships are often lasting, and almost lifelong.

GEMINI

Gemini women are social butterflies, outgoing, and they easily make friends, and then break off the friendship, if people do not hold their interest. A Gemini falls in love hard, is very creative, and often fantasizes about the object of her affection. She is uninterested in sex without any attachment, loves to flirt, and, for the most part, is not particularly affectionate. She dreams of a partner who is her friend, lover, and a romantic, all at once. A Gemini has no use for a man who brings nothing to the table intellectually. That is a tall order, so Geminis often divorce and marry several times. Others simply marry later in life. Once you have begun a life together, do not try to keep her inside – she needs to travel, explore, socialize, attend events and go to the theater. She cannot tolerate possessive men, so avoid giving her the third degree, and remember that despite her flirtatious and social nature, she is, in fact, faithful – as long as you keep her interested and she is in love. Astrologists believe that Geminis do not know what they need until age 29 or 30, so it is best to hold off on marriage until then.

Leo and Libra make the best matches. A relationship with a Cancer is likely, though complex, and depends solely on the Cancer's affection. A Gemini and Sagittarius can have an interesting, dynamic relationship, but these are two restless signs, which might only manage to get together after ages 40-45, once they have had enough thrills out of life and learned to be patient. Relationships with a Capricorn are very difficult, and almost never happen. The honeymoon stage can be wonderful with a Scorpio, but each partner will eventually go their own way, before ending things. A Gemini and Pisces union can also be very interesting – they are drawn to each other, and can have a wonderful relationship, but after a while, the cracks start to show and things will fall apart. An Aquarius is also not a bad match, but they will have little sexual chemistry.

CANCER

Cancers can be divided into two opposing groups. The first includes a sweet and gentle creature who is willing to dedicate her life to her husband and children. She is endlessly devoted to her husband, especially if he makes a decent living and remains faithful. She views all men as potential husbands, which means it is dangerous to strike up a relationship with her if your intentions are not serious; she can be anxious and clingy, sensitive and prone to crying. It is better to break things to her gently, rather than directly spitting out the cold, hard truth. She wants a man who can be a provider, though she often earns well herself. She puts money away for a rainy day, and knows how to be thrifty, for the sake of others around her, rather than only for herself. She is an excellent cook and capable of building an inviting home for her loved ones. She is enthusiastic in bed, a wonderful wife, and a caring mother.

The second type of Cancer is neurotic, and capable of creating a living hell for those around her. She believes that the world is her enemy, and manages to constantly find new intrigue and machinations.

Another Cancer, Virgo, Taurus, Scorpio, and Pisces make the best matches. A Cancer can often fall in love with a Gemini, but eventually, things will grow complicated, as she will be exhausted by a Gemini's constant mood swings and cheating. A Cancer and Sagittarius will initially have passionate sex, but things will quickly cool off. A relationship with a Capricorn is a real possibility, but only later in life, as while they are young, they are likely to fight and argue constantly. Cancer can also have a relationship with an Aries, but this will not be easy.

LEO

Leos are usually beautiful or charming, and outwardly sexual. And yet, appearances can be deceiving – they are not actually that interested in sex. Leo women want to be the center of attention and men running after them boosts their self-esteem, but they are more interested in their career, creating something new, and success than sex. They often have high-powered careers and are proud of their own achievements. Their partners need to be strong; if a Leo feels a man is weak, she can carry him herself for a while- before leaving him. It is difficult for her to find a partner for life, as chivalrous knights are a dying breed, and she is not willing to compromise. If you are interested in a Leo, take the initiative, admire her, and remember that even a queen is still a woman. Timid men or tightwads need not apply. Leos like to help others, but they don't need a walking disaster in their life. If they are married and in love, they are usually faithful, and petty gossip isn't their thing. Leo women make excellent mothers, and are ready to give their lives to their children. Their negative traits include vanity and a willingness to lie, in order to make themselves look better.

Sagittarius, Aries, and Libra make the best matches. Leos can also have an interesting relationship with a Virgo, though both partners will weaken each other. Life with a Taurus will lead to endless arguments – both signs are very stubborn, and unwilling to give in. Leos and Pisces are another difficult pair, as she will have to learn to be submissive if she wants to keep him around. A relationship with a Capricorn will work if there is a common denominator, but they will have little sexual chemistry. Life with a Scorpio will be turbulent to say the least, and they will usually break up later in life.

VIRGO

Virgo women are practical, clever, and often duplicitous. Marrying one isn't for everyone. She is a neat freak to the point of annoying those around her. She is also an excellent cook, and strives to ensure her children receive the very best by teaching them everything, and preparing them for a bright future. She is also thrifty – she won't throw money around, and, in fact, won't even give it to her husband. She has no time for rude, macho strongmen, and is suspicious of spendthrifts. She will not be offended if you take her to a cozy and modest café rather than an elegant restaurant. Virgos are masters of intrigue, and manage to outperform every other sign of the Zodiac in this regard. Virgos love to criticize everyone and everything; to listen to them, the entire world is simply a disaster and wrong, and only she is the exception to this rule. Virgos are not believed to be particularly sexual, but there are different variations when it comes to this. Rarely, one finds an open-minded Virgo willing to try anything, and who does it all on a grand scale – but she is rather the exception to this general rule.

The best matches for a Virgo are Cancer, Taurus, and Capricorn. She also can get along well with a Scorpio, but will find conflict with Sagittarius. A Pisces will strike her interest, but they will rarely make it down the aisle. She is often attracted to an Aquarius, but they would drive each other up the wall were they to actually marry. An Aries forces Virgo to see another side of life, but here, she will have to learn to conform and adapt.

LIBRA

Female Libras tend to be beautiful, glamorous, or very charming. They are practical, tactical, rational, though they are adept at hiding these qualities behind their romantic and elegant appearance. Libras are drawn to marriage, and are good at imagining the kind of partner they need. They seek out strong, well-off men and are often more interested in someone's social status and bank account than feelings. The object of their affection needs to be dashing, and have a good reputation in society. Libras love expensive things, jewelry, and finery. If they are feeling down, a beautiful gift will instantly cheer them up. They will not tolerate scandal or conflict, and will spend all their energy trying to keep the peace, or at least the appearance thereof. They do not like to air their dirty laundry, and will only divorce in extreme circumstances. They are always convinced they are right and react to any objections as though they have been insulted. Most Libras are not particularly sexual, except those with Venus or the Moon in Scorpio.

Leos, Geminis, and Aquarians make good matches. Libra women are highly attracted to Aries men - this is a real case of opposites attract. They can get along with a Sagittarius, though he will find that Libras are too proper and calm. Capricorn, Pisces, and Cancer are all difficult matches. Things will begin tumultuously with a Taurus, before each partner goes his or her own way.

SCORPIO

Scorpio women may appear outwardly restrained, but there is much more bubbling below the surface. They are ambitious with high self-esteem, but often wear a mask of unpretentiousness. They are the true power behind the scenes, the one who holds the family together, but never talk about it. Scorpios are strong-willed, resilient, and natural survivors. Often, Scorpios are brutally honest, and expect the same out of those around them. They do not like having to conform, and attempt to get others to adapt to them, as they honestly believe everyone will be better off that way. They are incredibly intuitive, and not easily deceived. They have an excellent memory, and can quickly figure out which of your buttons to push. They are passionate in bed, and their temperament will not diminish with age. When she is sexually frustrated, a Scorpio will throw all of her energy into her career or her loved ones. She is proud, categorical, and "if you don't do it right, don't do it at all" is her motto. Scorpio cannot be fooled, and she will not forgive any cheating. Will she cheat herself? Yes! But it will not break up her family, and she will attempt to keep it a secret. Scorpios are usually attractive to men, even if they are not particularly beautiful. They keep a low profile, though they always figure out their partner, and give them some invisible sign. There is also another, selfish type of Scorpio, who will use others for as long as they need them, before unceremoniously casting them aside.

Taurus is a good match; they will have excellent sexual chemistry and understand each other. Scorpio and Gemini are drawn to each other, but are unlikely to stay together long enough to actually get married. Cancer can be a good partner as well, but Cancers are possessive, while Scorpios do not like others meddling in their affairs, though they can later resolve their arguments in bed. Scorpio and Leo are often found together, but their relationship can also be very complicated. Leos are animated and chipper, while Scorpios, who are much deeper and more stubborn, see Leos as not particularly serious or reliable. One good example of this is Bill (a Leo) and Hillary (a Scorpio) Clinton. Virgo can also make a good partner, but when Scorpio seemingly lacks emotions, he will look for them elsewhere. Relationships with Lira are strange and very rare. Scorpio sees Libra as too insecure, and Libra does not appreciate Scorpio's rigidity. Two Scorpios together make an excellent marriage! Sagittarius and Scorpio are unlikely to get together, as she will think he is shallow and rude. If they do manage to get married, Scorpio's drive and persistence is the only thing that will make the marriage last. Capricorn is also not a bad match, and while Scorpio finds Aquarius attractive, they will rarely get married, as they are simply speaking different languages! Things are alright with a Pisces, as both signs are emotional, and Pisces can let Scorpio take the lead when necessary.

SAGITTARIUS

Sagittarius women are usually charming, bubbly, energetic, and have the gift of gab. They are kind, sincere, and love people. They are also straightforward, fair, and very ambitious, occasionally to the point of irritating those around them. But telling them something is easier than not telling them, and they often manage to win over their enemies. Sagittarius tends to have excellent intuition, and she loves to both learn and teach others. She is a natural leader, and loves taking charge at work and at home. Many Sagittarian women have itchy feet, and prefer all kinds of travel to sitting at home. They are not particularly good housewives – to be frank, cooking and cleaning is simply not for them. Their loved ones must learn to adapt to them, but Sagittarians themselves hate any pressure. They are not easy for men to handle, as Sagittarians want to be in charge. Sagittarius falls in love easily, is very sexual and temperamental, and may marry multiple times. Despite outward appearances, Sagittarius is a very lonely sign. Even after she is married with children, she may continue living as if she were alone; you might say she marches to the beat of her own drum. Younger

Sagittarians can be reckless, but as they mature, they can be drawn to religion, philosophy, and the occult.

Aries and Leo make the best matches, as Sagittarius is able to bend to Leo's ways, or at least pretend to. Sagittarians often end up with Aquarians, but their marriages do not tend to be for the long haul. They are attracted to Geminis, but are unlikely to marry one until middle age, when both signs have settled down. Sagittarius and Cancer have incredible sexual chemistry, but an actual relationship between them would be tumultuous and difficult. Capricorn can make a good partner- as long as they are able to respect each other's quirks. Sagittarius rarely ends up with a Virgo, and while she may often meet Pisces, things are unlikely to go very far.

CAPRICORN

Capricorn women are conscientious, reliable, organized, and hardworking. Many believe that life means nothing but work, and live accordingly. They are practical, and not particularly drawn to parties or loud groups of people. But if someone useful will be there, they are sure to make an appearance. Capricorn women are stingy, but not as much as their male counterparts. They are critical of others, but think highly of themselves. Generally, they take a difficult path in life, but thanks to their dedication, perseverance, and willingness to push their own limits, they are able to forge their own path, and by 45 or 50, they can provide themselves with anything they could want. Capricorn women have the peculiarity of looking older than their peers when they are young, and younger than everyone else once they have matured. They are not particularly sexual, and tend to be faithful partners. They rarely divorce, and even will fight until the end, even for a failed marriage. Many Capricorns have a pessimistic outlook of life, and have a tendency to be depressed. They are rarely at the center of any social circle, but are excellent organizers. They have a very rigid view of life and love, and are not interested in a fling, as marriage is the end goal. As a wife, Capricorn is simultaneously difficult and reliable. She is difficult because of her strict nature and difficulty adapting. But she will also take on all the household duties, and her husband can relax, knowing his children are in good hands.

Taurus, Pisces, and Scorpio make good matches. Aries is difficult, once things cool off after the initial honeymoon. When a Capricorn meets another Capricorn, they will be each other's first and last love. Sagittarius isn't a bad match, but they don't always pass the test of time. Aquarius and Capricorn are a difficult match, and rarely found together. Things are too dull with a Virgo, and while Leo can be exciting at first, things will fall apart when he begins showing off. Libra and Aquarius are both difficult partners for Capricorn, and she is rarely found with either of them.

AQUARIUS

A female Aquarius is very different from her male counterparts. She is calm and keeps a cool head, but she is also affectionate and open. She values loyalty above all else, and is unlikely to recover from any infidelity, though she will only divorce if this becomes a chronic trend, and she has truly been stabbed in the back. She is not interested in her partner's money, but rather, his professional success. She is unobtrusive and trusting, and will refrain from listening in on her partner's phone conversations or hacking into his email. With rare exceptions, Aquarian women make terrible housewives. But they are excellent partners in life – they are faithful, never boring, and will not reject a man, even in the most difficult circumstances. Most Aquarians are highly intuitive, and can easily tell the truth from a lie. They themselves only lie in extreme situations, which call for a "white lie" in order to avoid hurting someone's feelings.

Aquarius gets along well with Aries, Gemini, and Libra. She can also have a good relationship with a Sagittarius. Taurus often makes a successful match, though they are emotionally very different; the same goes for Virgo. Aquarius and Scorpio, Capricorn, or Cancer is a difficult match. Pisces can make a good partner as well, as both signs complement each other. Any relationship with a Leo will be tumultuous, but lasting, as Leo is selfish, and Aquarius will therefore have to be very forgiving.

PISCES

Pisces women are very adaptable, musically inclined, and erotic. They possess an innate earthly wisdom, and a good business sense. Pisces often reinvent themselves; they can be emotional, soft, and obstinate, as well as sentimental, at times. Their behavioral changes can be explained by frequent ups and downs. Pisces is charming, caring, and her outward malleability is very attractive to men. She is capable of loving selflessly, as long as the man has something to love. Even if he doesn't, she will try and take care of him until the very end. Pisces' greatest fear is poverty. They are intuitive, vulnerable, and always try to avoid conflict. They love to embellish the truth, and sometimes alcohol helps with this. Rarely, one finds extremely unbalanced, neurotic and dishonest Pisces, who are capable of turning their loved ones' lives into a living Hell!

Taurus, Capricorn, Cancer, and Scorpio make the best matches. She will be greatly attracted to a Virgo, but a lasting relationship is only likely if both partners are highly spiritual. Any union with a Libra is likely to be difficult and full of conflict. Pisces finds Gemini attractive, and they may have a very lively relationship – for a while. Occasionally, Pisces ends up with a Sagittarius, but she will have to fade into the background and entirely submit to him. If she ends up with an Aquarius, expect strong emotional outbursts, and a marriage that revolves around the need to raise their children.

Tatiana Borsch

Made in the USA
Columbia, SC
12 July 2023

20370311R00191